+ 09/06
29.95

D0826107

Retir

France

Retiring to France

Victoria Pybus

Published by Vacation Work,
9 Park End Street, Oxford
www.vacationwork.co.uk

RETIRING TO FRANCE

by Victoria Pybus

First edition 2006

ISBN 13: 978-1-85458-358-1
ISBN 10: 1-85458-358-1

Publicity by Charles Cutting

Cover design by mccdesign

Typesetting and text design by Guy Hobbs

Cover photograph: castle and grounds in the Loire Valley

Printed and bound in Italy by Legoprint SpA, Trento

Contents

PART I – BEFORE YOU GO

Setting the Scene

Basics

PART II – A NEW HOME IN FRANCE

Where to Retire

Your New Home in France

PART III – A NEW LIFE IN FRANCE

FOREWORD

Buoyed up financially by the high value of property in Britain, many of us can afford to follow the thousands of our countrymen and women already living permanently and happily in France. France is a beautiful and varied country with a rich culture, wonderful food and wine and welcoming inhabitants; attributes that have enabled many retired people to enjoy a laid back and comfortable lifestyle there, knowing that they would never have been able to reach the same level of satisfaction with so many aspects of their lives had they remained in Britain.

There are pitfalls. One of them is blowing the budget on renovating a charming French ruin. Knowing how much you can afford to spend, or buying property ready-renovated, is practically essential (unless you are a builder and it is a retirement project). Retirees to France should also consider that anyone coming from the Anglophone world is liable to experience culture shock, not least because of the very intrusive presence of the state in all aspects of daily life. It could be said, that the land that overthrew the tyranny of the aristocracy over two hundred years ago, is now subject to tyrannical bureaucracy. There are not many things you can do in France without filling in a form first. For that reason it is suggested that newcomers get sound advice and perhaps consider using lawyers, accountants and other experts where needed, so that they can face the challenge of setting up a new life in another country in a well-prepared way. On arrival, for initial and ongoing local support you cannot beat the émigré grapevines, either the one on the spot, or the cyber ones on expatriate websites. Online forums where subscribers swap useful information about dealing with aspects of daily life and French bureaucracy can be invaluable and informative.

Creating a better life in France demands a certain pioneering spirit; or does it? It is quite possible that some parts of the Dordogne may echo Britain of several decades ago; cricket matches on the lawn, a traditional English village shop stocking familiar British products, ladies' tea parties, amateur dramatic productions and Christmas bazaars. The alternative to creating a bubble of Englishness, is to involve yourself with the French community where you have chosen to live (this means learning the language) so as not to deprive yourself of the full richness of retiring to France.

Victoria Pybus,
Oxford
May 2006

ACKNOWLEDGEMENTS

A book such as this can only come about through the co-operation and assistance of other people. Generous thanks are given to my colleague **André de Vries** for his support and contributions to the regional guide and financial sections as well as furnishing me with his contacts in the Dordogne.

I would also like to thank the obliging and helpful retirees whose stories of retirement in France form such an integral part of this book: Julian Roberts, Keith Oakley, Bob and Annette Culshaw, Anne and Alan Barrett and Anne Scanlon; may they all continue to flourish in their respective domains and encourage others to do what they have done.

TELEPHONE NUMBERS

Please note that the telephone numbers in this book are written as needed to call that number from inside the same country. French numbers are easily distinguished from UK numbers. They are written as 10 digits laid out in 5 pairs (eg. 01 22 33 44 55). All French numbers begin with one of the 5 area codes in France: 01 to 05. To call these numbers from outside the country you will need to know the relevant access code.

To call France from the UK: Dial 00 33 and the number given in this book minus the first 0.

To call the UK from France: Dial 00 44 and the number given in this book minus the first 0.

Part one

Before
You Go

Setting the Scene

Basics

Setting the Scene

CHAPTER SUMMARY

O France has a well-deserved reputation as being a secure place to live and retire to.

O Many French adhere to traditional values and quality of life at any age is taken very seriously there.

O The average age for retirement in France is 57 years. The Government wants to raise it to 60 but the Unions have so far refused consent.

O Social security and healthcare provision are likely to deteriorate in the future as the population ages and becomes top heavy with retired people.

O France's fitness as a place to retire is due to a great extent to its wealth, culture, beautiful landscapes and historic architecture though there are considerable differences in lifestyle and wealth between regions.

O There are two main types of Britons in France: those who want to move to an area with a lot of British residents, and those who are Francophiles who want to integrate into the local community.

O France is the largest country in the EU and there is a lot of space for living in

O Corruption is rife in France from the highest levels and usually, it is who you know that ensures your smooth passage in French life.

O The French have huge respect for culture and learning and for artistic talent such as painting.

O France is one of the most bureaucratic countries imaginable. You can't do anything without filling in a form.

THE NEW 'OLD': CHANGING ATTITUDES TO RETIREMENT

At the start of the twenty-first century we are in the midst of a major social transformation. The post-war notion of retirement as a time to put your slippers on and settle in front of the telly with a nice cup of tea is fast becoming obsolete. The very word 'retirement', not to mention the images of encroaching decrepitude that it conjures, no longer fits the reality of how people are living their lives post full-time employment. Today's retirees are often younger, fitter and wealthier than their forebears and together they are reshaping the very meaning of 'old age' and 'retirement'.

Many social commentators suggest that these changes are being wrought by the baby boomer generation. Born between 1945 and 1965, they are a force to be reckoned with, making up almost a third of the UK population and responsible for nearly 80% of all financial wealth. The baby boomers grew up in an era of postwar optimism and new social freedoms, and as such, have always represented a force for social change. Indeed, they have spent a lifetime reconstructing social norms. In 2006 the first wave of this generation is approaching retirement age, and with such political and financial clout their approach to growing old is profoundly different. As *The Times* recently put it: *'the pioneers of the consumer society are unlikely to settle for an electric fire and a can of soup'.*

One of the main reasons that the concept of retirement is changing is that people are living far longer. Life expectancy in the twentieth century rose by 20 years due to better healthcare and greater health awareness. Around 18 million people in the UK are over 60. This is creating something of a crisis in the British economy and if the government had its way, then we would all work until we dropped, easing the pressure on the already over-burdened state pension fund. The new generation of retirees however, are not prepared to do this. Not only are people living longer, they are also leaving the workforce younger. Many are giving up work in their early fifties when they are still fit and active, in order to enjoy a new stage in life – not their 'retirement', according to the American website www.2young2retire. com, but their 'renaissance'.

A recent report by *Demos*, a democracy think tank, claims that the baby boomers are intent on having their time again; of creating a new life phase in which they can revisit their own desire for personal fulfilment, free from the pressures of overwork and childrearing. The report identifies a new 'experience economy' of travel, food, learning and lifestyle. The baby boomers do not want to retreat from the world as the word 'retirement' suggests, but to head out into it with renewed vigour.

The new retirement is all about finding a better life balance. This may not necessarily include giving up work – around half of the people who leave permanent 'career' jobs before state pension age move initially into part-time, temporary or self-employed work, be it in the UK or abroad. It would seem that people are no longer happy to compartmentalise their lives into linear stages – school, work, parenthood – with retirement at the end of the line. Retirees these days are demanding greater flexibility; preferring to see life as a never-ending cycle, in which they can choose to dip in and out of periods of work, education and leisure. Others have the funds behind them to pursue a hobby or interest full-time. And an increasing number of people have realised that they can do either of these things in a climate far removed from the dreary British winter.

Almost a million Britons already draw their state pensions abroad, and this figure does not include the many more who have retired early. According to a report from Alliance and Leicester, one in five older people (an extra four million) will be living outside the UK by the year 2020, lured by the warmer climate, a slower pace of life, health advantages and a lower cost of living.

It would appear that the prevailing gloom that people once felt about the ageing process is slowly being replaced by a sunny optimism. People no longer dread reaching retirement age, but eagerly anticipate a new life stage, in which, released from the shackles of full-time work, they can seek out new cultural experiences.

FRENCH ATTITUDES TO RETIREMENT

The French philosophy towards retirement or *le troisième âge*, is that it is a well-earned period of non-economic productivity that should permit individuals to live the latest period of their lives to the full and with financial security. Private pension schemes, which do not

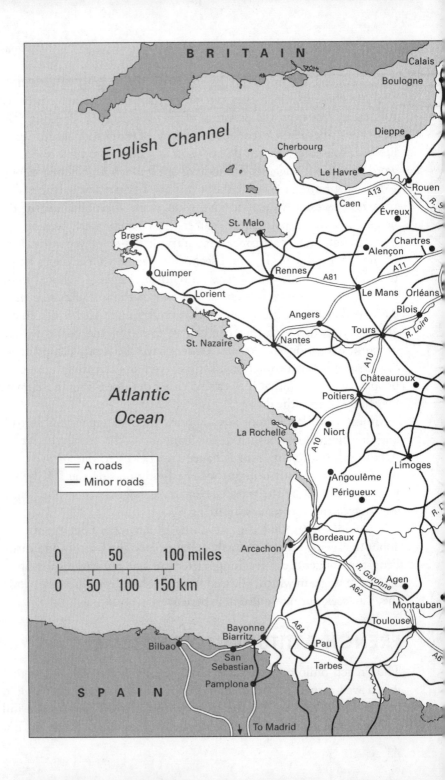

accord with France's socialist philosophy, have not needed to exist in France (although this may not be the case in the future). If proof were needed that retirement is better funded in France, UNESCO's quality of life index puts France in second place after Canada, another country with a strong French influence, and this is to a large extent gauged on France's healthcare and social security system, as well as the general *art de vivre*. No wonder then that so many foreigners, most of them British, are retiring there.

The security of the retired in France is funded partly by the state from employer/employee deductions, which citizens have paid from employment/earnings, and from compulsory supplemental pension schemes related to their occupational category, which ensures that the retirement pension is very generous. Higher taxes than the UK and a personal contribution element to the not-entirely-free health service means that there is an expectancy that the quality of facilities for the retired in France will be excellent and appreciably better than they are in the UK. However as France is divided into regions, which are responsible for a large chunk of their own funding, the quality of retirement (if defined by the standard and sufficiency of facilities) can be related to the overall wealth (or lack of it) in that region.

Grandparents in France are seen as the fundamental base of the family and a strengthener of ties between the generations. There is even a school for grand-parents (the *Ecole des Grand-Parents Européen/* EGPE) in Paris, which is open to people over 55. Its aim is to conserve an active role for grandparents through education, campaigning and example. It is common in France for several generations to live under one roof and for grandparents to be involved in family decisions and to help care for their grand-children when parents are working, as in Italy and Spain.

Such is the quality of life amongst retirees that the French government anticipates that by 2040 the average longevity of females will be a staggering 89 years (83 for men). Currently these are 83.8 and 76.7 years respectively. This means however that a growing problem looms over this otherwise utopian vision of retirement in France: namely that the population is no longer replenishing itself and there will be an excess of retirees by 2010 and insufficient workers paying into the social security system for the next generation to draw their pensions from.

Across the EU national pension schemes have been reformed to make them less extravagant and it is likely that people will be encouraged to carry on working after 65 in order to solve the imminent 'pensions crisis' and that pensions themselves will be less generous. The French government wants to raise the French retirement age to 60 but the Unions have put their collective feet down (so far).

Stats

o The average age of retirement in France is 57.

o Only 7% of French males are actively employed after 60 and only 4% of women (in the USA these figures are 27% and 14% respectively).

o In the age group 55-64 only 35% are employed in France, 50% in the UK and 67% in Sweden.

REASONS TO RETIRE TO FRANCE

Reasons for retiring to France are manifold and not a few of them are manifest the moment you arrive. For starters France has cheaper property, more space, better food, cheap wine, a more relaxed attitude to work, a more civilised population and a healthy resistance to the Americanisation of everything. Not least of the reasons to retire there, are the historical links between Britain and France. These links, if anything, have strengthened, due in no small part to the ease of travel between the two countries via the tunnel, as well as by the more traditional ferry services. Nowadays, a revolution in cheap flights has also augmented the possibility of hundreds of thousands of Brits decamping to different areas of France rather than just those within an hour's drive of a ferry port. The reverse is also true: many French people have settled in Britain to start businesses and find employment, particularly in the south east of England. However while thousands of French come to live in the UK to escape the over regulation of French business, high taxes and youth unemployment back home, many more Britons retire to France in anticipation of a potentially more enjoyable retirement there.

Of the estimated 600,000 Britons who now own homes in France there are two main types: those who want to retire to an area where there are already other Brits, preferably more than a few of them, or at least enough to play cricket matches. In other words, where there is a ready-made social circle of expatriates to mix with and there is no need to learn the language if you don't want to. When it comes to French paperwork they can get other Brits who have mastered the language to do it for them. The other type consider themselves true Francophiles and scorn the English colonists. The former have become synonymous with the Dordogne, which is the first region of France they are said to have 'colonised' but owing to the accessibility of most regions, colonies are forming in other parts of France. The francophiles can be found almost anywhere in France where the colonists are not. As Anne Scanlon, who is part of the Dordogne English-speaking community puts it:

If you don't want to mix with British people then you should avoid the Dordogne. It's not everyone's cup of tea; we had a couple move to the area from the UK and they said they didn't want to meet English people, only French people. They only lasted here a year.

For francophiles, one of the attractions of retiring to France is to integrate as much as possible into the local French landscape and become part of their local (French) community.

Bob and Annette Culshaw, who retired in the Dordogne are convinced that willingness to tackle the language is the key to integration:

The best thing about retiring in France is that we have been totally embraced by the local community. We were amongst the first English-speakers to move to this locality and considering how little French we spoke it is absolutely staggering how many French friends we have. Here I am, 61 years young and back in the schoolroom learning French. The French really respect you for trying to learn their beloved language.

Another oft quoted reason for wanting to retire in France is the gentler pace of life, which is also an essential facet of its quality. While the metropolitan French are as hyped up and frenetic as any people on the planet, move into the countryside, which the French call *La France Profonde* (essential France) and the pace of life slows to a pleasant amble. Even the French who deserted their own countryside in droves during the twentieth century (thus incidentally creating abandoned hamlets with houses suitable for conversion by Brits) are now rediscovering the charms of country living, especially now that this no longer means, being isolated from the mainstream. Thanks to modern technology you can run large chunks of your life from home and keep in touch more easily with family and friends and arrange your social life and plan your excursions. By contrast, in many parts of southern England it is increasingly hard to find tranquil areas of countryside where you can't hear the distant roar of traffic from the ground, or sky. In France there is a lot of space to live and breathe in and wonderful landscapes as far as the eye can see in any direction. As Julian Roberts, who first visited France 40 years ago, and retired to a tiny hamlet in the Dordogne two years ago, puts it:

For me, it is like turning the clock back to my boyhood; to the 1950s. Where we are, it is virtually crime free, and nearby towns seem to suffer only petty rather than major crime. There is no yobbish behaviour and you never see any litter. There is also a community spirit here which I remember, but that seems to have gone from England.

Everyone who has settled down in France has the same message: the language is the key to a more fulfilling lifestyle. Many Anglophone foreigners have created a better life for themselves in France. After years of paying into the system they reap the benefits and enjoy a quality of life that they would never have been able to achieve or afford in their own countries.

PROS & CONS

Pros

o Easy access thanks to Eurostar, TGV and cheap flights from regional UK airports to over 20 French regional airports; this means you can afford to visit the UK, encourage visits to your French home, or get back to the UK in a hurry for an emergency

o Land and property are much cheaper than in the UK and you may be able to retire to France early if you are lucky enough to have a valuable UK property that you can sell to fund retirement.

o France has many beautiful areas to choose from so you can find one that suits your requirements and your budget, even though it make take time to do so, as France is twice the size of Britain.

o The French lifestyle is more laid back and geared towards the art of living than the British one.

o French conveyancing is very thorough and it is relatively easy to get good advice (in English), from the numerous British and French legal firms and notaires used to dealing with Brits buying in France.

o Superb cuisine and wines are available at a fraction of the cost you would pay in the UK.

o The French health care system is reckoned to be one of the best in the world.

o French bureaucracy *vis-à-vis* foreigners from the EU living in France has been simplified in recent years.

Cons

o Retiring to France means creating a new social life and meaningful human interactions, which can be difficult if you don't speak French (though you can always learn).

o Taxes are much higher in France so if you are being taxed there it will be at a higher rate than in the UK.

o Eating out may be cheaper but other costs in France for goods and services are usually higher (as is the VAT rate of 19.6%).

o Some of the cheaper regions in which to buy property are cheap for a reason: they may be remote and slightly backward and the inhabitants may not be receptive to foreigners (even suspicious or hostile towards them).

o While the French may have a more relaxed lifestyle French officialdom can be frustratingly formal and officious; more so than in Britain.

o France is given to periodic crises of national confidence when the whole country appears to give itself over to gloomy introspection. Following a series of corruption and other government scandals, coupled with the French rejection of the European Constitution, one of these crises is in progress at the time of press.

INTRODUCING FRANCE

A brief history of France might seem unnecessary since most people have some idea of France and know a few basic facts. For instance that the Norman invasion of Britain took place in 1066 and began nearly a millennium of antagonism, rivalry, conflict and curmudgeonly cooperation between our two countries. The wider history of France is fascinating and it would take more than several retirements' worth of reading to exhaust all its subjects. There are hordes of French history titles and Amazon.co.uk or local libraries are good places to start.

Below is a chronology of some pivotal events in French history, which may help to set the scene of the country you have adopted for retirement.

KEY DATES OF FRENCH HISTORY

58–51 BC The Gallic Wars (Julius Caesar invades Gaul). Beginning of the Pax Romana (200 years of relative peace in the region). Lutetia (Paris) is founded.

43 BC Lugdunum (Lyon) is made capital of Gaul.

2ⁿᵈ Century Christianity arrives via the Romans.

3ʳᵈ Century Death throes of the Roman Empire

4ᵗʰ Century Barbarian hordes arrive from the east (Vandals, Visigoths and Franks) plunder former Gaul. Foundations of the feudal system created as people ally themselves to local rulers and come under their protection.

485-511 Reign of the Merovingian King of the Franks, Clovis I. Clovis converted from paganism to Christianity, which helped unite his kingdom loosely although it was in fact a collection of regional fiefdoms.

732 Charles Duke of the Franks defeated the Muslims at the battle of Tours (stopped the Arab invasion of Catholic Europe) and earned himself the sobriquet Charles Martel (Charles the Hammer).

751-768 reign of Pepin II (Pépin le Bref). King of the Franks. Carolingian dynasty.

755 Franks create strong links with papal states.

768-814 Charlemagne, son of Pepin II reigns over Franks .

800 Pope Leo III crowns

Charlemagne Holy Roman Emperor. Charlemagne is one of the most prominent figures in French/German history.

843 Treaty of Verdun partitions the Carolingian Empire amongst the sons of Louis the Pious.

987-996 Reign of Hughes Capet (begins the Capétien Dynasty).

1066 William Duke of Normandy invades England.

1077 Bayeux Tapestry is created.

1095 Pope Urban II preaches the cause of First Crusade in a dramatic speech at the Council of Clermont. Crusade takes place a year later.

1120-1140 Birth of Gothic architectural style (epitomised by French cathedrals such as Chartres) lasting into the beginning of the 13th century.

1154 Henry Plantagenet, Count of Anjou is crowned Henry II of England (married to Eleanor of Aquitaine).

1226-1270 Reign of Louis IX (he was canonised Saint Louis in 1297). Credited with uniting most of France.

1259 Anjou, Maine, Normandy and Poitou regions acquired from the English

1270 Eighth Crusade ends in Louis IX dying, along with most of his army, from plague in Tunis.

1305-1378 The Avignon Papacy. Seven popes, all of them French succeeded each other there. Lands around Avignon remained in the possession of the papacy until 1791 (i.e. The French Revolution).

1307 Members of the Knights Templar (pan-European order mostly run from France, whose history is that of the Crusades) arrested on the orders of Philip IV of France who feared their wealth and power. Their order dissolved by papal bull 1312.

1337-1443 The Hundred Years War between England and France.

1348-1352 Bubonic plague sweeps Europe.

1431 Jeanne d'Arc ('Maid of Orleans') was martyred as a heretic. Credited with uniting the French against the English which resulted in them being driven from France.

1453 English out of France, apart from last stronghold of Calais.

1470 First French printing press set up in Strasbourg.

1494-1559 The Italian Wars (between France and Austria) fought over Italian territories.

1515-1547 Reign of François I (Valois Dynasty). France's first Renaissance king, supporter of the arts and collector of Italian art and sculpture. Invited great painters including the ageing Leonardo da Vinci to come and work in France. More successful in bringing culture, fine architecture (including the Louvre and several Loire châteaux) and new ideas to France than at winning wars and diplomacy.

1562-1598 Rise of the Protestant Huguenots, leading to the Wars of Religion between Catholics and Protestants.

1572 St. Bartholemew's Eve Massacre (50,000 protestants slaughtered in Paris by order of the Queen Mother, Catherine de Medici, backed by Pope Gregory XIII).

1589-1610 Reign of Henri III of Navarre (1572-89). Crowned Henri IV of France at Chartres 1594. Died 1610. Beginning of the Bourbon Dynasty. Probably the most loved of all French kings. Converted to Catholicism and ended the Wars of Religion.

1598 Edict of Nantes gives Protestants full civil rights and freedom of conscience.

1608 Samuel de Champlain founds the French colony of Québec in Canada.

1610-1643 Reign of Louis XIII (with a regent until Louis crowned in 1617).

1624 Cardinal Richelieu appointed chief minister of France. Responsible for shifting the power of the monarchy from feudalism to an absolute monarchy.

1635 France's most eminent learned body, the Académie Française, founded by Cardinal Richelieu. It was suppressed in 1793 during the French Revolution and revived by Napoleon in 1803.

1642 Mazarin, succeeds his mentor Richelieu as chief minister of France.

1643-1715 Reign of Louis XIV 'The Sun King'. Court at Versailles was not only the most fashionable in Europe, but more importantly the focus of a highly ritualised life for the nobility and royalty which deprived them of the opportunity to foment insurgence. Involvement in wars and unbridled expenditure on luxury caused the near bankruptcy of France by the close of his reign. There was also the problem of the bourgeoisie who demanded more political rights but were ignored; a contributory factor towards full-blown revolution by the end of the 18th century.

1685 Edict of Nantes revoked. Major misjudgment by Louis XIV who wanted to make France wholly Catholic. Persecuted Protestants (Huguenots) fled France in droves leaving whole towns and cities depopulated and depriving the French economy of the invaluable contribution of these industrious and productive people.

1715-1774 Reign of Louis XV. An intelligent king much loved at the start of his reign but wholly despised by the end due to his inability to be decisive in European politics; probably because he could see all the possible consequences of his actions. This is the era of the influential Mme de Pompadour who embraced the liberal ideas of the Age of Englightenment and acted as a kind of minister without portfolio to King Louis.

1762 Publication of Rousseau's *Social Contract* (*'Man is born free and everywhere he is in chains'*). Rousseau's treatise on equality for all members of society under a just government; unjust governments which have broken the social contract have lost their authority, was intrinsic to the outbreaks of the American and French revolutions.

1763 Treaty of Paris ending the French and Indian wars. France surrenders its vast North American territories including Canada, to the British.

1770 The dauphin (the future Louis XVI) marries Marie Antoinette, an Austrian princess whose name was to become synonymous with profligacy and extravagance.

1774 Louis XVI crowned. His reign and his head were to be cut off by the French Revolution.

1778-83 American Revolution. France supports the Colonists in their war to gain independence from British rule in the American Colonies.

1788 Half of Paris is estimated to be without employment. The crops have failed in the countryside. In Paris and elsewhere food is short. Louis forced to reinstate the Estates General, France's National Assembly, which promptly curtails the king's powers.

1789 The Storming of the Bastille prison by the Paris mob (mainly for the vast stores of arms and ammunition within) marked the beginning of the French Revolution and the uprising of the people of France against the ruling class that had taxed them to starvation and ignored their plight. The legal status of nobility was abolished and all men declared equal. Beginning of the First Republic and Citizen Robespierre's Reign of Terror.

1791 The Royal Family is imprisoned in the Tuileries Palace.

1793 Louis XVI is tried and convicted of crimes against the people and guillotined, in the Place de la Concorde in Paris followed by his wife, Marie Antoinette some months later. The monarchy is abolished.

1793-1794 France is governed by the Committee of Public Safety. 16,000 people are guillotined as France is purged of 'enemies of the Revolution'. The terror ends with the overthrow and execution of Robespierre in 1794.

1794 Slavery abolished in France.

1799 The Revolution ends with General Napoleon Bonaparte's arrival in Paris where he is crowned First Consul.

1802 Slavery in France reinstated.

1804 Napoleon is crowned Emperor Napoleon I. Napoleon creates a powerful central administration and The Civil Code (which became the Code

Napoleon in 1807), which is the basis for several European countries' legal systems today.

1808 Napoleonic legal system of titles created but without any *ancien régime* type privileges of nobility (such as exemption from taxes).

1809 The baccalaureate examination is created.

1812 Napoleon's defeat in Russia halts his conquest of most Europe.

1814 Napoleon abdicates and is exiled to Elba. Monarchy (Bourbon line) reinstated with a charter under the constitution.

1814-1824 Reign of Louis XVII.

1814 Congress of Vienna begins reconstitution of Europe after Napoleon's downfall.

1815 Napoleon enters Paris and starts a '100 Days' comeback that precedes his final defeat.

1815 Battle of Waterloo ends Napoleon's rule over Europe. Napoleon sent into exile on the island of St. Helena.

1821 Death of Napoleon in exile.

1824-30 Reign of Charles X

1830-1848 Reign of Louis Philippe.

1830 Algeria becomes a French colony.

1839 Daguerre, the French photography pioneer invents the first practical camera.

1848 Another revolution in France (the Revolution of the Bourgeois Liberals) to defend privileges obtained during the 1789 revolution. Wanted to stop voting rights being limited to landowners only. Establishes the Second Republic.

1848 Slavery abolished for the second time. This includes slavery in all of France's overseas colonies where a policy of assimilation replaced mercantilist colonisation. However, while the natives of Senegal, Algeria etc were raised as French people, they had none of the democratic rights of French citizens.

1852 Napoleon III (a nephew of Napoleon I) masterminds a coup and makes himself emperor. End of the Second Republic.

1870-1871 Franco-Prussian War and the declaration of the Third Republic after France loses the war against Germany and Napoleon III is deposed. The regions of Alsace and Lorraine annexed by Germany. This was a factor that led cumulatively to the outbreak of the First World War in 1914.

1895 Lumière brothers invent the portable movie camera and Paris audiences flock to see the first publicly shown 'movie' *Leaving the Lumière Factories.*

1898-1906 The Dreyfus affair. Dreyfus was a Jewish army officer accused of spying. After convicting him and sentencing him to the notorious Devil's Island prison his supporters, who included writer Emile Zola protested his innocence. It became a cause célèbre and Dreyfus went from being a scapegoat to being used as a political pawn to discredit the rightist government. The case also exposed the depth of anti-Semitism amongst France's elite.

1914 The First World War breaks out in northeast France between the German and French armies and the allies of both countries are gradually sucked in until most of Europe is involved. Trench warfare adopted as a tactic by the French to halt the progress of the Germans. The Americans enter the war in 1917 and by weight of numbers help to end it. Enormous reparations demanded by the Allies from Germany make Germany bankrupt and are a major cause of the Second World War. Between the wars Paris becomes a leading centre of the Avant-Garde art movement and an international centre for painters and all kinds of artists including musicians and film makers.

1919 Peace Treaty of Versailles. France regains Alsace-Lorraine.

1939 Outbreak of the Second World War. France declares war on Germany.

1940 Third republic falls after France again loses to Germany and German armies enter Paris and the north and west of France which remain occupied parts of France (so called Vichy France after the puppet government established there with Marshal Petain as its nominal head) until 1944.

1944 Allies invade France via Normandy from Britain, Germany capitulates and the war in Europe ends. Fourth Republic established by Charles de Gaulle.

1946 France reinstalls colonial government in Indo-China. Viet Minh nationalist guerillas start attacking French troops in northern Vietnam. Beginning of the French war in Indo-China.

1954 France decides to make a stand against the Viet Minh at Dien Bien Phu and brings in garrison of 16,000 men. Viet Minh besiege Dien Ben Phu. 3,000 French killed and 8,000 Viet Minh plus 25,000 casualties. Dien Ben Phu falls much to the shock of the French. France's involvement in Indo-China ends.

1954-1962 War of Algerian independence. One of the bitterest in French history. By 1962, 1.7 million French soldiers had seen active service in Algeria. Over 3,000 Algerian prisoners had been tortured and executed. 25,000 French soldiers died and 60,000 were wounded. Over half a million Algerians died. The Pieds Noirs (white Algerian settlers) fled Algeria, which had been a French colony since 1830.

1957 Treaty of Rome establishes the EEC with France as one of the founding signatories.

1958 Fifth Republic launched after major constitutional changes under de Gaulle.

1968 French student unrest erupts in Paris over the continuing centralisation of education and lack of reform in the educational system. The 1968 riots marked the end of the de Gaulle era. Students came out on the streets building barricades and setting fire to them in battles with the police. 10 million French workers joined the students and these strikes bought the country to a grinding halt. De Gaulle was forced to make an ignominious flight to Gemany for his own safety. Such events marked the end of rightist politics and ushered in the Socialist era. Many of the '68ers' ended up running French government.

1969 De Gaulle resigns over failure to secure Senate and local government reforms. Georges Pompidou (Gaullist), becomes president.

1974 Pompidou dies in office. Valéry Giscard d'Estaing (Independent Republican) takes over presidency.

1981 François Mitterrand (Socialist) is elected president with 1.7 million unemployed in France.

1988 Mitterrand re-elected.

1992 France signs Maastricht Treaty pledging full European Union.

1995 Jacques Chirac (rightist) elected president. End of 14 years of Socialist presidency.

1996 France announces end to its programme of nuclear-testing in the Pacific after mounting international condemnation.

1997 March 1997 French unemployment reaches a postwar high of 12.8%. Lionel Jospin becomes prime minister on manifesto to creat 35,000 new jobs in the public sector for 18-25 year-olds.

2001 The 35-hour week is adopted in France.

2000 Chirac becomes embroiled in the state-owned Elf-Aquitaine scandal, one of the biggest corruption scandals in French history.

2001 Trial begins of Roland Dumas, France's ex-foreign minister on charges of corruption in relation to Elf-Aquitaine. Meanwhile President Chirac is investigated for alleged corrupt financing of his party when he was mayor.

2002 Euro currency adopted by France. President Chirac wins a second term by a landslide. In the same elections, Le Pen's extreme right party won 5.5 million votes nationally (without winning a single seat) causing nervousness over the rise of far right beliefs in France, and in Europe generally.

2003 French constitution changed to allow devolution to the regions and departments on economic development, transport, tourism, culture and further education matters.

2005 January French parliament starts debate on dismantling the 35-hour week. Trade unions organise public sector strikes against proposed labour, pension and welfare reforms. In May France rejects adoption of the European Constitution in a national referendum and Prime Minister Jean-Pierre Raffarin resigns as a result and is replaced by Dominique de Villepin, who is in for a rough ride from the Unions over reforms as above.

The French Economy

The French economy has for a long time been the fourth largest in the world, and the British the fifth, although for a while in 2002 the two countries exchanged places until the euro started to appreciate in value in 2003. France is basically a rich country; it generally posts a positive balance of trade of around £10-20 billion per year, while the UK has an annual deficit of some £30 billion. Although France is not a great trading nation like the UK, and has virtually no oil or gas, because of its greater land area and self-sufficiency in many products, it imports a lot less than it exports. France has traditionally been a difficult export market. One might also add that long-standing high unemployment has depressed consumer demand for foreign imports.

France's post-war history can be divided into two starkly different eras: *les trente glorieuses* or the 30 glorious years from 1944 to 1974, and *les trente piteuses* or 30 pitiful years from 1974 to 2004. The French call the last 30 years *la crise* or the crisis, which includes regular public sector strikes and a huge public deficit, and there is not much reason to suppose that this crisis is about to come to an end in the near future.

In the 1990s France became an industrial superpower, with some world-beating industries such as *Aérospatiale*, the company that makes the Airbus together with Britain, Germany and Spain. There have also been high-profile disasters such as the bank *Crédit Lyonnais* and *Alstom*, the maker of the Eurostar trains, companies that have had to be rescued by the French state. The French like *les champions* – huge companies that bring honour and glory to France, and they are keen to support them whether they make money or not.

The TGV or high-speed train is a well-known case in point: hugely successful and useful on the one hand and on the other hand bank-breakingly costly with a bill that will top over 100 billion pounds by 2020, when it is expected to have linked many of the important cities of Europe.

Periodic bursts of economic growth and the success of big companies have not helped solve the problem of high unemployment. There are simply too many disincentives for companies to take on more staff. Companies are penalised when they have 50 workers or more, so there are thousands of companies with 49 employees. The situation got to the point in the 1990s that the government brought in a 35-hour working week with the assumption that employers would automatically have to take on more workers. The idea had some initial success, but is not going to solve the unemployment problem, which is on the rise again (currently 9.9%) and is especially high amongst new graduates and other young people.

Population

The official population of France is estimated at 60.5 million (2004), but there may be as many as two million illegal immigrants in addition to that figure. Three-quarters of the population are urban dwelling. It is estimated that nearly a quarter of the population will be aged 65 and over by 2030. However, whereas the populations of other European countries are in decline owing to negative birth rates, France's has been increasing since 1992 due to a combination of a slightly higher birth-rate than the EU average, and immigration. The increase is about 25% higher than the EU average.

The population includes a million immigrants from the former French colony of Algeria and just over two million immigrants from other EU and European countries of which approximately half are from Portugal and the remainder are from Italy, Spain, former Yugoslavia and Poland. The rest of the immigrant population is derived from the Mahgreb (Morocco and Tunisia) and more recently from Asia. France is home to Europe's largest Islamic community (a factor in France's refusal to support America's war against Iraq). The potential for conflict within France's borders is minimised by a policy of upholding France's strongly secular traditions (banning the wearing of the Muslim headscarf and prominent Christian crosses in state schools) and ensuring the integration of French immigrants into the wider French community. This does not prevent French immigrants, particularly those from Arab and African countries from being amongst the most socio-economically disadvantaged part of the population.

Paris is one of Europe's largest conurbations with 11.1 million people. Other large urban areas are Lyon (1.6 million), Marseille (1.4 million), Lille (1.1 million) and Toulouse (920,000).

Geography

France is the largest country in the EU with a surface area of 544,500 square kilometres. It is also one of the most thinly populated, with a mere 109 inhabitants per square kilometre (compared with the UK's 243 per sq. km). Most of the land is habitable, being less than 200 metres above sea level. The three main mountain ranges are the French Alps, including Europe's highest mountain, Mont Blanc, the Pyrenees, running along the border with Spain, and the less mountainous Massif Central, in south-central France. The English Channel (*La Manche* to the French) is just 22 miles wide at its narrowest point and it is possible for either country to see the coast of the other on a clear day. France has land borders with Belgium, Luxembourg, Germany, Switzerland, Italy, Andorra and Spain.

The main rivers are the Loire, the Rhône, the Seine and the Garonne. In total there are 8,500 km of navigable rivers and waterways.

Other European Territories Linked to France

The Principality of Monaco is neither a department of France, nor a truly independent country. The head of state is an hereditary Prince, but France controls many aspects of the government. The small mountain principality of Andorra in the Pyrenees recognises the French President and a Spanish bishop as heads of state, but is more or less independent.

Climate Zones

France has substantial variations of climate, given its great size. The northwest, bordering the Atlantic has a similar climate to southwest England, if somewhat warmer. The dividing line between north and south as far as climate goes is the Loire valley.

Continental. The north and east of France have a continental climate, characterised by predictably warm summers and cold winters, with fairly high rainfall, similar to southern England. Continental weather also characterizes the Auvergne, Burgundy and Rhône Valley.

Mediterranean. Roussillon, the Riviera and Provence which comprise the south and southeastern corner of France experience a Mediterranean climate, with regularly hot summers and mild winters, and unpredictable low rainfall. The south is subject to strong winds like the *mistral*, and sudden storms.

Mountainous. The mountain regions of the Pyrenees, Alps and Massif Central have cool summers, frequent rain and very cold winters with long periods of both sunny weather and rain or snow.

AVERAGE MONTHLY TEMPERATURES (CENTIGRADE) AND RAINFALL (MM)

	Jan	Feb	Mar	Apr	May	Jun	Jul	Aug	Sep	Oct	Nov	Dec
Bordeaux												
Max	9	11	14	16	19	23	26	26	23	18	13	10
Min	2	3	4	6	10	13	15	15	12	9	5	3
rainfall	76	64	66	66	71	66	53	58	71	86	89	86
Cherbourg												
Max	8	8	10	12	15	18	19	20	19	15	12	10
Min	4	4	5	7	9	13	15	14	13	10	8	5
rainfall	110	75	61	50	37	36	52	73	77	100	125	118

	Jan	Feb	Mar	Apr	May	Jun	Jul	Aug	Sep	Oct	Nov	Dec
Dijon												
Max	5	6	12	16	20	23	26	25	22	16	9	6
Min	-2	-1	2	5	9	12	14	13	11	6	2	0
rainfall	48	41	48	51	58	69	64	64	53	74	71	58
La Rochelle												
Max	9	10	13	16	19	23	24	25	23	18	12	8
Min	3	3	4	7	9	13	14	14	12	9	6	3
rainfall	63	59	64	57	54	50	44	49	52	90	97	93
Lille												
max	6	6	9	12	17	19	22	23	19	14	9	7
min	1	1	3	4	8	11	13	13	11	7	4	2
rainfall	48	41	43	43	51	56	61	58	56	64	61	58
Marseille												
Max	11	12	14	17	21	26	29	28	25	20	14	12
Min	3	3	6	8	12	16	19	18	16	11	7	3
rainfall	48	41	46	46	46	25	15	25	64	94	76	58
Paris												
Max	6	7	11	14	18	21	24	24	21	15	9	7
Min	1	1	3	6	9	12	14	14	11	8	4	2
rainfall	53	48	37	43	54	52	55	61	53	50	51	50
Tours												
Max	6	8	12	16	19	23	24	24	21	16	10	7
Min	1	1	3	6	9	12	14	13	11	7	4	2
rainfall	60	55	48	46	60	48	48	60	58	60	62	65

CULTURE SHOCK

Latin V Anglo-Saxon Mentality. The British and the French are close in many ways, but are a gulf apart in mentality. Foreigners choose to go and live in France because they like the lifestyle, not necessarily because they like the French. There is a crucial difference between a foreigner who goes to live in the UK or the USA and who over time is accepted as a Brit or an American because they have adopted British or American habits and so successfully blend in with the locals, and an Anglo-Saxon who goes to live in France. Somehow, he or she never seems to be quite accepted by the French as one of them. Someone who has no Latin ancestry is never likely to metamorphose themselves into a Frenchman or Frenchwoman. The gulf between the Germanic and Latin cultures is simply too great for this ever to happen, and why should it? There are areas of France where a more Germanic mentality tends to prevail. The people of northwest France, in the former Flemish-speaking areas of the Nord have a lot in common with their stolid cousins over the border in Belgium. The area of Alsace-Lorraine, where German is still in everyday use, is in many ways more German than French. In the southwest of the country, the Basques have an entirely different mentality.

Culture Shock – Essential Franco/British Differences

○ France is a country with a strong tendency towards uniformity thanks to a long tradition of centralization.

○ French social customs seem old-fashioned by British standards with a lot of etiquette and formality surrounding social occasions.

○ The French are well known for their touchiness about personal criticism, or even worse criticism of France, by foreigners. Though it is usually all right to do this if it is between one French person and another.

○ The French are very volatile and to foreigners often appear inconsistent. This is because they like to have drama and excitement in their daily lives; it is not usually meant to be taken seriously.

○ The French respect anyone who is self-confident and who is proud of their country; while the British are the complete opposite making jokes at their own expense and disparaging the land of their birth; neither of which go down well with the French.

O The French have a huge respect for learning, and artistry such as painting. It goes without saying if you want to earn their respect you have to master French and read literature in the French language. Then you will never be at a loss for a topic of conversation. The more you know about French *Lettres et des Beaux Arts* the better. If you are a painter, you will also be regarded with respect. Improving your painting skills, or studying French arts and letters make great retirement occupations in any case.

O It is extremely important to address people verbally by their titles e.g. Madame, Mademoiselle, Monsieur, with or without their surnames (in the case of Mademoiselle with or without a Christian name). Also *Madame le Professeur, Monsieur le Docteur Monsieur le Directeur, Madame la Directrice* etc are voiced forms of address, not just for envelopes.

O France is one of the world's most bureaucratic countries. You can't do anything without filling in a form. French bureaucrats run the country and the state interferes in every aspect of its citizens lives.

O France is without doubt one of Europe's most corrupt countries. If you happen to know the right person anything becomes possible and many a little difficulty with planning etc. has been solved by a word to the wise.

O Because France is excessively regulated there is a backlash towards defiance of authority. A prime example is the number of traffic laws. This has resulted in a film stunt style of driving (and also a very high accident rate) that is quite terrifying to Anglo-Saxons used to a more placid exhibition of driving skills. However, it is best to leave rule-breaking to the French as they know how to do it.

O Because France is basically a socialist society there are a lot of rules designed to protect weaker members of society. Other laws however are arbitrary and designed to make life difficult such as having to submit certified copies of your degrees and qualifications every time you apply for a job.

O The standard measure for bottles or draught beer in France is either 250 or 330 ml and it is usually consumed with food. This is quite different to beer consumption customs in Britain, which usually entail drinking several pints after work with bar snacks or crisps and which results unsurprisingly in drunkenness.

○ Banquets and wedding feasts can go on for hours and involve ten courses with a wine for each. Outsiders can be shocked by such gluttony, even though there may be dancing between courses at weddings. It is considered very bad form to leave before the end, which may be at 5am. No matter how close to collapse you are you have to try and stay awake (though it is acceptable for grannies to nod off).

Basics

- Cost of living analyses indicate that France is 15%-20% cheaper than the UK but many services are much more expensive than in Britain because of higher social costs.
- Land and property, eating out, alcohol, tobacco and car-running costs are lower in France than in the UK.
- Knowledge of how to use the internet and other computer services will make your life in France, and staying in touch with friends and relatives much simpler; knowledge of the French language is also very important.
- It is advisable to have a trial period of living in France for a few months to make sure that you really want to make the move and to get to know the locality to which will be moving.
- Alternatives to moving to France include extended renting and homeswaps.
- It is not a legal requirement for EU nationals living in France to have a residence permit (*permit de séjour*) but you can apply for one voluntarily as it is useful proof of ID for many official procedures in France.
- For driving to France you can download route maps, town plans and instructions for following your route, free from the internet.
- Before you depart the UK permanently you should arrange to have your UK pension paid into your bank account in France.
- If you are taking cats and dogs to France they must be micro-chipped and vaccinated against rabies; the latter within specified time parameters.
- The cardinal rule before arranging removals is to have a massive house turnout and reduce the items for removal to France to a minimum.

THINGS TO CONSIDER

Is it Affordable?

The basic point here is that if you can afford retirement (i.e. non-income generating activity) in the UK, then you will be able to afford it in France. However it may be a mistake to assume that it will be cheaper to live in France as it depends on your lifestyle and how much you spend on goods and services to create and maintain it, how regularly you want to make trips back to the UK, whether your pension and any other income amounts to a secure, regular long-term income and what happens if your funds are linked with the fate of the euro which is likely to fluctuate in value.

Bob and Annette Culshaw found their general shopping cost slightly more than in the UK :

> *Our cost of living expectations were not fulfilled. We thought shopping would cost less here, but although we use the local hypermarkets, prices are slightly higher than the UK's. Prices are higher in general except for local wines (€3 a bottle direct from the viticulteur) and diesel petrol is also cheaper at €1.03-€1.17 a litre.*

The economic pundits and official purveyors of statistics tell us that the cost of living in France is 15-20% lower in France than in Britain. Eating out, wine and property are all cheaper, but essential tradesmens' services such as plumbing, repairs and renovations, are much more expensive. Public transport is excellent value, but many retirees are living in rural areas where at least one car is a necessity to reach an embarkation point for public transport. Motoring costs come to less than in the UK; Bob Culshaw again:

> *Motoring (but not the cost of buying a car) is one of the few things that costs less than in the UK. The cheapest place to get petrol is from hypermarkets where it is 12-15 cents cheaper. Diesel petrol costs €1.03 a litre there. There is no road fund tax in France and car insurance is surprisingly inexpensive compared with the UK. I pay €280 for comprehensive insurance.*

The Bare Necessities of Life Comparison of UK and France

NB The figures quoted below were gathered in 2005 (Source: *EIU Worldwide Cost of Living*) and refer to costs in the larger cities. In rural areas the cost of living is considerably cheaper.

Alcohol & Tobacco. Much cheaper. In the case of cigarettes not by much; French cigarettes are the third most expensive in Europe after Britain and Norway; in the case of alcohol it depends what you are drinking but local wines are usually very good value.

Product	France price (€)	UK price (£)	France price in £ sterling equivalent
Cigarettes – Marlboro (20)	4.70	5.20	3.34
Cigarettes – Local brand (20)	4.50	4.80	3.20
Table wine (750 ml)	2.73	4.99	1.94
Beer – known brand (330 ml)	0.71	0.92	0.50
Scotch (6 yrs old – 700 ml)	12.47	12.34	8.86

Books and Newspapers. More expensive than the UK. In the case of books because they carry VAT at 5.5%. VAT on audio books, videos and DVDs is 19.6%.

Product	France price (€)	UK price (£)	France price in £ sterling equivalent
Daily local newspaper	0.93	0.60	0.66
Imported daily newspaper	1.85	1.20	1.31
International weekly news magazine (Time)	4.23	2.50	3.00
Paperback novel	11.50	6.99	8.17

Cars. Car expenses are lower generally, because there is no road fund tax to pay and petrol is slightly cheaper (€1.10-€1.20 per litre for diesel). However, buying a second-hand car in France is much more expensive than in the UK.

Product	France price (€)	UK price (£)	France price in £ sterling equivalent
New low priced car (900-1299 cc)	13,075	8,995	9,290
Annual road tax	n/a	160	n/a
Low price insurance premium in the city	957	685.65	680.33
Cost of a tune up	96	150	68.21

Clothing and Footwear. Mostly more expensive; think chic and good quality. Factory outlets and other cut-price outlets exist but are more geared to the young and very young. Probably cheaper to stock up in the UK on trips back there.

Food. As bought in supermarkets and shops things cost about the same as in the UK. In the plentiful open-air markets prices are cheaper than supermarkets and you can bargain for large quantities, or as the market winds down. Your property may well come with some land where you can grow your own vegetables, keep chickens etc. and be partly self-sufficient and barter produce with your neighbours. All of which can keep down costs and could make France cheaper than the UK.

Product	France (supermarket) price (€)	UK (supermarket) price (£)	France price in £ sterling equivalent
Pasteurised Milk (1 litre)	0.94	0.49	0.67
Eggs (12)	2.77	1.02	1.98
Orange Juice (1 litre)	1.93	1.22	1.37
Butter (500g)	3.17	1.96	2.25
White Bread (1 kg)	2.22	0.55	1.58
Ground Coffee (500 g)	4.55	3.30	3.24
Tea bags (25 bags)	1.42	0.30	1.00
Potatoes (2 kg)	2.09	1.50	1.49
Onions (1kg)	1.13	0.64	0.81

Furnishings. Secondhand furniture is usually very inexpensive because the French prefer new and it can be fun to hunt down the items you need. For modernists, Ikea has 18 stores in France.

Rents. Much lower than in the UK generally, but can depend on location. The figures below compare London with average prices in Paris. Rents are considerably cheaper outside the major cities.

Product	France price (€)	UK price (£)	France price in £ sterling equivalent
Furnished moderate 1-bedroom apartment (pcm)	1,100	700	781.58
Furnished moderate 3-bedroom house	2,800	2137.50	1,989.47

Repairs and Renovations. These are some of the major expenses of retiring to France and have caused many a bankruptcy. All trades people are much more expensive than in the UK because of higher taxes on businesses and higher social costs for employees.

Transport. Public transport is cheaper than the UK and very efficient. However, this is not hugely helpful if you are retiring to a rural area, although it may help speed up your visits to the UK (depending where you are in France) and other parts of France if you don't like flying. There are special reductions for *les retraités* (seniors) on most forms of transport.

Utilities. Gas, electricity and water bills are slightly cheaper for most people than they are in the UK. However if you are rurally-based away from mains, and rely on suppliers for diesel boilers, wood-burning stoves and bottled gas this works out more expensive.

Product	France price (€)	UK price (£)	France price in £ sterling equivalent
Phone line – average monthly rental	13	10.66	9.24
Phone – average charge per local call from home (3 mins)	0.13	0.14	0.10

Electricity, monthly bill for family of four	69.80	45	49.60
Gas, monthly bill for family of four	67.50	45	47.96
Water, monthly bill for family of four	32	25.83	22.76

Leaving Family and Friends

In the excitement of realising that you can afford to retire in France as you have always dreamed of doing, it is easy to forget that moving to another country means leaving your circle of friends and family behind; close families can find the idea of this quite daunting. On the other hand you may be giving family and friends a whole new dimension to their lives in the form of a unique holiday home, which they can visit as often as commitments permit for as long as they like. Potentially more problematic, is leaving behind elderly and frail relatives especially elderly parents. The consequences of you moving to France in this instance need to be considered carefully as they may be too frail to visit you in France.

Main Considerations Before Moving Abroad

○ You will need contingency plans to stay in touch with and assist close friends, children, grand-children elderly parents and relatives, and to deal with any emergencies that may arise in the UK when you are living in France and to have somewhere for any of the above to stay with you when they want or need to.

○ Are you familiar with computer technology? If not, you should attend a computer course before leaving the UK in order to familiarise yourself with the internet, e-mail and computer linked gadgets that will help you maintain your links with the UK and enable you to run your life in France smoothly.

○ Are you going to take your right-hand drive car to France or are you going to buy one there? It is generally considered safer to have a left-hand drive in France, especially for overtaking.

○ Are you going to be dependent on Ryanair or other budget airline operating to a small airport in proximity to your French property?

If so, it is important to bear in mind that routes can be axed and fares rise, so you will need to ensure that you are within easy access of alternatives.

○ Are you going to sever all your financial links with the UK and become wholly liable to French taxes. This is something that requires expert advice as it may not be financially beneficial. At the very least, most people find it useful to maintain a UK bank account for ordering supplies from UK outlets, and for use on their regular trips back to the UK.

○ If you are a couple, have you considered what will happen if one of you dies? Will the other one want to stay on or return to the UK? This ties in with whether or not you sever all links with the UK tax and national insurance system. If you have wholly left the British system and then want to return to it, you may find it financially punitive to do so, unless you have made plans for this contingency.

○ Who will you leave your French property to? Under French law inheritance automatically passes directly to the children of the deceased. If you want to bypass French inheritance law and leave the property to your partner or grand-children you will need to set up legal remedies for this to happen (see *Wills and Inheritance*) in the *Personal Finance* chapter.

ALTERNATIVES TO PERMANENT RETIREMENT IN FRANCE

If you are not quite sure whether permanent retirement to France is for you, but you plan to spend a large part of your retirement period in France without actually severing your ties to the UK, it is not essential to own your own French property. There are several possible alternatives including extended renting of holiday homes, timeshare and home exchanges. The advantages or disadvantages of each of these possibilities compared with each other and compared with buying and having your own retirement property will have to be weighed up in order to ensure that you make the right choice for your circumstances.

The obvious advantage of any of these alternatives is that it relieves you of the worry of having to buy and maintain your own property. It could also allow you to stay in a very expensive region such as Provence, where you might not be able to afford to buy, or if you did buy you would worry a lot about forest fires and damaging storms, which pose a regular threat to property in some southern and mountainous regions.

Main Points of Extended Renting

- Holiday rentals are charged by the week and longer rentals are regarded as any period longer than a month. Some rental companies only rent up to a maximum of three months, others will consider a year or longer though contracts are usually reviewed annually.
- Expensive if done through a rental company. Many French properties have been renovated by foreign owners with rental income in mind and have been finished and furnished to the high standard this demands, including having a swimming pool. The cheapest low season rent for a Provençal home that sleeps 4 is about £500 per week before discount. Discounts on longer rentals are not huge, usually 10%.
- Renting from a French landlord is a possibility but you will probably need help to find a suitable place and with the contracts and negotiations (if you don't speak French) and there will be the usual French run around of paperwork. This is probably a cheaper way to rent, but more complicated and time consuming. The tenancy agreement for a furnished property rented for three or more months is a *Contrat de Location, Habitation Meublée.*
- Longer rentals are much more common in Spain than in France where spending retirement wintering there and returning to the UK in summer, is firmly established, but there has been a rising interest in France mostly for rural properties of character.
- The best deals are likely to be obtained by negotiating with the owner direct and to do this you will probably have to trawl the small adverts on expat websites and in French property magazines. However, if a rental property is not being managed by an agency it may not be fitted up to the highest standards. You would have to be as thorough as possible in finding out exactly what you were getting. The owners will probably want to meet and interview you. The rental agreement will be a French one governed by French

law the same as for renting from a French landlord. The cost of drawing up the contract is usually split between the tenant and the landlord.

Companies that Offer Long-Term Rentals in France

Cottages4you: ☎08701-57160; www.cottages4you.co.uk. All over France. Up to 3 months. 10% disount.

French Locations: ☎01275–856691; www.french-locations.co.uk. Long-term rental specialists for France.

Serendipity Rentals: ☎029-2044 3844; www.serendipityrentals.com. Dordogne, Lot, Gironde, Haute Provence. Up to a year. Discount depends on owner.

French Property Magazines

French Property News: ☎020 8543 3113; www.french-property-news.com. Monthly

Living France: ☎01242-216087; www.livingfrance.com. Monthly.

French News: ☎05 53 06 84 40; www.French-news.com. Monthly newspaper for residents of France.

The Mostly Lows of Timeshare

○ Timeshare has as bad a reputation in France as anywhere else but owing to strict laws governing its sale there is less timeshare property available in France than in Spain or Portugal.

○ The principal behind timeshare is that you buy a share in a timeshare company, which gives you a lifetime's use of the property for a fixed number of weeks per annum. The catch is that you never own a brick of it; it is merely a rental right, which other people who have bought into the company also have; so it is in fact a multi-rented property. As there are other people using the property throughout the year, it will never feel yours.

○ Under the French system, you are buying shares in a timeshare company. You can sell these shares on if you wish (which may or may not be at a loss); or you can leave the timeshare to your heirs. You can rent out the property for the weeks that you have bought which could make you a profit over time.

○ If the timeshare company goes bust, you lose not only your right to the property, but you may also be liable for a part of the timeshare company's debts.

○ In addition to the usually very poor investment potential that a timeshare offers, there will be costs involved with the day-to-day running of the property which will be passed on to you as management fees; probably in the region of £200-£300 per year.

Main Points of Home Exchanges

○ Although one of the oldest home exchange organisations, Homelink was established over 50 years ago, the internet has opened up the possibilities for home exchanges (also called home swaps) enormously with instant communication, virtual tours and thousands of homes worldwide offered for holiday and longer-term slots.

○ Most home exchange organisations charge an annual fee for posting your details and a photograph of your home and for use of their database. Fees vary but start at £29 per annum.

○ Differences in style of housekeeping can make or break a home-swap, so it is best to swap with someone who shares a similar lifestyle or who is at a similar stage of life to you. It is also essential to get to know your exchange partner via email, telephone and if possible a meeting, before agreeing to the exchange. Also ask for references (business and personal).

○ If you decide to buy a holiday home in France, you can then exchange yours with other holiday homes in France and spend your retirement in France visiting other parts of it on a no cost basis.

○ Most (but not all) home exchanges come with a car, which is essential if you are planning to explore or even look for a property to buy.

Home Exchange Organisations	
www.homelink.org.uk	Established 1953. 13,500 members worldwide. Publishes 700+ page directory twice a year. US and UK offices.
www.gti-home-exchange.com	home exchange vacations worldwide. Multi-lingual website.

www.homeexchange.com	8,000 listings in 85 countries.
www.seniorhomeexchange.com	The only home exchange exclusively for over 50s
www.swaphouse.org	5000 members worldwide. £34 year's subscription.

A TRIAL PERIOD

There will always be people who decide on the spur of the moment after a two-week holiday to retire to France, but the majority of us are better off treating this as a project and approaching it in a methodical way. One possibility is to have a trial period, so that all the disadvantages and advantages can be weighed up having been experienced at first hand. Or it can even be a way of easing yourself into retiring in France as the first step. A trial period can take the form of several 'reconnaissance trips' staying in different regions for more than the usual holiday length of one to three weeks. Ideally, you should plan to stay for several months continuously by renting either in one location or several different ones. It is also essential to spend part of a winter in the place where you intend retiring to as many areas undergo a complete change of character in the cold months; coasts may be desolate and deserted, and countryside, especially the Midi and the north liable to lengthy periods of bone numbing cold. You also need to see if you can survive with minimal French language skills, or better still you can use the reconnaissance period to brush up and improve your French so that you are ready to handle dealing with every day bureaucratic and financial matters in a foreign language. It also gives you the time to get to know the facilities and attractions of the region where you intend living. You can also use a trial period to meet the neighbours so that you have a network of contacts in place before you take the final plunge.

LEARNING FRENCH

It may be acceptable for tourists not to speak French when they are holidaying in France. Anyone intending to live there for all or part of the year should, as a matter of courtesy as much as practicality, make an effort to learn French. Bob Culshaw thinks it is essential because

'Not learning the language is one of the biggest causes for sell-ups and failures, as it leaves you isolated.'

The French have a reputation for being quite censorious if you mangle their language out loud, but you should absolutely not be put off by exhibitions of francophone pedantry. Perseverance will be rewarded by patient correcting, advice and being told that you speak French with a charming accent. There are other advantages as Bob Culshaw, who started learning French at the age of 61, explains:

One of the biggest advantages of understanding French is the way that it opens up the whole culture to you, and that is immensely stimulating. My wife had 'O' level French, and I not even that; we arrived with a pile of phrase books and dictionaries. We tried to find classes locally but were put off by the teachers changing every week. In the end we found a Dutch woman teacher who gives one-to-one lessons. We can understand the radio quite well now, but find the gabbling delivery of television presenters too fast.

More French people now speak English than used to be the case. English is the first foreign language choice in French state schools and not just in schools; a large number of the French police now have a basic grasp of English, and French people generally are more aware of the need to speak English and are more interested in learning English than formerly, particularly if it gives them a business advantage.

There is no excuse for not learning French however old you are and however rusty your school French might be. Many municipalities, particularly any with a large number of foreigners run free French courses. Junette Earnshaw, who retired to Bergerac where her daughter had already been living for 20 years took up French in her seventies.

When I arrived in Bergerac I had only very rusty school French. I am learning it now though. I go to classes in Bergerac that a friend told me about. There are French people there who want to learn English and we speak in French for half the class and English for the other half.

Top Tips for Learning French

o **French Lessons by Phone.** Not as naughty as it sounds, this is surprisingly popular; but then you don't pay petrol costs and you can arrange lessons to suit. Many native French teachers are willing to do this. You have to concentrate because there are no visual clues, but this is probably an advantage in speeding up the learning process. 25 minutes is the maximum as it is quite intense. Usually followed up with homework and e-mail as arranged with your teacher. Can be started before you leave the UK and continued once in France. Especially practical if you have a free internet telephone service (see *Communications* section).

o **Watch French Television and Films.** You won't understand at first because media stars gabble like mad or have character accents, but you will pick up French more quickly if you keep at it. As well as watching French movies try classic British and American series like *Columbo* and *The Avengers* dubbed into French on the French television channels, which can be an amusing way of absorbing yet more French.

o *Accueil des Villes Françaises.* Hundreds of these exist across France for helping newcomers settle in. Useful source of info on French courses and many other things local (more info on functions of AVFs under *Where to Get Information* in the *Quality of Life* chapter).

o *Les Petites Annonces.* Once in France (or before you go) there is nothing to be lost by posting a small advert in the local newspaper asking for French tuition or a French/English tuition exchange. You can also put up a *petite annonce* in a local college, shop or community centre in your new place of residence in France.

o *SELs.* Across France there are community websites (*Systèmes d'Echanges Locals*) set up to swap services locally. You can advertise English lessons for French lessons on them.

o **Read Children's Books in French.** A good example is the classic *Le Petit Prince.* The books of the comic character *Asterix,* and even Agatha Christie translated in French are also useful as they are entertaining easy reads, and will help you with your written French. The local bookshop or library is a useful source of such material. Publishers of children's books include *Folio Junior, Pocket Jeunesse* and *Le Livre de Poche Jeunesse.*

Self-Study and UK French Classes

BBC Online Courses: www.bbc.co.uk/languages. Lots of online courses at different levels plus online practice and details of course books, videos and more.

Grant & Cutler: ☎020-7734 2012; www.grantandcutler.com. Famous London language bookseller. Stocks every French Course imaginable. Catalogue available online.

Alliance Française: www.alliancefr.org. Worldwide organisation promoting French language and culture. Courses all over the UK.

RESIDENCE REGULATIONS

The good news about residence regulations is that since 2003 a residence permit has not been a statutory requirement for EU nationals staying longer than three months in France. Pre-2003 pioneers of living and retiring in France, who had no choice but to obtain one of these documents can tell you that it represents an huge amount of time in assembling and certifying the dossier of documents necessary to qualify for a *carte de séjour*.

However, you can still apply for a *carte de séjour* voluntarily for the very good reason that it acts as a useful personal ID and is still recognised in some parts of the country for various official documentation and services. However, no official can insist (at least with legal justification) that you must have one.

If you decide to apply voluntarily for a residence permit you will need a minimum of eight personal documents and you have to know the full names, dates and places of birth of your parents and grandparents, as you do for most official documents in France. If you do not know these details (and most of us don't) you can obtain them from the Public Record Office in London.

Obtaining Copies of Birth, Marriage and Death Certificates

You can order these from the Public Record Office in London (☎0845 603 7788; www.familyrecords.gov.uk). You can visit in person or you can order certificates online.

Main Documents Required for a Carte de Séjour

○ Passport, with copies of the main pages, stamped '*copie certifiée conforme*' by the prefecture or town hall.

○ Four passport photographs (of each member of your family).

○ Birth certificate (with an official translation if requested), notarised by a French Consulate or French lawyer.

○ Marriage certificate/divorce papers/custody papers (officially translated and notarised only if requested).

○ Certificate from the town hall stating that you are living in *concubinage notoire* if you live with a common-law partner.

○ Proof of residence: *certificat* from the notary who handled your house purchase, or rent receipts, or *attestation d'hebergement* from the person you are staying with.

○ Proof of entry. Your travel ticket may be sufficient; or ask the immigration police when you enter the country.

○ Proof of financial resources.

○ You may be asked for proof that you have no criminal record.

○ You may be asked for a medical certificate though this is usually for non-EU citizens.

Main Points – Carte de Séjour

○ Not a legal requirement since 2003, but useful as ID for many official procedures to do with daily life in France.

○ Applications for a residence permit have to be accompanied by at least eight personal documents but it is no longer necessary to make official translations of them in advance.

○ If you decide not to have a *carte de séjour* you will also not have to prove that you have financial resources to support your retirement in France. If you voluntarily apply for this document, you will need to show proof of income. The minimum acceptable for a couple is about £800 per month (but realistically £1,100 is the minimum you should budget to live on).

○ Applications, as well the forms for application, are handled by the *préfecture de police* (police station) or *mairie* (town hall.

○ The time between application and receipt of a carte de séjour can vary from a few weeks to several months.

o The ritual and the documents required for a carte de séjour vary greatly from office to office and region to region and some regions may not even offer them any more.

British Embassy & Consulates in France

Embassy Paris(consular services) ☎01 44 51 31 00

Consulate Bordeaux   ☎05 57 22 21 10;

                                    postmaster.bordeaux@fco.gov.uk

Consulate Lille   ☎03 20 12 82 72; consular.lille@fco.gov.uk

Consulate Lyon   ☎04 72 77 81 70

Consulate Marseille   ☎04 91 15 72 10;

                                    marseilleconsular@marseille.fco.gov.uk

French Consulates in the UK

Consulate London   ☎020 7073 1200;

                                    www.consulfrance-londres.org

Consulate Edinburgh   ☎0131-220 6324;

                                    www.consulfrance.edimbourg.org

---

GETTING THERE AND AWAY

Flying

Over the last few years many new air services between the UK and France have sprung up and it is possible to fly from the UK direct to most large French cities. Stansted-based Ryanair flies to the most French places (18 cities in France) and has permanently low fares mostly around £29 (one way) Flybe flies to nine French cities from a range of UK airports and has similar fares to Ryanair. Several other low cost airlines fly to France including easyJet and BMI, but they only go to a few destinations; for instance Thomsonfly go to just Lyon and Nice. As you might expect, the national carrier Air France goes to the most destinations (38), but has the priciest fares starting from £83 return London-Paris. Additional choice is provided by special offers from scheduled airlines including BA, which has met the challenge of Ryanair with its own no frills prices starting at £69 (return). For cheapest fares to a destination in France you can do a comparison on a website such as www.opodo.com. A dedicated website that compares prices for flights only is www.skyscanner.net.

Budget Airlines Flying to France

British Airways: ☎0870 850 9850; www.ba.com. Fares from £69 return.

British Midland: ☎0870 264 2229; bmibaby.com. Nice and Paris from East Midlands Airport. Tiny fares.

easyJet: www.easyjet.com. Paris, Lyon and Nice from several UK airports.

Flybe: ☎0871 700 0535; www.flybe.com. Nine French cities from several UK regional airports.

Jet2: ☎0871 226 1737; www.jet2.com. Flies to Chambéry, Nice and Paris from Manchester and Leeds Bradford airports. One way fares from £21.

Ryan Air: ☎0870 156 9569; www.ryanair.com. Flies to 18 cities in France. Very low fares.

Thomsonfly: ☎0800 107 1517; www.thomsonfly.com. UK regional airports to Lyon and Paris. From £23 (one way).

Rail

Getting to and from France via the Channel Tunnel from the UK involves taking the Eurostar from London Waterloo Station (unless you are taking your car on Eurotunnel/Le Shuttle from Folkestone). There are 13 trains a day from London to Paris Gare du Nord and passengers have to travel via the metro to Gare du Lyon or Montparnasse to connect with the TGV (high speed trains) to other parts of France.

Train Services

Eurostar: ☎08705 186 186; www.eurostar.co.uk. Passenger only service. London Waterloo to Gare du Nord Paris.

Eurotunnel: ☎08705 353 535; www.eurotunnel.com. For passengers with vehicles. From Folkestone. Journey time is 35 minutes.

Rail Europe: ☎08705 848 848; www.raileurope.co.uk. Booking subsidiary of French Railways based at Waterloo Station.

SNCF: www.sncf.fr. French railways booking site.

Seat61: www.seat61.com/France.htm. Excellent website that tells you all you need to know about getting to France by train and has lots of useful links.

Sea Crossings

Getting to and from France by sea is an age-old method much challenged by the new cheap airfares and fast trains to France. The ferry companies have responded by increasing their fleets and in many cases revamping ferries to provide passengers with swish, on board facilities. The longest crossings are the overnight ones from Portsmouth to the Breton Ports and the fastest are the seacats (high speed catamarans) out of Dover that can cross the narrowest part of the Channel in 45 minutes. Ferry fares can seem pricey when compared to cheap airfares though Norfolk Line has a £19 overnight car and passenger fare. Brittany Ferries operates a third off discount fare scheme for owners of property in France. You can compare ferry prices on www.ferrycheap.com.

Ferry Services

Brittany Ferries: ☎08703-66533; www.Brittany-ferries.com. Portsmouth to St.Malo/Caen/Cherbourg. Poole to Cherbourg; Plymouth to Cherbourg/ Roscoff.

Condor Ferries: ☎0845 345 2000; www.condorferries.co.uk.Pool/ Weymouth to St Malo via Channel Islands May to September only.

Hoverspeed: ☎0870 240 8070; www.hoverspeed.com. Dover to Calais; Newhaven to Dieppe. High-speed SeaCat only operates Apr-Sept. Normal ferry service in winter.

Norfolkline: ☎0870 870 1020; www.norfolkline.com. Dover to Dunkerque.

P&O Ferries: ☎08705 711 711; www.poferries.com. Dover to Calais; Portsmouth to Le Havre.

Sea France: www.seafrance.com. Dover to Calais.

By Road

Getting to and from France is done via the Tunnel or car ferry route most appropriate for your destination. You will arrive by road at least once as you will probably bring a load of belongings from the UK to your new home. You can find out all you need to know about French *autoroutes* at www.franceautoroutes.com. Some residents prefer the driving route to and from the UK, especially if their relatives live at a

UK ferry port. Anne Scanlon who is widowed and lives in the hamlet of Faux in the Dordogne is one such:

I drive to Roscoff (it takes about 8 hours direct from here) to get the ferry to Plymouth, where my son lives. I love driving because I am completely free to stop when I want to. I often take longer on the way back, sometimes days, making detours and visiting interesting sounding places.

Route planning is especially easy if you have internet access as there are websites which can supply you with route details starting from your own street in the UK all the way to your French destination. Some also provide town plans and estimate the time and the cost of your journey.

Route Planner Websites	
www.mappy.fr	www.theaa.com
www.viamichelin.co.uk	www.rac.co.uk

PREPARATIONS FOR DEPARTURE

Making a permanent move to France requires preparations which will normally entail weeks, or months as you contemplate every aspect of daily life and decide what has to be cancelled in the UK and what has to be transferred to France and how it should be done. For such an arduous undertaking checklists are virtually essential in order to bring a degree of organisation into the process. How your checklists pan out depends on your personal requirements. The items below are the essential ones.

Banking

At some stage it will be appropriate and necessary to open a bank account in France but not necessarily before you go. Estate agents usually advise you to open an account when you are looking for a property to buy so that the financial part of the process can take place quickly and smoothly. The drawback is that it is best to know where you will be living first, so that you can deal with a local branch. If you are spending a trial period in France, you can withdraw money from your UK bank account with a cashpoint card with the Visa or Cirrus symbol but there is a charge and you may not get a good exchange rate. You will need to know your PIN number or you may not be able to use your card.

For details of banking in France including Post Office banking services see the banking section in the chapter *Settling Into Your New Life*.

Arranging to Have Your Pension Paid in France

You should arrange for your occupational and state pension payments to be paid into your bank account in France. To do this you need to contact the pensions service in the UK (www.thepensionservice.gov. uk; ☎0845 60 60 60) and search/ask for details of Overseas Direct Payment in local currency. For occupational pensions contact your provider. For more details see *Pensions and Exportable UK Benefits* in the *Personal Finance* chapter.

Medical Matters

The medical system in France is slightly different to the UK in that there you own your own medical records and X-rays. In the UK access is limited and you are not usually allowed to have all the records to take with you to France. However access to these records by a medical practitioner in France can be arranged. Once you have a doctor in France you can contact your UK doctor/medical practice and ask for your records to be sent to your new doctor in France. The same applies to dental records. You may be asked to pay for this.

Medical records in France are in the process of being computerised so the system for sending medical records around the EU may be simplified in future. For more information about French healthcare and entering into the French health system, see the chapter *Healthcare*.

You should also ensure that you know what the French equivalents are of any regular prescriptions that you are taking. Ask your doctor for advice before you depart.

Main Points – Medical Matters

○ If you are on a reconnaissance trip to France, which lasts for less than three months, or you have just moved to France you should take an EHIC (European Health Insurance Card) with you. Application Forms (ask for a T6 leaflet) are available at UK post offices. The EHIC entitles you to 90% of the costs of emergency treatment. It is advisable to take out health insurance to cover the remaining 10% of costs as these could be considerable. The EHIC runs out after three months by which time you should have entered the French health system.

○ It could be financially disastrous if you fall ill in France before you are integrated into the French health system if you do not have an EHIC.

○ If you forget to apply for an EHIC before departure, the Department of Work and Pensions will send it to you, or you can download the forms from their website www.dh.gov.uk.

○ If you are retiring to France and are entitled to UK state benefits (pension, invalidity, bereavement) ask for form E121 from the UK Department for Work and Pensions before you leave so that you can register with French social security and receive the same benefits as the French in France.

○ If you retire early from the UK to France and have paid Class 1 or 2 NI contributions up to the time you leave (or at least up until some months before you leave), then you will be entitled to benefit from the same entitlements as a French resident for an extended period (the length of time is not entirely clear). If there is too long a gap between the time you stopped paying NI contributions and your application for E106, then you will be turned down. This type of E106 is obtainable from the Medical Benefits Section of the DWP and you should do this before you go.

DWP and Private Health Insurers

Department for Work & Pensions: The Pension Service, International Pension Centre, Medical Benefits Section, Tyneview Park, Whitely Road, Newcastle-uponTyne NE98 1BA; ☎0191 218 7547; www.dh.gov.uk.

Agence Eaton: ☎ 02 97 40 80 20; www.French-insurance.com.

Expacare: ☎01344 381663; www.expacare.net.

Mail Forwarding

You may need to have snail mail forwarded to you in France. If you are keeping your UK home and therefore address, this is likely to generate more post than if you have sold up your UK assets and quit the UK entirely. If you have a trusted neighbour, or your tenants are friends you can ask them to check your post, throw away obvious junk and read-dress any important looking mail to you in France. If you have no UK address you should arrange to have your post redirected by The Royal Mail via airmail. You can arrange this at any post office. The time limit for redirecting mail is two years and it costs £60 per surname, per year. Special Delivery and signed for mail cannot be forwarded. A more flexible service can be provided by having an Accommodation Address. Your mail is forwarded to a commercial address provider and you can customise the service to your requirements. Obviously, this is going to work out far more expensive than Royal Mail. There are dozens of accommodation address mail forwarders and you can find them via an internet search.

Pets

All cats and dogs entering France must first be micro-chipped and then vaccinated against rabies, (which periodically makes an appearance in France, usually arising from illegally imported animals). The vaccination has to be given at least 21 days and not more than 12 months before leaving the UK. Your vet will give you an EU pet record book which you must have with you when you enter France. The French authorities do not require cats and dogs to be treated for ticks and tapeworm before they enter the country. This is however a requirement for pets entering the UK from France.

If you want to bring in pets other than cats and dogs, there are other rules. If you want to bring in a parrot or similar you will have to swear that you are not going to resell it in France and agree to a veterinary inspection. The local French consulate will advise you of formalities for other types of animals. The UK Department of Food Environment and Rural Affairs/DEFRA (www.defra.gov. uk) can provide forms for France. If you are thinking of exporting animals other than cats and dogs the PETS Helpline (☎0870 241 1710) will give you the section you need to call.

Removals

The cardinal rule for removals is to take as little as possible with you. This means having a massive turnout of your whole house from basement to attic or as appropriate. If you are renting initially in France then the same rule applies for storage. Removals will cost at the very least around £600 to northern France within easy distance of the Channel Ports.

Removals Checklist

○ Before moving you should make an inventory of all the possessions and household effects that you think you should take with you and then reassess it and pare it down (several times if necessary).

○ You should dispose of all items that you will never use again if you have not used them for years. You can give them to charity shops, local homeless shelters, sell them on E-bay, have a garage sale or participate in car boot sales, give them to your relatives or take them to the council tip as appropriate. If you are not selling your UK home then you can probably skip this step, though not if you are renting it out.

○ Furniture and other large items from your English home might not be suitable for your cottage on the Brittany coast or chalet in the Alps. Bear in mind that it is easy to buy cheap second-hand furniture in France.

○ UK electrical appliances should work in France with adaptors, but it may be difficult to get spare parts for them in France. On the other hand electrical equipment is generally more expensive in France.

○ If you want to be ultra cautious choose a removal company with an office in France as well as in the UK as they will be the safest bet if more expensive.

○ Decide what smaller items you want to transport yourself by car to France.

There are numerous removal firms: many of them advertise in French property magazines. Membership of the BAR/British Association of Removers (www.bar.co.uk) provides a guarantee that you are dealing with a reputable company that is not likely to go bust suddenly. This is an important point as you normally have to pay the company up front for the removal. BAR has set up International Movers Mutual Insurance so that any clients of any of its member companies will be compensated for loss or damage, or in the case of bankruptcy, the removal will be completed by another BAR member. A list of members can be obtained from the website or telephone 01923-699480.

Odds and Ends Checklist

- O Cancel any regular subscriptions to newspapers, magazines, book, wine etc clubs, or arrange to have them redirected if this is possible and appropriate.
- O Cancel gym or other UK club memberships.
- O Return library books.
- O Cancel any regular deliveries of groceries etc.
- O Cancel contracts with gas, electricity and telephone companies and settle accounts.
- O If you are renting out your UK home take meter readings for gas and electricity and settle bills before tenants move in and make an inventory of items left in the house to be attached to the tenancy agreement.

Part two

A New Home
in France

Where to Retire
Your New Home in France
Housing Finance

Where to Retire

CHAPTER SUMMARY

O It is important for potential visitors that you are within easy reach of an airport, port or TGV station. If you are more than one and a half hour's drive from any of these your visitor rate drops by 50%.

  O Unfortunately properties with good transport links are invariably pricier than those off the beaten track.

O Demand for property in the **Dordogne** is so great that even new town houses on estates are being bought by foreigners.

O **Puy-de-Dôme** and **Haute-Loire**, departments in the **Auvergne** were more or less ignored by retirees until recently. The French call this area the wilderness because of its long-term depopulation. Cheap land is the big attraction, but it gets very cold in winter.

O One of the biggest influxes of retirees in recent years has taken place in **Languedoc-Roussillon** where prices have been shooting up at the rate of 30% a year.

O **La Creuse** and **Haute Vienne** in the **Limousin** region are attracting increasing interest from foreign buyers as property there is the cheapest in France (at the moment).

O **Aveyron, Haute-Pyrénées,** the area southwest of Toulouse has great potential with plenty of properties in good condition. The climate is sunny and dry which makes it attractive to retirees and in the winter there is skiing in the Pyrenees.

O **Lower Normandy** is a good place for retirees who need an income because there is good potential for running gîtes.

O The **Vendée** in the **Pay de la Loire** is currently a very trendy and pleasant place to retire. It has a warm climate and the departmental capital La Roche-sur-Yonne is rated as one of France's best places to live.

CHOOSING THE RIGHT LOCATION

France is in many ways an ideal country to retire to as the climate is is near ideal in many areas and there is excellent health care provision throughout the country. There has been a long tradition of the rich and famous retiring to the 'South of France', meaning the Côte d'Azur, now out of reach for all but the very well off.

The area you choose to retire to requires some thought. Most of northern France is as wet and cold as England and not really suitable. If you are a sun worshipper, the greyness of the sky will soon pall. Normandy is muddy and foggy for much of the year. Brittany is subject to violent storms in the autumn and winter. The most obvious area to retire to is in the southwest, near the Pyrenees, where there is less rainfall and guaranteed sunshine for much of the year. Provence and the southeast are also attractive but subject to strong winds and violent storms. Anyone who suffers from arthritis or rheumatism will be better off in the drier parts of the south and anyone who wants to be physically near Britain will have to choose somewhere closer to the Channel ports. In the end though, your choice of location is likely to be a combination of what pleases you and what you can afford.

Easy Access is Crucial

'Location is everything', as Conrad Hilton, founder of the eponymous hotel chain, said. Nothing could be truer. The first thing to look at is where your potential property is in relation to airports and motorways. This becomes more and more vital as you get older. Being close to an airport or Channel port is a must: it is estimated that if you live more than an hour from an airport or port, 25% of your potential visitors won't come; if you are more than one and half hours away, the figure rises to 50%. The eastern Pyrenees, in particular the up-and-coming Ariège, is an ideal area in this respect, since there are cheap flights from London to Carcassonne, Perpignan and Toulouse. This is assuming that such cheap flights continue indefinitely.

Proximity to a TGV stop is also pertinent. Properties near TGV stations are worth considerably more than those which are not. There is always a rush to buy property once it becomes known that a new

TGV station is going to be built somewhere. A property on a main road is generally cheap to buy and very difficult to resell.

You also need to consider accessibility by car. Although driving along twisty mountain roads may be no problem when you're 50, by the time you're 80 it may become a daunting challenge.

Blots on the Landscape & Noise Pollution

The next point to consider is whether there are any nuclear power stations in your area. There are 20 locations in France with nuclear reactors, some of them in tourist areas. See the website http://nucleaire.edf.fr to make sure you are not near one. Another point is to check whether there are any small airfields nearby. Noise from neighbouring farmyards can also be hard to cope with for city-dwellers though you could become used to it in time. Wind farms are being built in many parts of France. Although they are not bad for your health they can ruin your view.

Friends and Neighbours

There is more than one kind of social deprivation and another major consideration is your social life after you have left the UK. Some are happy with the company of a small circle of other foreigners and will try to find a location where there are other English-speakers, but in most of France you will have to find friends among the locals. Is your French good enough to talk about more than the weather and the price of vegetables? Isolation and the lack of clubs and societies can spell trouble. It is essential that both partners can drive. You should also consider what happens to the partner left behind if one dies. Would the surviving partner have a social network of support locally, or would they be quite isolated.

Ideally, you need to spend several months renting a property in your chosen area to see how you like it out of season. French holiday spots by the coast can be desolate places to live out of season. Buses may not run, and services may be reduced. Many shops and restaurants close down for the winter; there are few people about, and the place could be dead for several months. As Julian Roberts, who retired in August 2004 and who spent several months travelling around before finding what he and his wife wanted puts it:

We wanted to find the best property for us; that usually takes time. Being retired means you can take all the time you need. We looked at places on the Mediterranean during the winter, and in the Charente where we rented basic accommodation, before deciding on the Dordogne.

Everyone who has successfully settled down in France has two pieces of advice: learn French as soon as possible, preferably before you leave home, and do spend some time renting in an area before you buy.

Getting Information on the Regions

To help you find out more about the region or regions you are considering for retirement you have the resources of the tourist industry at your disposal. Tourism is France's biggest money-earner – generating 12% of GDP – and every region has lavish brochures on offer to advertise its uniqueness. If you can, it is worth visiting the French Government Tourist Office in London (www.franceguide.com), where there are brochures for every part of France, otherwise you can order the information by e-mail (info.uk@franceguide.com).

Since the SNCF took it over from British Rail, Rail Europe has run from the same building as the French tourist office in London, so you can book a train ticket at the same time as looking at brochures. The main city in every region has a *Comité Régional du Tourisme* (CRT) who organise information facilities. *Départements* have a *Comité Départemental du Tourisme,* which may be more informative than the regional office. Towns and cities have their own *Office du Tourisme*; in smaller places the equivalent is the local *Syndicat d'Initiative*, which may have a small welcome office, but their opening hours are generally shorter than those of the Office du Tourisme, and their function is more to promote business in general in their area. The syndicats are still not all on the web. For more practical information about living in France, the best starting point is the French Embassy's website: www.ambafrance-uk.org. Each *département* has its own website: just search on *Conseil Général* + the name of the département. The regional websites are under *Conseil Régional*.

French Government Tourist Office

Maison de la France Great Britain: 178 Piccadilly, London W1V OA1; ☎0891-244 123; fax 020-7493 6594; e-mail info.uk@franceguide.com; www. franceguide.com or www.tourisme.fr or http://uk.franceguide.com.

THE REGIONS OF FRANCE

ALSACE

CRT: ☎03 88 52 28 28; www.tourisme-alsace.com; www.strasbourg.com.

Percentage of population: 2.88%; percentage of GDP: 2.88%.

Départements: Bas-Rhin (67),Haut-Rhin (68)

Alsace borders Germany in the northeast of France. The greatest appeal of Alsace lies in the Vosges mountains, good for skiing in winter and walking the rest of the year. Fishing and horse-riding are also popular. The region is 45% forest; the climate is fairly wet.

The main city, Strasbourg (pop. 388,000), houses the plenary sessions of the European Parliament, as well as being home to the Council of Europe. Both Strasbourg and Mulhouse have very high crime rates. There are flights from Strasbourg to London.

Property. The classic Alsace house has half-timbering (*fachwarik*) with a hipped and sometimes mansard roof. The massive German style with all the functional spaces under one roof is common. There is only a limited second homes market in Alsace; houses to renovate are few and far between. Property is expensive compared with most of France.

Location	Type	Description	Price
Ittenheim (67) nr Strasbourg	Fermette 85 sq.m.	3 bedrooms, spacious living room, kitchen, bathroom. 350sqm. land.	€199,000
Strasbourg (67)	Apartment	2 room 37 sq.m. apartment in *copropriété*.	€94,000
Mulhouse (68)	Villa 350 sq.m	5 bedrooms, 2 bathrooms, swimming pool, sports room, garage, cellar. 30 km from Basel, Switzerland.	€950,000

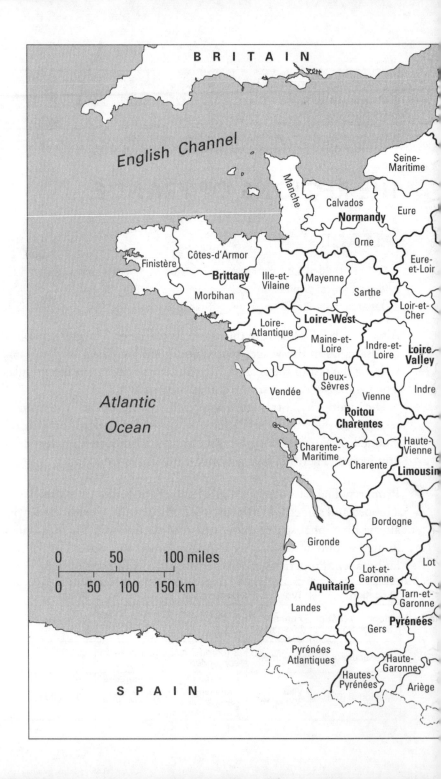

BRITAIN

English Channel

Seine-Maritime

Manche

Calvados

Normandy

Eure

Orne

Finistère

Côtes-d'Armor

Brittany

Ille-et-Vilaine

Mayenne

Eure-et-Loir

Morbihan

Sarthe

Loir-et-Cher

Loire-Atlantique

Loire-West

Maine-et-Loire

Indre-et-Loire

Loire Valley

Vendée

Deux-Sèvres

Vienne

Indre

Atlantic

Ocean

Poitou Charentes

Charente-Maritime

Charente

Haute-Vienne

Limousin

Dordogne

Gironde

Lot

0   50   100 miles

0   50   100   150 km

Lot-et-Garonne

Aquitaine

Tarn-et-Garonne

Pyrénées

Landes

Gers

Pyrénées Atlantiques

Haute-Garonne

Hautes-Pyrénées

Ariège

SPAIN

Regions and Departments of France

Nord-Pas-de-Calais
Pas-de-Calais
Nord
BELGIUM
GERMANY
Somme
LUXEMBOURG
Picardy
Ardennes
Aisne
Oise
Paris
Meuse
Moselle
Seine-et-Marne
Marne
Lorraine
Alsace
Région parisienne
Meurthe-et-Moselle
Bas-Rhin
Paris et Région
Champagne-Ardenne
Aube
Haute-Marne
Vosges
Haut-Rhin
Loiret
Yonne
Haute-Saône
Cher
Côte-d'Or
Franche Comté
Belfort
Burgundy
Nièvre
Doubs
SWITZERLAND
Saône-et-Loire
Jura
Allier
Creuse
Ain
Haute-Savoie
Puy-de-Dôme
Loire
Rhône
Auvergne
Savoie & Dauphiné
Savoie
Corrèze
Cantal
Haute Loire
Rhône
Isère
ITALY
Ardèche
Drôme
Hautes-Alpes
Lozère
Aveyron
Alpes-de-Haute-Provence
Alpes Maritimes
Gard
Vaucluse
Côte d'Azur
Tarn
Languedoc
Provence
Bouches-du-Rhône
Var
Haute-Corse
Hérault
Aude
Corse-du-Sud
Pyrénées-Orientales
Mediterranean Sea

AQUITAINE

CRT: ☎ 05 56 01 70 00; www.crt.cr-aquitaine.fr; www.bordeaux-tourisme.com.
Percentage of population: 4.85%; percentage of GDP: 4.24%.
Départements: Pyrénées-Atlantiques (64), Landes (40), Gironde (33), Lot-et-Garonne (47), and Dordogne (24).
Regional Capital: Bordeaux (pop.700,000).

The Aquitaine region is a large area of southwestern France, stretching from the borders of the Massif Central down to the Spanish border and the Pyrenees. Bordeaux is the prefectural town of the Gironde (www.tourisme-gironde.cg33.fr).

Bordeaux has been rated second for economic dynamism and quality of life after Toulouse in a survey conducted by *Express* magazine amongst managers. A new tramway linking city and suburbs is helping the property market. The rebuilding of the waterside, *Les Quais de la Garonne*, to be completed in 2008, and the extension of the TGV from Tours (perhaps not until 2016) and then on to Spain, will certainly cause property prices to rise.

Pyrénées-Atlantiques incorporates the French Basque country bordering on Spain. Sprayed graffiti in Basque, or defaced road signs are the norm. Biarritz, close to Spain, is a popular and expensive resort for surfers. The prefectural town of Pyrénées-Atlantiques is Pau. The main attraction is the mountainous scenery, excellent for walking and camping.

The Landes (www.tourismelandes.com) is a flat, rather empty region of forests and sandy soil and the longest and straightest beach in Europe, the Côte d'Argent, stretching from the Gironde estuary down to Biarritz.

The Dordogne and Lot-et-Garonne are two *départements* strongly associated with homes for Anglos. The presence of foreigners looking for retirement and second homes has pushed prices up. The main Bordeaux-Toulouse railway and motorway bisect the Lot-et-Garonne département.

Dordogne

The Dordogne (www.dordogne-perigord-tourisme.fr) is known as Périgord to the French; foreigners tend to use the word Dordogne for a wider adjoining area. Certain areas of the Dordogne are being taken over by foreigners, the heaviest concentration being around Ribérac, Sarlat to the southeast and Eymet in the southwest In the village of Bouteilles-St-Sébastien, outside Verteillac in Périgord Vert, 60% of the houses are owned by foreigners, but 90% of these are rented out to holidaymakers and remain shuttered in winter. In the wake of this invasion, some Britons have bought bars and hotels, or started art galleries or antique shops. The Périgourdins are naturally friendly and sociable, and this has certainly been a factor in drawing foreigners here. Even those who tried to avoid the Dordogne may find themselves 'drawn inexorably' into it as retired financial services executive, Julian Roberts did:

Initially my wife and I wanted to avoid the Dordogne. We looked at places on the Mediterranean, but it was too expensive. We also checked out the Charente, and liked bits of it, but it was still not quite what we wanted. By this time, we found that we were approaching the edge of the Dordogne almost by default. We saw our future house advertised in an estate agent's in Angoulême, and here we are, living in a hamlet between Riberac and Bergerac, the Chiantishire of France.

Property. The demand for property in the Dordogne is so great, that even new houses on estates in the towns (*lotissements*) are being bought by foreigners. Newer holiday homes reflect the prevalent liking for the Provençal style of ochre rendering and Spanish tiles. Because of the price inflation in Dordogne, foreigners are prepared to consider doing up any building that is still standing up, and the locals are quite happy to try to offload a collapsing barn (*grange*) for an apparently paltry sum on an unsuspecting foreigner.

Location	Type	Description	Price
Perigord (24)	Perigourdine farmhouse 200 sq.m.	3 bedrooms, 210 sq.m. of outhouses, 5 ha. Land	€365,000
Bordeaux (33)	19th century apartment 91 sq.m.	2 bedrooms, interior patio, cellar.	€225,000
St Caprais de Lerm (Agen) (47)	Stone house with gîte business	3 bedrooms. Separate gîtes for 2 with solar energy, barn.	€387,500
Urcuray (64)	Basque-style house 140 sq.m.	4 bedrooms, 2 bathrooms, terrace. 1500 sq.m. grounds.	€350,000

AUVERGNE

CRT: ☎04 73 98 65 00; www.auvergne-tourisme.info.
Percentage of population: 2.18%; percentage of GDP: 1.77%.
Départements: Allier (03), Cantal (15), Haute Loire (43) and Puy-de-Dôme (63).

The Auvergne is in the Massif Central, a thinly-populated region, much of it above 3000 feet. The typical landscape features are the dome-shaped extinct volcanoes (*puys*). As young people desert central France for the cities, the countryside becomes more and more a preserve of the elderly. On the other hand, Auvergne is traditional and more genuinely French than much of the country. Clermont-Ferrand is the regional capital.

The departmental capital of the Ardèche département, is Aurillac. The capital of the Allier département is Moulins. The main attractions

Up and Coming Region: Puy-de-Dôme and Haute-Loire

The Puy-de-Dôme and Haute-Loire are two départements that were more or less ignored by second home-buyers until recently. The French call this *le désert* (the wilderness) – as long-term depopulation has caused havoc here. Their cheapness is one reason why more British people are looking at this area as a place to live and even for a holiday home. Direct flights from London to Clermont-Ferrand and Saint-Etienne have made the area reasonably accessible. The main attraction is the plentiful and cheap land. On the plus side there is peace and quiet and not too many expats in your vicinity. The rather dour locals and cold winters are the downside.

Areas that are hot with Britons now are around Ambert, such as the Livradois and Craponne-sur-Arzonne. About 50km south of Clermont-Ferrand, check out the Brioude region; Vieille-Brioude is spectacularly located in a gorge and the modern town of Brioude has good facilities and is close to the E11 motorway to Montpellier. The altitude of your is a major consideration; above 3000 feet (900 metres) and you are looking at an extra month of winter. Prices are rising fast, as local people realise that they can sell renovated properties to the British which no one would have looked at a few years ago. It is essential to haggle; you can reasonably try to get the price down by 15%. Expect to pay from €100,000 for a substantial farmhouse with several acres of land.

of the Auvergne for property buyers are cheapness and space, the main drawbacks remoteness and poor public transport. Railway lines have been replaced by buses in many areas. There are direct flights from London to Clermont-Ferrand and St Étienne, some way to the east.

Location	Type	Description	Price
St Pourçain (03)	14th century tower	3 floors, terrace, garage, orchard. Potential to expand.	€55,000
Le Claux (15)	Modern basalt house	3 bedrooms, garage, cellar, 800 sq.m. garden. View of extinct volcano.	€160,000
Langeac (43)	House 110 sq.m.	3 bedrooms, central heatng. 750 sq.m. garden.	€145,000
Brioude (43)	Villa 230 sq.m.	5 bedrooms, 3 bathrooms, garage for 3 cars.	€320,000
St Anthème (63)	Stone house 200 sq.m.	In need of renovation. At 1000 metres.	€28,003

BRITTANY (BRETAGNE)

CRT: 1 rue Raoul Ponchon, 35069 Rennes; ☎02 99 36 15 15; fax 02 99 28 44 40; e-mail tourism-crtb@tourismebretagne.com; www.tourismebretagne.com; www.tourisme-rennes.com.
Percentage of population: 4.85%; percentage of GDP: 3.92%.
Départements: Finistère (29), Côtes-d'Armor (22), Ille-et-Vilaine (35), and Morbihan (35).

Bretons usually refer to Haute and Basse Bretagne (Upper and Lower Brittany); the dividing line runs between St Brieuc in the north and Le Croisic on the south coast. Ille-et-Vilaine is often called 'Haute-Bretagne'. The most popular tourist spots are along the north coast of Ille-et-Vilaine and Côtes-d'Armor, which has a ferry port at Roscoff with services to Plymouth and Cork. The main town of Ille-et-Vilaine (www.bretagne35.com), and its regional centre is Rennes, which is considered a good retirement spot because of its high quality of life. The TGV will be extended from Le Mans to Rennes by 2013, and bring Brittany much closer to Paris. The département of the Côtes-d'Armor (www.cotesdarmor.com) was until quite recently known as the Côtes-du-Nord.

To the west is Finistère (www.finisteretourisme.com). The properties are some of the cheapest in France. Brest has direct flights to London Stansted. Inland Finistère has the highest rainfall in France: over 50 inches a year. The area is subject to severe storms in winter.

Along the south coast is the département of Morbihan (www. morbihan.com). The port of Lorient holds the annual Inter-Celtic Festival. The prefectural town is Vannes, which is rated as one of the best places to live in France.

Property. Brittany is one of the most attractive areas of France, and some 20% of properties are second homes. The main drawback is the wet climate in much of the area, especially in winter. Closer to Poitou-Charentes around Vannes the climate is drier and sunnier and a very active second homes market. The cheapest properties are in Finistère and Côtes-d'Armor. Reckon on a minimum of €70,000 for a 2-bed house. There is some hostility in Brittany towards so many outsiders buying properties and forcing up prices.

Location	Type	Description	Price
Plourhan (22)	House 90 sq.m.	2 bedrooms, next to golf course, 10 mins from the sea, large garden.	€124,000
St Brieuc (22)	Breton *longère* 140 sq.m.	3 bedrooms, gas central heating, Jacuzzi	€275,000
Dinard (35)	18th century stone town house 200 sq.m.	5 bedrooms, 2 bathrooms, close to sea. 200 sq.m. garden.	€550,000
Séné (56)	Villa	5 bedrooms, 2 bathrooms, 1ha. garden.	€440,000

BURGUNDY (BOURGOGNE)

CRT: ☎ 0380 280 280; www.burgundy-tourism.com; www.dijon-tourism.com.
Percentage of population: 2.7%; percentage of GDP: 2.34%.
Départements: Côte-d'Or (21), Saône-et-Loire (71), Nièvre (58), and Yonne (89).

Burgundy is one of the three main centres of French wine production; the other two are Bordeaux and Champagne.The regional capital is Dijon. The western part of Saône-et-Loire (www.cg71.com) is cattle country. Montceau-les-Mines was the centre of a coal-mining industry that has died out. Digoin, to the west, is the centre of pottery manufacture in France.

The underpopulated Morvan plateau region stretches over the northern half of the Saône-et-Loire and into the Nièvre next door. The emptiness attracts retirees who like to leave the rat race behind. The creation of the Parc Naturel du Morvan in 1970 (www. parcdumorvan.org) has given the area a better image. The main attractions are fishing, canoeing and rafting. There is a TGV stop at Le Creusot, about 20 km away; the regular train service from Paris is scenic, but slow.

The département of the Nièvre (www.cg58.fr), west of Saône-et-Loire, is sleepy and with few inhabitants. The prefectural town is Nevers.

The Yonne, north of Nièvre, is also quite thinly populated. The prefectural town is Auxerre.

Property. The areas closer to Paris of the Yonne and Nièvre now have a high proportion of second homes, and there are opportunities for renovating old farmhouses. Southern Burgundy does not present the same phenomenon of flight from the land, and cannot be characterised as poverty-stricken. There are not that many derelict properties to do up. House prices are cheapest in Morvan. Prices are determined by the closeness to Paris, and the TGV. Expect to pay from €70,000 for a 2-bed house in an isolated area.

Location	Type	Description	Price
Nuits St Georges (21)	Villa	4 bedrooms, oil central heating, 500 sq.m. wooded garden	€300,000
Chaulgnes (58)	House 105 sq.m.	2 bedrooms, 1800 sq.m. garden, good views, swimming pool.	€198,000
Menou (58)	Fermette 40 sq.m.	2 bedrooms, stable, barn, 2,400 sq.m. land.	€69,500
Louhans (71)	Renovated farmhouse	4 bedrooms, stable, barn, 4,750 sq.m. land.	€160,000

CENTRE (VAL-DE-FRANCE)

CRT: ☎02 38 24 05 05; www.visaloire.com; www.coeur-de-france.com.

Percentage of population: 4.2%; percentage of GDP: 3.5%.

Six Départements: Eure-et-Loir (28), Loir-et-Cher (41), Indre-et-Loire (37), Loiret (45), Indre (36), and Cher (18).

The Centre region includes the pre-revolutionary counties of Touraine, Berry and Orléanais. To the Anglo-Saxons this is 'the Loire Valley'. The main attractions are the châteaux and churches. The Loire has given its name to several départements, in several different regions; in the Centre you are never far from water, or marshlands. There is also the Loir river, which runs north of the Loire parallel to its bigger sister.

The prefectural capital of the Eure-et-Loir, Chartres, home to a UNESCO world heritage site cathedral. The Loire Valley châteaux are the other great tourist draw.

The regional capital, Orléans (population 245,000), is within commuting distance of Paris. The Sologne area south of Blois straddles the Loir-et-Cher and Loiret; consisting mostly of wetlands; it has little scope for house-buying but is very popular amongst the French hunting fraternity.

Further downriver, the city of Tours stands at the centre of the traditional county of Touraine (www.tourism-touraine.com), as well as being the prefectural town of the Indre-et-Loire.

Bourges, the capital of the Berry region, or Berrichonne, and prefectural town of the Cher, is another pleasant town with a UNESCO designated cathedral.

Property. There is an active market in second homes in the northern part of the Centre, particularly Eure-et-Loire, which is within easy reach of Paris. It only takes 45 minutes by train from Chartres to the Gare de Montparnasse. In spite of the competition from the Parigots, prices are not unreasonable. About 17% of properties are second homes. The relative flatness of the landscape is a factor in dissuading Anglos from buying here, but there are plenty of cultural festivals to make up for the indifferent scenery.

Location	Type	Description	Price
St Symphorien (18)	Fermette 70 sq.m.	2 bedrooms, bare beams, bread oven, needs renovation.	€45,000
Chartres (28)	Restored farmhouse 270 sq.m.	12 rooms, 3 toilets, soundproof music room, garages, workshops, well, 2410 sq.m.	€402,800
Blois (41)	Restored stone 240 sq.m.	5 bedrooms, 2 bathrooms, garage workshop.	€335,000
Neuville-aux-Bois (45)	Wooden villa	4 bedrooms, in a forest, 5 ha. garden, part-furnished.	€270,000

CHAMPAGNE-ARDENNE

CRT: ☎03 26 77 45 00; www.tourisme-champagne-ardenne.com; www.reims-tourisme.com.

Percentage of population: 2.23%; percentage of GDP: 2.02%.

Départements: Ardennes (08), Marne (51), Aube (10), and Haute-Marne (52).

The Ardennes borders on the Belgian provinces of Hainaut and Luxembourg. The prefectural town of Charleville-Mézières is the world centre for marionettes, and there is a large festival every three years devoted to them. The main attraction of the area is the fact that properties are cheap.

The regional departmental capital is Reims (pronounced 'Rengss') is also the capital of champagne, at least as far as tourism is concerned. The real centre of champagne-production is the town of Epernay, 26km to the south of Reims.

South of the Marne is the Aube, a region of undulating wheatfields that rises up to the Plateau de Langres on the border with Burgundy. Troyes, the traditional capital of the champagne region and prefectural city, is architecturally very rich. In most respects the Aube is a rather deserted region, and not much visited by tourists. One can get from Troyes to Paris in about 90 minutes.

Property. The Ardennes has been more or less ignored by foreign buyers; its main selling point is the cheapness of the properties and the accessibility from the Channel ports. Broken-down farmhouses can be picked up for next to nothing. Both Ardennes and Champagne are wet and humid areas, with a climate similar to southern England. There is never likely to be a great market for second homes here, but at least you won't be surrounded by English-speakers.

Location	Type	Description	Price
Charleville-Mézières (8)	Town house	4 bedrooms, 100 sq.m. terrace + two separate apartments for rental to tenants.	€350,000
Reims (51)	Terrace house 90 sq.m.	3 bedrooms, high class housing estate, shared swimming pool, tennis courts, 100 sq.m. garden.	€220,000
Boult-sur-Suippe (51)	Building land 1,400 sq.m.	All utilities already connected. Private access road.	€150,000
Laferte-sur-Aube (52)	Stone farmhouse 100 sq.m.	Sheds, stables, barn, on 1200 sq.m. land.	€82,000

CORSICA

Agence du Tourisme de la Corse: ☎ 04 95 51 00 00; www.visit-corsica.com.
Percentage of population: 0.43%; percentage of GDP: 0.34%.
Départements: Haute-Corse and Basse-Corse.

The island of Corsica (*La Corse*) has more associations with Italy than with France. The French bought the island from the Genoese in 1768. Napoleon Bonaparte, born in Ajaccio in 1769, made the island a lot more noticed.

A mere 180km long and a maximum of 80km wide, Corsica is sparsely populated and very mountainous, with deep gullies and tree-covered slopes. The interior is covered with *maquis* (a mix of wild flowers, herbs and dense scrub). Viewed from the sea the island looks like a mountain. The 600-mile long coastline has Europe's finest beaches, which bring in the seasonal tourist hordes to the western coast. The cost of living is considerably higher than in mainland France.

The usual access is by ferry from Nice, Toulon or Marseille. There are direct flights during the tourist season from London to Ajaccio and Bastia, on Air France and from London to Bastia on British Airways. Otherwise one has to change at Paris or Nice. There is also an airport at Calvi.

Property. Recently, more and more Italians have been buying holiday villas, and they are better accepted than the French. One can still pick up a small apartment by the sea from €110,000. Houses for renovation inland can be as little as €80,000. Building land with a sea view costs some €120-160 per square metre near towns; without a sea view the cost is €30-50 per sq.m.

Location	Type	Description	Price
Calvi (2B)	Duplex apartment 150 sq.m.	3 bedrooms; air-conditioning.	€470,000
Nessa, nr Calvi (2B)	Traditional house	4 storeys; 6 bedrooms.	€90,000
Porto Vecchio (2A)	Apartment	2nd floor apartment with 3 bedrooms in town centre.	€180,000
Vico (2A)	Traditional village house 300 sq.m.	6 bedrooms, swimming pool, 1,200 sq.m. land.	€660,000

FRANCHE-COMTÉ

CRT: ☎03 81 25 08 08; www.franche-comte.org.
Percentage of population: 1.86%; percentage of GDP: 1.57%.
Départements: Haute-Saône (70), Territoire de Belfort (90), Doubs (25) and the Jura (39).

The Franche-Comté region became part of France in 1678. The city of Belfort has changed hands many times. It was made a separate département in 1922, the Territoire de Belfort. It is 10 miles away from the Swiss border and there is a strong Swiss influence on the architecture.

Besançon (www.besancon.com), the regional capital, stands on the River Doubs. Besançon is also the departmental capital of the Doubs (www.doubs.org), named from the river that rises near the Swiss border and briefly enters Switzerland before turning back into France.

The Jura (www.jura-tourism.com) is in the pre-Alps. It has chalet-like houses with steep roofs and colourful window-boxes, landscape interspersed with meadows and pine forests and is similar to Switzerland.

Franche-Comté is remote from the UK; the region is also devoid of airports or TGVs. This could easily be a region to retire to if you don't mind being a bit cut off from the UK. There are very good recreational possibilities: many areas are close to ski stations and there is white-water rafting, fishing and walking.

Property. Timber-framed farmhouses are standard in the Belfort region and the Haute Saône. In the Jura there are stone-built vine-grower's houses with the storerooms on the groundfloor. In the Vosges area of the Saône red sandstone is used, with red sandstone roof slates. The higher Doubs has inclusive farm buildings, with lower storeys of stone with white rendering, and planks covering gable ends for insulation. Building land is cheap. Houses start from about €70,000.

Location	Type	Description	Price
Chenecey-Buillon (25)	Village house	3 bedrooms, 2 garages, 1,700 sq.m. mature garden.	€228,673
Chappelle Voland (39)	Bungalow 80 sq.m.	3 bedrooms, detached, village centre.	€85,000
Arsure Arsurette (39)	Renovated farmhouse 190 sq.m.	3 bedrooms, exposed beams and stonework (18th century). 1550 sq.m. garden. High elevation.	€190,000
Lure Luxeuil (70)	Renovated farmhouse 1,400 sq.m.	2 bedrooms, 10 ha. of land. Fine views.	€295,000

LANGUEDOC-ROUSSILLON

CRT: ☎04 67 22 81 00; www.cr-languedocroussillon.fr/tourisme; www.
sunfrance.com.

Percentage of population: 3.82%; percentage of GDP: 2.87%.

Départements: Lozère (48), Gard (30), Hérault (34), Aude (11), and Pyrénées-
Orientales (66).

Languedoc derives its name from *langue d'oc*, that is the Occitan language of the south, while Roussillon is another word for French Catalonia. Generally, the idea of Occitan identity is still very strong here, even though few people can speak the language.

Languedoc-Roussillon has a distinctly extreme climate, rain is adequate but it tends to be infrequent and falls mostly in October and November. The Gard is particularly prone to flash flooding. In September 2002, 27 people were killed and a large area between Nîmes and Alès was cut off from civilisation after several days of torrential downpours. Flooding is a real risk in the area and should be taken into account when buying property.

Pyrénées-Orientales. This département (www.cg66.fr), formerly known as Pyrénées d'Or, includes part of the grape-growing region of Corbières in the north, and the former Catalan county of Cerdagne in the west, around Fort-Romeu. The coast between the capital, Perpignan, and the Spanish border is known as the Côte Vermeille (Vermillion Coast). Generally, the coast has been over-developed.

Aude. Carcassonne, prefectural town of the Aude (www.audetourisme. com), is one of France's big tourist destinations thanks to its huge citadel that evokes the Middle Ages better than anywhere in Europe.

On the western end of the Aude is the Lauragais, a farming region that spreads out into the Tarn, Ariège and Haute-Garonne. North of Carcassonne is the area known as La Montagne Noire (Black Mountain), whose people suffered severely during the anti-Cathar crusades of the early 13th century. The national park of the Haut Languedoc extends over the southeast of the Tarn into the Hérault and Aveyron.

Hérault. Above the Aude is the département of Hérault (www.cdt-herault.fr). The surrounding country is known as *garrigue,* a stony landscape almost bare of trees, originally forest degraded by overgrazing and bushfires. The coastline of the Hérault, the Côte d'Améthyste, is equally arid. The prefectural capital, Montpellier, is one of France's most dynamic cities and is a top medical research centre. It is also the region's main city (it shares the title with Narbonne and Béziers) and focus of investment in new industries.

Gard. The neighbouring département of the Gard (www.cdt-gard.fr) is noted for its Roman ruins, and has only a short coastline. The Gard does, however, have a part of the Cévennes national park. The prefectural city is Nîmes. The Gard has always been popular with British property buyers, especially the pretty hilltop town of Uzès, northeast of Nîmes.

Lozère. North of the Gard, the Lozère (www.lozerefrance.com) includes most of the Cévennes national park and few people. The Cévennes is remote: two and a half hours driving from Nîmes airport. The northern Lozère is about 120 miles from St Étienne, which also has flights to London Stansted. Train and bus services are limited, but if you want to get away from it all this is the place to be.

Up and Coming Region: Pyrénées-Orientales

Pyrénées-Orientales is French Catalonia or Roussillon, rather than Languedoc. The typical older buildings are of Pyrenean granite. In the mountains one can find ski chalets. One can see the Catalan influence in the flat roofs and arched shutters. In the mountains there are even crude stepped gables, or *pignons à redents*. The hot and dry climate and Catalan culture have a lot of attractions for retirees. In summer one can go to take the waters at spas such as Amélie-les-Bains; in the winter there is skiing. There are direct flights from London to Perpignan; in other respects this is a remote area. The current property market is fairly flat, with not that many properties on the market, so one should not expect prices to rise. Expect to pay from €60,000 for a basic village house.

Property. Second homes make up 30% of the total housing stock in Languedoc-Roussillon. Of the five departments that make up the area the Hérault is seen by the French as the most desirable area to live in France, and it has had spectacular property price rises; currently 30% per year.

Kim and Gill Bethell run La Châtaignerie, a luxury bed and breakfast in Céret, located 900 metres up in Roussillon or French Catalonia. Their website is www.ceret.net.

I was looking to retire with my husband, and we found this place in a chestnut grove – which is why it's called La Châtaignerie – with superb views of Mont Canigou and over the plains of Roussillon to the sea from all the rooms. Subsequently two of my daughters decided to come and live here as well. The location is ideal; you can be on the Costa Brava, or go ski-ing in the Pyrenees, or go the French coast, all within an hour's drive. The nearest airport is in Spain at Girona, and Perpignan is also close by.

We set up a Société Civile Immobilière to own the house. A SCI exists to buy and run property, so if we sell the house the money has to be reinvested in a similar business. It was very complicated actually going through the process of buying it and setting up the company; I had to sign my name 34 times. When we set up the company we were not aware of the potential difficulties caused by French inheritance laws. My husband was in the process of switching the business from the UK to France when he passed away, and things became very complicated. I could not have the whole property, even if the rest of the family wanted me to, so now I have 50% and I can remain here as long as I want. I strongly recommend all women coming to France to go to a lawyer and sort out the best way to own the property to avoid the kind of problems that we have had to deal with.

The first owner built the place as a hotel, and then retired. When we acquired it in 1996 we intended to run it as a bed and breakfast, because it's too small to really be a hotel. We did a conversion job, and used the best local builder's co-operative with the best electrician, the best plumber, etc. I believe very strongly that one should use local craftsmen, and not import them from other countries. They did a superb job.

We are only allowed to extend the house by 20% even though we have 1 hectare of land around it. There is a lot of semi-abandoned agricultural land around here – the name Céret means cherries – and there are vineyards as well. In the spring you have all the cherry blossom, and almonds and peaches in bloom too. While the owners of the land may have died a long time ago, it

88   A NEW HOME IN FRANCE

is still impossible to build on it (for the moment at least). The rules are very strict. Since we only did internal work we didn't require a permis de construire anyway.

Mont Canigou is a magical mountain and is more or less sacred to the Catalans. The locals consider themselves Catalan, not French. We are in the middle of Catalan, French and Spanish culture. The area is very popular with northern Europeans. It is very evident how in the winter the people in the market place are quite short, and then when it gets warmer there are all these people who are 6 foot tall, Germans, Dutch, Norwegians, Americans and so on. This is a wonderful spot, with great walking, riding, swimming, skiing and much else to do. The donkey trail used by allied airmen to escape to Spain during World War II runs through our property. You couldn't find a better place to live.

Location	Type	Description	Price
Minervois (11)	Village house	5 bedrooms, 2 bathrooms, 2 kitchens, for *chambres d'hôtes*.	€220,000
Cabardès (11)	Village house	4 bedrooms, view to Pyrenees.	€130,000
Uzès (30)	Villa	140 sq.m. on 900 sq.m. garden; 3 bedrooms, 2 bathrooms, swimming pool. Near golf course.	€635,000
Béziers (34)	Apartment	2nd floor apartment with 3 bedrooms, balcony, lift, double-glazed, garage.	€145,000
Font-Romeu (66)	Chalet 155 sq.m.	2 floors; 2 separate apartments entirely furnished. Loft conversion possible.	€395,000

LIMOUSIN

CRT: ☎ 05 55 45 18 80; www.tourismelimousin.com; www.crt-limousin.fr.
Départements: Corrèze (19), Creuse (23), Haute-Vienne (87).

The eastern Limousin is considered a desolate region where tough, dour farmers make a living from breeding Limousin cattle. Tourism is a seasonal industry; the beauty of the landscape is the main attraction, although there are the usual cultural and gastronomic festivals. The regional government has poured money into new roads; the Paris-Toulouse motorway runs past Limoges. The east-west A89 from Clermont-Ferrand will eventually meet up with the A20 at Brive. The train services are scenic but limited; a lot of lines are only served by buses. There are 14 flights a week from the UK to Limoges and this will probably encourage Brits to keep buying property there.

The prefectural capital of the Haute-Vienne (www.tourisme-hautevienne.com) is Limoges which is also the regional capital of the Limousin. South of Aubusson is the Plateau de Millevaches, the lofty source of several major rivers, including the Vézère and the Vienne. The département of La Creuse (www.cg23.fr) is very green, and it is known as La Verte for this reason.

The southwestern corner of the Limousin tends to be lumped in with the Dordogne in the minds of Britons. Brive is an attractive old town and a main railway junction on the line from Paris. Its new airport is due to open in 2007. A little to the north, the town of Uzerche on the upper reaches of the Vézère is a lot more attractive. Tulle, the departmental capital of the Corrèze (www.cg19.fr), deep in the valley of the river of that name, is known for its stitched lace.

Up and Coming Region: La Creuse and Haute Vienne

These are two départements that are attracting increasing interest from foreign property buyers who have been priced out of the Dordogne and Lot. Southwest Haute-Vienne has been made into a regional park, the Parc Naturel Régional Périgord-Limousin. The area has strong associations with Richard the Lionheart; there is a route one can follow.

La Creuse is a fairly empty region. There is just one golf course at Gouzon. Haute Vienne has three, and Corrèze two 18-hole courses. In La Creuse there are still small farms for renovation for as little as €15,000. Even the tourist town of Aubusson has some extraordinarily cheap properties in quite good condition. In the Haute Vienne the prices are a little higher. The main consideration for those thinking of retiring here is whether one would want to remain here all the year round. The valleys can be gloomy in winter with lingering fogs.

Property. The Limousin countryside has more to offer in terms of personal space, empty roads and cheap property that many areas of France. A few thousand Brits have already retired there and now British tradesman such as plumbers and small businesses are moving in too. Rural depopulation is a serious issue here and property prices are about the lowest in France, but may not stay that way as the Brits keep coming.

Location	Type	Description	Price
Naves (19)	Traditional house 180 sq.m.	5 bedrooms, 900 sq.m. of land.	€150,000
Bonnat (23)	Water mill 180 sq.m.	4 bedrooms, orchard, on river. 5,800 sq.m. land, great views.	€300,000
La Nouaille (23)	Stone house	5 bedrooms, in need of renovation.	€62,000
Nexon (87)	Fermette.	2 bedrooms, barn, 2 ha. land.	€178,000

LORRAINE (LORRAINE-VOSGES)

CRT: ☎ 03 83 80 01 80; www.crt-lorraine.fr.
Percentage of population: 3.85%; percentage of GDP: 3.06%.
Départements: Meuse (55), Meurthe-et-Moselle (54), Moselle (57) Vosges (88).

Lorraine is a region with strong Germanic influences. The conurbation of Nancy, with some 335,000 inhabitants, is less of an industrial city than it used to be, but has developed in the areas of banking and technology. It has a major university.

The other major town in the region, Metz, the departmental capital of the Moselle, has some 195,000 inhabitants. As well as the main rivers, there is a canal connecting the Rhine to the Marne (Canal de la Marne au Rhin) and the Canal de l'Est, connecting the Meuse up to the Moselle which provided transport arteries until the railways came, and are kept up now for holidaymakers.

The departmental capital of Meuse (www.tourisme-meuse.com) is Bar-le-Duc. Meurthe-et-Moselle (www.cdt-meurthe-et-moselle.fr) separates the Meuse and Moselle *départements*. Metz, the capital of Moselle (www.cdt-moselle.fr) is more or less due south of Luxembourg and there are regular trains to Germany. Lorraine does not have any direct air links with the UK, however, the nearest airport with flights to London being Strasbourg in Alsace.

The southernmost département, Vosges (www.vosges.fr) with the attractive town of Epinal, is a land of lakes, forest and spectacular gorges, and good skiing in winter. There is a tradition of taking the waters here,

Property. The typical farmhouse is the *usoir*, usually with an arched entrance for carts. Lorraine has a number of notable châteaux, if not the kinds of wrecks that Anglos like to do up. As with Alsace, there is not a great market here for second homes, the main interest coming from the Germans. The Vosges attracts the most interest for holiday homes. Houses start from about €95,000.

Location	Type	Description	Price
Bar Le Duc (55)	Farmhouse 180 sq.m.	4 bedrooms, barn, stables, outhouses, orchards, 2 ha. land.	€200,000
Fresnes en Saulnois (57)	Fermette 195 sq.m.	4 bedrooms, vast barn, 4,600 sq.m. land.	€150,000
Gérardmer (88)	Chalet	3 bedrooms, double glazing, 780 sq.m. land.	€192,230

MIDI-PYRÉNÉES

CRT: ☎05 61 13 55 55; www.tourisme-midi-pyrenees.com.
Percentage of population: 4.25%; percentage of GDP: 3.6%.
Départements: Ariège (09), Haute-Garonne (31), Hautes Pyrénées (65), Gers (32), Tarn (81), Tarn-et-Garonne (82), Aveyron (12), and Lot (46).

Most of the Midi-Pyrénées, especially the Ariège, has experienced severe rural depopulation and an excess of abandoned houses. It is reckoned that half of the houses in Ariège are now second residences. The region's capital, Toulouse, is one of France's most dynamic cities in terms of economic opportunities and lifestyle.

All areas of the Midi-Pyrénées should interest second-home buyers. Toulouse is in the Haute-Garonne (ww.cdt-haute-garonne.com). The Gers (www.gers-gascogne.com) is already a well established area for second home-buyers.

The Lot (pronounced lott) covers a large part of the old county

Quercy, a wilderness of gorges and limestone plateaux (*causses*) that has an irresistible appeal for foreign buyers (see www.quercy-tourisme. com/le-lot). Next to the Dordogne, the Lot, in its widest sense, is the place where most British buyers would like to find a house. The prefectural town, Cahors, on the Lot, is a typical sunny, sleepy southern town. The most attractive town in the Lot is Figeac, east of Cahors.

The prefectural city of the Tarn-et-Garonne is Montauban. The Tarn is one of the most popular areas for British property-hunters; suitable properties in the so-called 'golden triangle' of Gaillac, Cordes-sur-Ciel and Albi are becoming scarce and expensive. Only the out-of-the-way corners of the Tarn have cheap properties nowadays. It can take a good two hours to get here from Toulouse or Bordeaux airport. Most tourists head for Albi, the prefectural town

The Aveyron (www.tourisme-aveyron.com), in the southern Massif Central has few inhabitants, and is popular with French campers and walkers. The prefectural town of Rodez stands at the centre of a remote and wild region where properties are still cheap and fairly plentiful.

Up and Coming Regions: Aveyron, Hautes-Pyrénées

Southwest of Toulouse, towards the Pyrenees, is an area with few estate agents that has plenty of potential for second-home hunters. The Comminges region, between Bagnères de Luchon and Toulouse, is likely to become popular soon; it tends to be overlooked by foreigners, but there are plenty of properties in good condition. During the winter there is skiing in the Pyrenees. The rest of the year there is climbing, fishing, sailing and walking for the active. Hautes-Pyrénées is generally tipped as one of the up-and-coming regions for British house-buyers, mainly because of the very sunny climate; with luck you can be sunbathing for 10 months of the year here. The property market is geared to outsiders; the failing economy has left the département virtually dependent on tourism. The dryness of the climate makes it especially attractive to retirees. Hautes-Pyrénées has very cheap property on the plains around Tarbes; closer to the ski-fields expect to pay €150,000 upwards for renovated properties.

The Aveyron has been opened up thanks to direct flights from London Stansted to Rodez. The building of the huge motorway bridge at Millau has made road access easier as well. The remoteness of the area is both an attraction and a drawback. The property market could go down if Ryanair stopped flying to Rodez, but as it is prices have gone up rapidly and you may have to look at more remote locations. Expect to pay at least €100,000 for a small farmhouse.

Property. The Midi-Pyrénées has 260,000 second homes out of 1,320,000 units. The property market around Toulouse has generally been transformed by the opening of the A20 motorway from Toulouse to Limoges and Paris, and cheap flights to the UK. The Tarn has recently become fairly expensive, and one has to look in the more out-of-the-way areas for a bargain. The Ariège was a well-kept secret until about 2000, but is now very fashionable. It combines views of the Pyrenees with charming hilltop villages. The extension of the motorway from Toulouse to Foix has stoked up property prices.

Location	Type	Description	Price
Baraqueville (12)	Farmhouse 240 sq.m.	Needs renovation, 3 ha. of land.	€150,000
Vieille-Toulouse (31)	Villa 200 sq.m.	5 bedrooms, one storey, swimming pool, 3 ha. garden.	€540,000
St Lary (32)	Stone house 120 sq.m.	3 bedrooms, central heating, 4,800 sq.m. land.	€270,000
nr Figeac (46)	Country seat	3 bedrooms, barn, stables, guest house, 3 ha. land.	€575,000

NORD-PAS-DE-CALAIS

CRT: ☎03 20 14 57 57; www.crt-nordpasdecalais.fr; www.northernfrance-tourism.com.
Percentage of population: 6.65%; percentage of GDP: 5.25%.
Départements: Nord (59) , Pas-de-Calais (62).

A triangle of territory running with the Belgian border in the north and the English Channel on the west is made up of two departments. This is one of the smaller regions, but very densely populated. Flemish culture survives in the centre of the Nord département (www.cdt-nord.fr) in place-names and family names.

The regional capital, Lille, joins up with the towns Roubaix and Tourcoing to form the only real urban sprawl in France, spilling over into Belgium. The industrial heritage of this area, once the main coal-mining and textile region of France gives the Nord-Pas-de-Calais its special identity. The Lille conurbation counts as France's fourth largest city, with 960,000 residents. The Nord-Pas-de-Calais has the highest unemployment in France, at 20%. A great deal of money has been spent on beautifying the city centres – Lille was European Capital of Culture in 2004 – but no amount of money seems to be able to deal with the endemic industrial decline here.

Pas de Calais (www.pas-de-calais.com) is well known to the English as the entry point to France if you come through Calais, Boulogne or Dunkerque. In most ways, it tends to be overlooked by tourists and property-hunters. The Côte d'Opale has fine flat beaches, particularly suitable for families, but is fairly wild when the weather closes in from the sea. South of Le Calaisis and Le Boulonnais is the area of Canche-Authie, with the high-class resorts of Montreuil-sur-Mer and Berck-Plage. There are now cheap flights direct from Brighton and Lydd in Kent to Le Touquet, reviving a tradition that goes back to the 1950s. The golf course is still one of the best in France, and there are several others in the vicinity.

The prefectural town of Arras was at the centre of World War I trench warfare. The Nord has one great advantage in that it is easy to reach from London: only two hours by train to Lille. Moreover one can get to Brussels in 40 minutes, and Paris in 60. TGVs from Lille go virtually everywhere in France, bypassing Paris.

Property. The Nord-Pas de Calais is France's most industrialised region, but there is still enough countryside left to find some attractive properties, particularly along the canals. Naturally enough, the coast is expensive.

Location	Type	Description	Price
Loon Plage (59)	Seaside house	2 bedrooms, garage, 305 sq.m. garden. Sitting tenant.	€130,000
Lille (59)	Town house 85 sq.m.	2 bedrooms, garage.	€150,000
Hesdigneul-les-Boulogne (62)	Villa 200 sq.m.	5 bedrooms, 2 bathrooms, nr beach, 1,100 sq.m. garden.	€300,000

NORMANDY

CRT: ☎ 02 32 33 79 00; www.normandy-tourism.org.
Upper Normandy Départements: Eure (27) and Seine-Maritime (76).
Upper Normandy Percentage of population: 2.97%; %age of GDP: 2.83%.
Lower Normandy Départements: Calvados (14); Orne (61); Manche (50)
Lower Normandy Percentage of population: 2.37%; %age of GDP: 1.92%.

While Upper and Lower Normandy are two separate regions, they have much in common, and are treated together here. There is a possibility that they could be combined into one region in the next few years.

Upper Normandy

Upper Normandy – *Haute Normandie* – is a region rich in history linking it to England and is dairy country with rolling hills reminiscent of southern England. Closeness to England and the good ferry connections from Dieppe and Le Havre make it popular with Britons especially those who want to divide their lives between England and France. Rouen is the capital of the region.

Further north Le Havre is France's second largest port after Marseille, with 245,000 inhabitants. Dieppe is conveniently close to Rouen and has regular ferries to Newhaven. Upper Normandy's most attractive towns and villages are situated in the Eure département,

Lower Normandy

Lower Normandy – *Basse Normandie* – has strong ties with both Britain and North America. Once you cross the estuary of the Seine you are on the Côte Fleurie or Norman Riviera with the twin resorts of Trouville and Deauville.

The city of Caen, inland from the ferry port of Ouistreham (ferries to Portsmouth) rose from the rubble after World War II. The département of Calvados, of which Caen is the capital, gave its name to the potent liqueur. To the northwest of Bayeux is the rustic and remote Cotentin peninsula which has a ferry port at Cherbourg. Brittany Ferries sail here from Portsmouth and Poole.

Lower Normandy has some advantages over Upper Normandy: the climate is somewhat warmer, but it is also wetter. For anyone who wants to start *gîtes* or *chambres d'hôtes,* prospects are good if you are within reach of the *plages du débarquement,* the landing beaches, which guarantee you a steady stream of American tourists.

Property. The archetypal Norman property is the half-timbered *longère* or farmhouse. Anything advertised as a *maison normande* will have half-timbering (*colombages*), One may still find properties to do up in the Eure, and to a lesser extent, Seine-Maritime. There is competition from the Parisians for holiday homes. Starting prices are €60,000 in Eure, and €80,000 in Seine-Maritime. The cheapest properties are in Calvados, starting from around €40,000. In the Manche and the Orne there is not much under €85,000.

Because it is a holiday region, most new construction in Normandy is for second homes. Prices of property depend on two things: the distance from Paris and the distance from the sea. A sea view adds 50% or more to the price. A good railway link to Paris is also a plus point. Note that the climate here is much like southern England. Good insulation is a must, as is an adequate heating system.

Location	Type	Description	Price
Honfleur (14)	Half-timbered longère 115 sq.m.	3 bedrooms, double glazing, renovated, close to shops, 1,500 sq.m. land.	€229,000
Gatteville Le Phare (50)	Granite house	2 bedrooms, shower room, fine garden, close to sea.	€210,000
Roncey (50)	19th century house	2 bedrooms, loft conversion + extension possible.	€119,000
Vimoutiers (61)	Norman half-timbered house	5 bedrooms, guest bungalow, propane gas central heating from cistern.	€218,000
Caudebec Les Elbeuf (76)	House 150 sq.m.	4 large bedrooms, 50 sq.m. lounge, 2 ha. garden.	€229,000

Vineyard in Provence

Harbour at Menton, Alpes-Maritimes

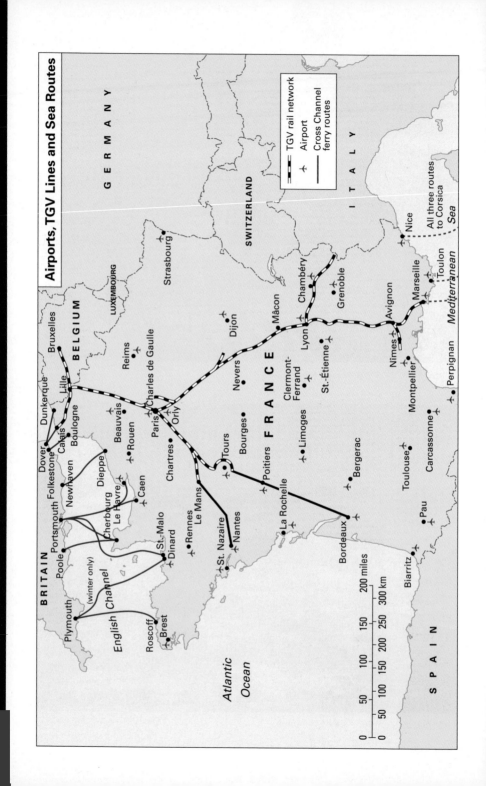

Airports, TGV Lines and Sea Routes

Legend:
- TGV rail network
- Airport
- Cross Channel ferry routes

BRITAIN

Plymouth
Poole
Portsmouth
Newhaven
Dover
Folkestone

English Channel

(winter only)

Roscoff
Brest

Atlantic
Ocean

Dunkerque
Calais
Boulogne
Lille

BELGIUM

Bruxelles

Cherbourg
Dieppe
Le Havre
Caen

St.-Malo
Dinard
Rennes
St. Nazaire
Nantes

Beauvais
Rouen
Chartres
Le Mans

Tours
Poitiers
La Rochelle

Bordeaux

Biarritz
Pau

SPAIN

Paris
Orly
Charles de Gaulle

Reims

LUXEMBOURG

Strasbourg

GERMANY

Nevers
Bourges
Limoges

Clermont-
Ferrand

FRANCE

Dijon

Mâcon
Lyon
St.-Étienne

SWITZERLAND

Chambéry
Grenoble

Avignon
Nîmes

Montpellier

Perpignan

Toulouse
Carcassonne

Marseille
Toulon

Nice

Mediterranean
Sea

ITALY

All three routes
to Corsica

0 50 100 150 200 miles
0 50 100 150 200 250 300 km

PARIS AND ILE-DE-FRANCE

CRT: ☎08 92 68 3000; www.paris-ile-de-france.com; www.parisinfo.com; http://english.pidf.com.
Percentage of population: 18.25%. Percentage of GDP: 27.3%

The nation's capital, with its surrounding area, forms one region known as Ile de France. The central core of Paris is home to 2.1 million people; the Paris agglomeration has a population of 11.1 million, more than half as much again as Greater London. As with any huge urban conglomeration. Paris has a well-integrated and cheap public transport system, which is even cheaper for seniors. The downside to Paris is partly to do with its size and the cost of living, which is much higher than the rest of France. If you want high excitement and a cutting-edge cultural experience, this would be the place to go for.

Most people live in apartments; there are few houses on the market within the Boulevard Périphérique which delimits the city. Property prices are 40% to 65% of those in London, but there are vast differences between the 20 *arrondissements.*

Outside Paris is a large area of suburbs as well as countryside. Central Ile de France is known as *la petite couronne,* and includes Hauts-de-Seine, Seine-Saint-Denis and Val-de-Marne. Paris is also a département. The rest of Ile de France is *la grande couronne,* comprising Seine-et-Marne, Yvelines, Essonne and Val-d'Oise.

Property. Almost all residential property in central Paris dates back to the 19th century. There are plenty of modern villas and mansions outside the inner city. As far as Paris central goes, the only property you could expect to afford would be an apartment. Out in the suburbs, prices are very reasonable by British standards. A three-bedroom house in a good area can be had for £180,000. There are very expensive suburbs: wealthy Americans live in a sort of enclave in St Cloud. Versailles, Fontainebleau and St-Germain-en-Laye are very up-market.

Location	Type	Description	Price
St Germain-en-Laye (78)	House	3 bedrooms, situated in 2.5 ha. park with tennis courts and sports grounds, intercom, caretaker.	€600,000
Corbeil Essonne (91)	Row house 133 sq.m.	3 bedrooms, 2 terraces, loft conversion, remote control garage doors, close to main roads.	€255,000
Sèvres (92)	Apartment 78 sq.m.	4 rooms, centre of town, close to Lycée International, newly rendered, *copropriété*	€320,000
Bobigny (93)	House	5 bedrooms, fitted kitchen, 320 sq.m. garden.	€290,000
Amenucourt (95)	Traditional house 150 sq.m.	3 bedrooms, double glazed, garage, 3,210 sq.m. garden.	€265,000

PAYS DE LA LOIRE

CRT: ☎ 02 28 20 50 00; www.paysdelaloire.fr.
Percentage of population: 5.37%; percentage of GDP: 4.6%.

The western part of the Loire Valley has been made into a region covering the old counties of Maine and Anjou. The capital, Nantes (www. nantes.fr), is a pleasant place to live and is popular with foreign workers. It was rated third in a survey of French cities by *Express* magazine, for economic dynamism and quality of life.

The départements of Loire-Atlantique (www.loire-atlantique-tourisme.com) and Vendée offer flat sandy beaches and excellent sailing and golf, but parts of the coast have been spoilt by overdevelopment. La Baule is the most up-market (and therefore expensive) beach resort on the Atlantic coast.

The département of Maine-et-Loire including the city of Angers and the area round about are worth considering for property; the proximity of airports and the TGV to Paris and Lille make it a convenient place. One could say this is an up-and-coming region.

In the north of the Pays de la Loire lies the wild and thinly populated département of Mayenne (www.lamayenne.fr). The departmental capital of Laval is further south. Mayenne's remoteness makes it attractive to foreigners who want to get away from it all without being too far from the Channel ports. The Maine is both flat and somewhat arid, and lacks the kind of scenery that attracts foreigners.

The capital of the Sarthe département (http://tourisme.sarthe.com), Le Mans, lies on the motorway from Paris to Rennes and is famous for its 24-hour race. Le Mans is also connected by TGV to Paris.

The Vendée (www.vendee-tourisme.com) is attracting a lot of attention now from foreign property buyers (see below). The fine sandy beaches and some up-market resorts attract Parisians in droves The departmental capital, La Roche-sur-Yon is rated as one of France's best places to live.

Property. About 20% of properties are second homes, mainly concentrated along the coast. Mayenne is famous for its châteaux; there is scope for finding stone farmhouses to renovate. Sarthe is an area of small stone-built farmhouses. Habitable properties start from €60,000. One may also find something situated next to a river quite cheaply. Nantes, the regional capital, is one of the trendiest places to live in France, and is experiencing something of a housing shortage as a result, while Le Mans is a lot cheaper. Angela Bird, the author of the guidebook *The Vendée* has set up a useful webpage for visitors and prospective buyers: see www.the-vendee.co.uk. The main attraction of Vendée is the very mild climate, with sunshine on a par with the Riviera.

Location	Type	Description	Price
Nantes (44)	House 120 sq.m.	4 bedrooms, terrace, 2 garages, 1 ha. garden.	€335,000
Nozay (44)	Farmhouse 250 sq.m.	5 bedrooms, oil heating, 6 ha. land.	€228,000
Ingrandes-sur-Loire (49)	Village house 180 sq.m.	5 bedrooms, oil heating, 70 sq.m. courtyard.	€198,000
Angers (49)	Bungalow 100 sq.m.	3 bedrooms, town centre, 350 sq.m. garden, near hospital.	€183,000

PICARDY

CRT: ☎03 22 22 33 66; www.picardietourisme.com; www.cr-picardie.fr.
Percentage of population: 3.1%; percentage of GDP: 2.46%
Départements: Somme (80), Oise (60), Aisne (02).

The Somme area is dotted with memorials and cemeteries of World War combatants. Around the bay of the Somme, the region has one of the best stretches of unspoilt sandy coastline in France. The departmental capital, Amiens, will be familiar to anyone who travelled by train from the coast to Paris in the days before the Eurostar and cheap flights.

The prefectural town of Oise is Beauvais. It is only a short distance from here to Paris, and a short drive to Charles de Gaulle Airport at Roissy-en-France. There are flights from Beauvais to London and Birmingham.

The Aisne was heavily fought over in World War I; the front line stayed static here for most of the war. The Aisne has a short stretch of border with Belgium at the far northeast corner. The region at one time had its own language, *picard.* Picardy generally prides itself on its literary traditions and holds some major literary festivals.

Property. The Somme is not of much interest to foreign property buyers. The climate is wet and the landscape flat, and heavily farmed. The after-effects of the coal-mining industry are still in evidence, with many slagheaps that are gradually being returned to nature. Away from the main roads to Paris, the Aisne and the Oise have a lot more scope; generally they are more hilly and green, with more space.

Location	Type	Description	Price
Saint-Gobain (02)	18th century mansion 270 sq.m.	6 bedrooms, vast rooms, outhouses, 2 ha. land.	€300,000
Chantilly (60)	House 220 sq.m.	5 bedrooms, 60 sq.m. lounge, covered heated swimming pool, 900 sq.m. garden.	€480,000
Compiègne (60)	Detached house 90 sq.m.	2 bedrooms, loft for conversion, outhouse, 600 sq.m. garden.	€230,000

POITOU-CHARENTES

CRT: ☎05 49 50 10 50; www.poitou-charentes-vacances.com.
Percentage of population: 2.73%; percentage of GDP: 2.11%.
Départements: Charente-Maritime (17), Deux-Sèvres (79), Vienne, (86), Charente (16).

Two regions rolled into one: the coastal area of Charente-Maritime and the inland Poitou. Poitiers, the capital, has become a popular tourist haunt thanks to the theme park, Futuroscope, about 8 km outside the city. The building of the TGV station means you can get here from London with only one change of train at Lille; it also means fast connections to Bordeaux and Toulouse.

Charente is one of the popular areas with foreigners buying second homes, and borders on the Dordogne. The Vienne (www.cg86.org) is one of the poorer regions of France.

The neighbouring small département of Deux-Sèvres (www.deux-sevres.com) is poor agricultural land with low rainfall, like the Vendée. The prefectural town of Niort is the centre of the insurance industry in France.

Charente-Maritime is a holiday region. The prices of holiday homes in the prefectural town and port of La Rochelle (www.ville-larochelle. fr), have rocketed in recent years. The coast of the Charente (www. poitou-charentes-vacances.com) benefits from one of France's sunniest climates, over 2,250 hours a year, on a par with Provence.

Up and Coming Region: Deux-Sèvres

The small département of Deux-Sèvres, inland from the Vendée, is likely to see more interest from British home-buyers in the next few years. The climate is dry, and there are still farmhouses for renovation available. Small houses start from €35,000. This is an area of plentiful stone for building, mainly granite and gneiss. The improvements in communications make this a more easily accessible area than it was: there is a TGV as far as Poitiers, as well as flights from London. While the Vendée is becoming more and more popular with Parisians, Deux-Sèvres, which has no coast, remains cheap. There is the possibility of finding a house in the wetlands, next to water.

Property. The Charente is already popular with foreign house-buyers; the area bordering on the Dordogne is the most attractive: Aubeterre-sur-Dronne is particularly expensive. Charente-Maritime, with its two large islands and seacoast is already well established with Parisian holiday-makers.

Location	Type	Description	Price
Perignac (16)	Country house	6 bedrooms, 4 bathrooms, exposed beams, individual gas heaters, 3 terraces, swimming pool, 3,500 sq.m. garden.	€390,000
Ile d'Oleron (17)	Traditional *longère* 200 sq.m.	Includes wine stores and outhouses. For restoration.	€220,000
Parthenay (79)	Country house 170 sq.m.	5 bedrooms, oil central heating, 3,400 sq.m. land.	€260,000
Lussac-les-Châteaux (86)	Traditional house 160 sq.m.	4 bedrooms, 510 sq.m. garden.	€186,300

PROVENCE-ALPES-CÔTE D'AZUR (PACA)

CRT: ☎04 91 13 89 00; www.crt-paca.fr; www.visitprovence.com.
Percentage of population: 7.51%; percentage of GDP: 6.62%.

The Provence-Alpes-Côte d'Azur region, or PACA as it is usually called, has everything that the retiree might want in terms of sunshine and natural beauty. There is a sharp contrast between the overdeveloped coastal region and inland Provence, an area of poor agricultural land and high unemployment. The French equivalent of Silicon Valley centres around Sophia-Antipolis, Antibes.

The capital of the PACA region, Marseille, is France's oldest city. It has been superseded as France's second city by Lyon. The surrounding area is one of the most industrialised in France. By some criteria, Aix-en-Provence is reckoned to be the best place to live in France.

The PACA attracts large numbers of outsiders from elsewhere in France, and from abroad. It is reckoned that the population will increase by 20% by 2020, because of high birth rates and immigration.

The départements are: Vaucluse (84), Bouches-du-Rhône (13), Var (83), Alpes-de-Haute-Provence (04), Hautes-Alpes (05), and Alpes-Maritimes (06). The first four of these départements make up Provence; the region's capital was traditionally Aix-en-Provence, but this has been taken over by Marseille nearby. The Vaucluse represents one typical image of Provence: namely sunflowers, lavender fields, and Roman remains.

The prefectural walled city of Avignon is heavily touristic with its trademark bridge that stops halfway across the Rhône. The tourists also draw crime; Avignon has the highest rate in France.

Michael Frost runs a luxury bed & breakfast near Miramas in the Bouches du Rhône, about 15 km from the Etang de Berre.
I had been working in Burgundy and was looking for somewhere with more or less good weather all the year round. I deliberately looked in January to be sure. Not everyone realises that it can get quite cold in winter inland; e.g the Lubéron. It's always nice here. Where I am there are virtually no holiday homes owned by French people. It's not fashionable here. I spent 3 months looking, full-time. I had no preconceived ideas; I had just retired. I bought the place because it was in a nice location; but it is a modern building. It's halfway between Aix & Arles. I wanted to be reasonably close to an airport and the TGV so my children would come and visit. If you are up some country track then people are less keen to come and visit you. One great thing about the property is that it has air-conditioning; when I bought it I didn't care about this but now it is very convenient. Particularly if you're cooking for people it is very useful to have air-con. I didn't plan to run a B&B; in the first place I had a lot Bosnian refugees staying here. When they left, I realised that I liked having people around, and I didn't feel that I was ready to do nothing at all, so I started on B&B. The crucial thing is that you must like having people around you; you can't view them as intruders.

There was a problem with the land itself. The seller showed me the garden, which was fenced off, and I assumed that all of it belonged to him, but in fact a part of it did not belong to him. So I had to find out who actually owned it. I went to the Section des Domaines, part of the Ministry of Finance, and they went through a long process of finding out who owned that bit of land. They put up notices: 'Does this land belong to you?', and 'Has anyone paid taxes on this land recently?' As there were no claimants the land was forfeited to the state and they could then sell it to you. So I got it at 4 francs the square metre. But of course the state made money out of it for nothing. For this reason it's important to check that all the land you are shown is actually owned by the seller.

Bouches-du-Rhône (www.visitprovence.com) is named after the delta of the Rhône, which spreads out into the Camargue region. The town of Arles, located next to the Rhône gets the full force of the *mistral,* a biting wind that blows down from the Alps for much of the year.

The Var (www.tourismevar.com), east of Marseille, can boast the celebrity beach playground of St Tropez, and the Roman town of Fréjus, amongst other things. This is also the stronghold of the neo-Fascist Front National.

Behind the Alpes Maritimes lies the département of Alpes-Haute-Provence (www.alpes-haute-provence.com). The prefectural town of Digne-les-Bains lies at a comfortable 1,800 feet above sea level. The border with the next département – Hautes-Alpes (www.hautes-alpes.net) – once marked the frontier between Provence and Dauphiné. Hautes-Alpes is tourist country; ideal for outdoor pursuits and sports.

Property. The Riviera around Nice is expensive as it is not subject to the mistral wind that affects the Rhône delta. The Alpes Maritimes hinterland has many second homes. The population in the upper valleys has fallen by more than half since 1900, leaving plenty of abandoned old houses for renovation.

Location	Type	Description	Price
Luberon, nr Apt (30)	Villa 120 sq.m.	4 bedrooms, facing south, on 1,500 sq.m land.	€325,000
Uzès (30)	Provençal *mas* 230 sq.m.	4 bedrooms, swimming pool, on 2,300 sq.m. land.	€980,000
Tourtour, Draguignan (83)	Villa 200 sq.m.	3 bedrooms, jacuzzi, swimming pool, 3 ha. land.	€1,150,000
Fontaine de Vaucluse (84)	1800s house 210 sq.m.	4 bedrooms, garage, flood-free zone.	€435,000

RHÔNE-ALPES

CRT: ☎ 04 26 84 74 74; www.crt-rhonealpes.fr; www.lyon.fr.
Percentage of population: 9.4%; percentage of GDP: 9.5%.

The Rhône-Alpes region revolves around two main natural features: the River Rhône and the Alps. The capital, Lyon, is France's second largest city (population 1,600,000). Lyon has excellent transport connections: the TGV runs through on the way to Geneva beyond Lyon), and there are frequent flights to the UK from the Satolas airport to the east of the city. By 2018 Lyon will have a full TGV service to Turin via a 35-mile tunnel under the Alps.

Rhône-Alpes is a very varied region, stretching from the Massif Central in the west to the Italian border in the east, and down to Provence in the south. The Rhône is less an artery of commerce than a place to dump industrial effluent, and also serves to cool the nuclear reactors along its banks. Because of the concentration of chemical and other industry around the Rhône pollution is a factor here.

The region encompasses eight départements: Rhône (69), Loire (42), Ardèche (07), Drôme (26), Savoie (73), Haute-Savoie (74), Isère (38), and Ain (01). North of Lyon, in the Rhône, starting from Villefranche-sur-Saône, one enters Beaujolais country, named after the small town of Beaujeu. Properties in the wine region are hard to come by; the most active market is around Lyon itself. The Rhône (www.rhonetourisme.com) is the smallest département in France after Paris; it is basically rural, and quite hilly.

The département of the Loire (www.loire.fr) stands on the eastern edge of the Massif Central. The prefectural town of St Étienne has an airport with daily flights to London. The Loire does not stand out as a touristic region; it is more an extension of the wine-growing country of Beaujolais.

Ardèche (www.ardeche-guide.com) can be divided into two halves, the north and east with good transport connections to the outside world, and the rather remote western half. The northern end is a mere 50km from St Étienne airport and Lyon. The eastern boundary of the Ardèche is formed by the Rhône; the prefectural town of Privas is a short distance from the river.

Property. The Rhône Valley is a vast region with a great variety in prices and types of property. The Ardèche tends to attract interest from foreign buyers who are looking for a permanent move to France rather than a holiday home, and there is a well-established British community. There are few cheap properties available now for renovation. Many properties are handled by estate agents in Montélimar, which is on the other side of the Rhône in the Drôme.

Location	Type	Description	Price
Annonay (07)	Renovated farm 400 sq.m.	3 bedrooms, dressing room, on 900 sq.m.	€350,000
Veauche (42)	Traditional house 90 sq.m.	2 bedrooms, gas and electric central heating, 900 sq.m. land.	€250,000
Villefranche (69)	2-storey house 160 sq.m.	2 adjoining houses, 4 bedrooms, pool house, barbecue, on 2,000 sq.m.	€480,000

SAVOIE AND DAUPHINÉ

CRT: ☎04 76 42 41 41; www.grenoble-isere.info.

GDP/Population: see under Rhône-Alpes.

Départements: Drôme (26) , Isère (38).

Although officially part of the Rhône-Alpes region, Savoie and Dauphiné are quite different in character from the Rhône Valley, and so are treated separately here. In the Dauphiné, the Drôme (www.drometourisme.com) is a deserted and scenic region; south of the prefectural capital, Valence. Straddling the Drôme and the département of the Isére is the dramatic Vercors plateau. The Isère stretches from the Rhône to the Alps, with the prefectural city, Grenoble in the middle. Grenoble is considered as one of the best places to live in France; the downside is pollution.

Savoie takes in two-thirds of the French section of the Alps – the Alpes du Nord – including Europe's highest peak, Mont Blanc (15,719 feet) on the Italian border. Chambéry is the gateway to the ski fields and prefectural town. It is on the TGV line to Paris and

Lille and is also served by direct flights from several British cities. The departmental capital, Annecy, is an up-market tourist destination. The star attraction, however, must be the old resort town of Mégève, stunningly located under the Alps. At the northern edge of Haute Savoie lies Lac Léman/ Lake Geneva.

Property. Skiing resorts such as Chamonix and Morzine have become very popular with British buyers, who see that these are attractive places to live and also run a business all the year round. Some of the most expensive properties in France are large ski chalets, which can provide a high rental income, which will set you back over £350,000. Much of the ski accommodation is in unattractive concrete apartment blocks; they are a good investment but the initial purchase costs are steep.

Location	Type	Description	Price
Panossas (38)	Traditional house 200 sq.m.	5 bedrooms, terraces, covered swimming pool.	€374,000
Lanslevillard (73)	Chalet 150 sq.m.	2 separate apartments with 5 bedrooms in all, balconies, foot of the ski pistes.	€480,000
Annecy (74)	Chalet	3 bedrooms, fine views, 1,800 sq.m. land.	€460,000
St Gervais-les-Bains (74)	Traditional villa 155 sq.m.	Renovated in local style; 2 separate apartments, view of Mont Blanc, 375 sq.m. land.	€775,000

Your New Home in France

CHAPTER SUMMARY

- Property purchase fees can be more than 10% of the purchase price but the average is around 8%.
- Land and property are considerably cheaper in most areas than in the UK, but new homes include VAT at 19.6%.
- Mortgages do not have an upper age limit but if you are over 65 you will have to take out life insurance cover. Mortgages run for five to twenty years and may be for up to 85% of the purchase price.
- French property purchase is highly regulated and dealt with by a notaire, a legal official qualified in conveyancing.
- A seven-day cooling off period is allowed after signing the deed of sale during which the buyers can change their minds.
- The cost of renovating an old property usually far exceeds the purchase price and can be a ruinous road to go down.
- If you decide to rent a French property, bear in mind that shorter rentals are not very common; a year is typical. However, if you are renting the holiday home of a fellow expatriate, duration of occupancy can be more negotiable.
- If you decide to buy a plot of land to build on, there are various restrictions and pre-emptive rights which have to be checked off before you buy or build.
- Pre-Contracts to buy are binding and difficult to get out of, so think very carefully before signing one.
- If possible have the contract checked for you by a lawyer, especially if it is in French.

Don't buy French Property...

FRENCH LEGAL CONSULTANTS

Before taking advantage of our comprehensive range of skills which include:

- Free information about all aspects of buying and selling French property
- French wills from only £100
- French estate and tax planning
- SCIs and other appropriate ownership structures
- All other French legal and tax matters
- Strength in depth and breadth
- Personal service
- Active communication
- Informal and approachable staff
- Extremely good value

It costs you nothing to find out more about our services.
Please contact Stephen Smith at stephen@stephensmithfranceltd.com or telephone (01473) 437186 fax (01473) 436573
website: www.stephensmithfranceltd.com

BUYING PROPERTY

Overview of the Property Market

France is the second most popular European country for Britons to retire to after Spain and though the market has gone quieter in the last couple of years, there is still a steady demand for properties. It is surprising to find that in a highly regulated country like France the French authorities are not certain how many foreigners are full or part-time residents there. Recent estimates put the number of Britons with French properties at around 600,000. There were about 120,000 registered British residents (i.e. holding a *carte de séjour*) in the whole of France in 2004, the last year that the carte de séjour was obligatory, which means the rest are holiday or second homeowners who may eventually retire to France.

Cheap flights from the UK to places all over France have made most areas accessible to potential property buyers. It is worth bearing in mind that cheap flights may not be permanent, and routes may be axed at short notice. Channel ports in Normandy and Brittany are immune to such risks. The Pas de Calais is not popular with retirees and second homebuyers, as the climate is too similar to that of the UK. Provence and the Côte d'Azur (or French Riviera) remain popular with certain buyers, even if the coast is overdeveloped. Properties with a good view of the sea command a 50% premium over those without one. To get away from tourists and live in the 'real France', it is becoming more and more necessary to head inland. During 2003 there was an exceptional boom in property buying by Britons, with estate agents reporting an increase of 75% in enquiries compared with 2002. Britons bought 66,000 properties in France in 2003, up from around 15,000 a year in the early 1990s. France has seen unusually rapid rises in property prices in popular areas. Annual increases of 30% are normal in the Hérault, the département most favoured by the French. Corsica has also been seeing 25% annual rises. In 2003 prices nationally went up 14.2%, in 2004 the rise was 11.5% and in 2005 15%. The huge influx of Britons has certainly affected prices in France.

The traditional bastion of British homeowners, the Dordogne, has become very expensive, and many are now buying in Charente instead. The Lot and Tarn have already become almost as expensive as the Dordogne. The Ariège and Aude had their boom years in 2002 and 2003, and are no longer all that cheap. The British still perceive the Pyrénées Orientales as 'too far away'. Attention has shifted to the previously unfashionable central regions of Limousin and Auvergne; these are not that well served by budget flights from the UK, but are more attractive to those who would like to remain in France for the longer term.

There is still scope for further price rises, given that French property is still considerably cheaper than in neighbouring countries, but the exchange rate is no longer that favourable for buyers from outside Euroland

The French view of property as an investment has also changed recently. In the past the stock market has always handsomely outperformed property. Since 2001, property has outperformed the stock market, but capital gains tax still discourages speculation. For French residents there are attractive incentives to buy to let, via the Loi de Robien, which offers generous tax incentives to invest in new rental property, but tenants cannot easily be got rid of once they move in.

One of the biggest changes to the French property market is the rise in specially built developments especially in the Alps and in coastal areas. In 2003 their proportion of the property market was almost nil; in 2006 it represents a third of the market.

FINDING A PROPERTY

Estate Agents

Estate Agents (*agences immobiliers*) are not as highly developed in France as in the UK. Until recently, property sales were handled by *notaires*. On the plus side French estate agents tend to be more laid back and less cut throat than they are in the UK though this can also translate as 'more amateurish'. For dealing internationally with British buyers, French agents often rely on a property search agent who channels potential clients to them in return for a commission, or they establish partnerships with British estate agents who handle the English-speaking clients for them.

The number of agents immobilier in operation has grown rapidly in recent years. Most UK-based agents do not deal directly with properties themselves, but rather put you in touch with immobiliers. Some French estate agents speak enough French to negotiate a sale in English and more and more British estate agents are setting up in France. There are also independent property consultants who get a commission from French agencies for introducing clients to them and offer clients a 'hand-holding' service through the buying process for which they charge fees.

According to British estate agents, many people hope to buy a property in France during their holidays and generally there is not time to do this. It is far better to search in a leisurely fashion while spending several months living in rented accommodation in the area where you wish to settle. This is something that retired, or nearly retired people can usually do more easily. Keith and Hannah Oakley did just this:

Nine years ago, we had a camping van and we came to France to look at a property in Cognac we thought we might be interested in. We didn't like what we saw, so we kept on going until we reached Riberac and went into an estate agents there. We were shown the farmhouse, where we now live. It had been beautifully restored by a previous (French) owner for personal use. Some retired people like to buy a property that needs restoring as a retirement project, but not us; we had already done all that in the UK.

Only half of property sales in France are conducted through immobiliers. The rest are sold privately, through notaries or at auctions. Going around villages asking if there are any properties coming on the market (usually because someone has died recently) or even paying a local to keep an eye open for you could save you a lot of money. Whether you need another intermediary is up to you.

Estate Agents – How They Operate

o Unlike in the UK, French-based estate agents must have professional qualifications and be licensed by the local chamber of commerce with a *carte professionelle* which is renewable annually. They should have a diploma in law (e.g. DEUG) or baccalaureate or other degree and a year's experience in an estate agency. Alternatively, they must have ten years' experience in an estate agency.

o The English-speaking agent receives commission from the immobilier, which is up to half of the total commission on the sale for established partnerships. For less established partnerships their commission from the immobilier is less, and they will charge the client 1% or 1.5% extra commission.

o Clients should establish at the start how much commission is charged by intermediaries. It is more usual now for the seller to pay, but this is by no means universal.

o The asking price that is advertised must by law, include the agent's commission if the buyer is to pay it. However there are still ways to slip in extra charges so you should always request a precise breakdown of all the components of the price.

o Estate agents are legally required to have a minimum guarantee or bond of €110,000 if they maintain a blocked account for payments, as well as professional indemnity insurance.

Useful Contacts: Estate Agents & Property Developers and Consultants

The French national body for estate agents is the confident sounding *Chambre des Experts Immobiliers de France* (FNAIM), and you can use their website to find members in your area. The UK-based Federation of Overseas Property Developers (FOPDAC) unites agents, developers and specialist consultants in a body restricted to companies and individuals who agree to Fopdac's high professional and ethical standards. Fopdac has 23 members operating in France.

Vive La France is a major and expanding exhibition held at Olympia, London every January. The whole upper level is devoted to estate agents, developers, builders, surveyors, insurers, banks, lawyers, mortgage providers and more and is a great starting point for contacts and ideas. Many people also find estate agents that deal with France, by searching on the internet.

> ### Estate Agents Contacts
>
> **FNAIM:** *Chambre des Experts Immobiliers de France.* French Association of estate agents. ☎01 53 76 03 52; www.experts-fnaim.org.
> **FOPDAC:** Federation of Overseas Property Developers, Agents and Consultants. ☎0870 3501233; www.fopdac.com.
> **Vive La France:** ☎0870 380 0144; www.vivelafrance.co.uk.

WHAT TYPE OF PROPERTY?

Buying your French property is an investment in your future life. It should fulfil or exceed your expectations, and the pluses of living in it should outweigh the minuses. It would be disingenuous to say that no one has ever bought the wrong type of property for themselves, either in the wrong location, or by not setting a realistic limit on their budget. Asking yourself a list of simple questions makes it easy enough to see whether a property is the right one for you:

- What is my budget?
- How much work does it need, and what will it cost?
- How easy is the property to get to?

○ Are there any airports nearby?
○ Do I want to live there all the year round?
○ Is the climate bearable in the winter?
○ How close is it to tourist attractions?
○ Will I or my partner be able to pursue our hobbies there?
○ Will we or our family still want to use it in 20 years' time?

As a general rule, it is wise to decide on your budget and stick to it, no matter how tempted you might be to spend an extra €20,000 or whatever. If the property needs renovating, ask for some quotations beforehand (and be realistic about actual cost nearly always exceeding the quotations). You should have outline planning permission – a *certificat d'urbanisme* – before buying if you are planning a change of use or large-scale renovations. Your notaire will advise you on whether you need this.

Old versus New

It is an oddity of the French property scene that the French consistently prefer new-build, or completely renovated property, leaving the ruined character farmhouses to the foreigners. The French have seen what the British and other foreigners can do with old properties and sometimes buy them after the foreign owners have nearly bankrupted themselves restoring them, but not that many are interested in imitating them. Old barns are of no interest whatever to the local people, who are amazed that foreigners are willing to take them on. Incomers look for a beautiful location, and authenticity, while what the French really want is elegance and convenience. The most telling statistic is the fact that an average new property is worth 40% more than an old one. It is therefore important to understand that it may be very difficult to recoup the investment that you make in renovating an old property in a remote area, unless you are lucky enough to find another foreigner who happens to like it.

Advantages of the Old
○ The property has an authentic feel and rustic charm.
○ There will probably be more land attached to it.
○ The garden will be well-established.

○ You know from the outset what you are buying.
○ The view will probably be better than from new property.
○ There will be more craftsmanship in the construction.
○ You are more likely to be able to rent it out to holiday-makers.

Advantages of the New
○ There will be a garage or parking spaces already built.
○ The kitchen will be more modern.
○ The wiring and plumbing won't need replacing.
○ The building is guaranteed for 10 years from construction.
○ You can design the property yourself.
○ The heating will be more efficient.
○ There should be insulation.
○ On some developments, there are shared sports facilities.

Buying Off Plan

It is common in France to buy property on the basis of plans – *achat sur plan* – or which has not yet been completed – *vente en l'état futur d'achèvement* (VEFA). A developer – *promoteur constructeur* – buys a piece of land, arranges for planning permission, and then looks for potential buyers before the property is built, or when it is partially built. The dwelling can be an apartment, or an individual house, as in the case of a *lotissement* or estate. The first step in the process is to sign a preliminary contract, or *contrat de réservation*, with a developer. The contract must contain certain information, as well as any get-out clauses in the sale:

○ The habitable surface area.
○ The number of main rooms.
○ A list of any attached rooms, or spaces.
○ The location of the building in the estate.
○ The technical quality of the construction, with a list of the materials to be used.
○ The provisional price of the building, and any conditions that allow for the price to change.
○ The date by which the final contract can be signed.

○ Where relevant, any loans that the developer intends to obtain for the buyer.
○ The conditions for paying the deposit.

The buyer has the right to ask for changes to the contract. Once the contract has been received by registered post, there is a 7-day cooling-off period during which buyers can change their mind.

The deposit – *dépôt de garantie* – depends on the length of time before the completion of the project: 5% if within one year, under 2% if between one and two years, and no deposit if beyond two years. The deposit will be returned if:

○ The sale does not go through.
○ The sale price exceeds the provisional price by 5%.
○ The buyer fails to obtain a mortgage.
○ Equipment that has been promised is not installed.
○ The property falls 10% in value.

The developer is legally required to present a guarantee that the project will be finished, or a guarantee of full reimbursement if it is not completed. In most cases the developer will have their own guarantor, a bank or co-operative society, as a backer. The second, final, contract is signed once the building programme has been decided on, and construction can commence. A draft of the *contrat définitif de vente* is sent to the buyer at least a month before the signing date.

Agents Offering Off-Plan Properties

ApartForSale: www.apartforsale.com

Latitudes French Property: ☎020 8951 5155; www.latitudes.co.uk.

VEF: ☎020 7517 1031; www.vefuk.com.

Payment. Under normal circumstances, the buyer pays in four instalments, which include the deposit:

1. 35% when the foundations are completed.
2. 70% when the roof has been built and the terraces are no longer exposed to water.

3. 95% when the building has been completed.
4. The final 5% is payable at the handing-over stage, unless there is a dispute.

When the property is ready to be handed over, there has to be a formal *réception des travaux* between you (or your representative) – the *maître d'ouvrage* – and the developer – the *maître d'œuvre*. The *réception des travaux* (acceptance of the works), can take place with or without reservations. The final 5% of the payment is known as the *retenue de garantie* and this can be withheld until any defects have been put right, or to cover your own expenses in putting them right if the builder fails to do the work. If the 5% is withheld, it should be deposited in an escrow account held by a notaire.

Before the handing-over the buyer should inspect the building, with the help of an expert if necessary, to determine if there are any faults that need correcting. Electrics and heating should be tested. At the *réception des travaux* you will sign a document – a *procès-verbal* – accepting the handover. You can only refuse to take over the building if there are serious defects or equipment is missing. At the handing-over the developer has to show that they have the necessary insurance policy to cover their *responsabilité décennale* – the compulsory 10-year guarantee against major construction errors. There is also a 2-year guarantee – *garantie biennale* – against faults in the equipment, such as the fitted kitchen, heating and double glazing.

VAT on New Buildings

There are both advantages and disadvantages to buying a new property, as far as taxes go. The downside is that 19.6% TVA is payable, although this can be avoided in some circumstances. The costs associated with the purchase, to be paid to the notaire, are reduced to about 2-3% of the price (instead of the usual 8%+) before TVA. There is a 20% reduction if you buy a unit in a development of more than 10 units. On the other hand, there is the *taxe de publicité foncière* – at 0.615% of the price before TVA, and another €900 in charges. TVA is also payable if you buy a property within 5 years of its completion. Professional advice is essential if you are looking for ways of avoiding TVA.

Buying Land for Building

It is not unusual for the French to buy a piece of land with the intention of building a property on it themselves. There are, naturally, a lot of formalities involved; this is not something you could do while sitting at home in England, but in many ways, it could be an ideal solution. Building land is cheap in the countryside, and you will have complete control over the design of your property.

Land Legislation – How it Works

- A lot of land cannot be built on, especially on the coast. Agricultural land is also protected.

- Many *communes* have a PLU – *Plan Local d'Urbanisme* – which states which pieces of land may be built on.

- Linked to this is the COS – *Coéfficient d'Occupation des Sols* – a figure giving the maximum amount of square metres of surface area that can be built on each square metre of land.

- If you want to build a property with a higher surface area than the COS permits, you will have to pay a penalty, if permission is granted at all.

- If the *commune* has no PLU, then the use of the land is decided by central government.

- The required outline planning permission – the *certificat d'urbanisme* – will only be granted where there are adequate access roads, drains, water and electricity supplies and so on.

Finding the Plot. A usual way to buy land for building is to buy a plot in a *lotissement* or new estate; otherwise you may find a single plot or *parcelle* by looking in the usual property magazines. If you are thinking of buying land for building, it is vital to be aware of any plans on the part of the local authorities to construct new roads, industrial parks, etc. Look in the local *Plan Cadastral* or Land Registry, to see what the precise measurements of your piece of land should be. If the boundaries are not clearly defined then you will need the services of a *géomètre-expert* – see www.pagesjaunes.fr – to carry out the *bornage*, that is put in markers to show the boundaries. For companies selling land see the following websites which are all in French: www.allobat.fr, www.terrain.fr and www.villesetvillages.fr.

Losing the Plot

○ In many areas, the state, or state organisations can have pre-emptive rights (*Droit de Préemption*) on land purchase.

○ Even after you buy a piece of land, the state can make a compulsory purchase order; you will receive 10% compensation.

○ It is also conceivable that a private person has a pre-emptive right, or some other right, such as the use of the land for a fixed period, or rights of way.

○ In order to avoid pointlessly acquiring land, it is essential to conduct a search of all the possible servitudes or obligations attaching to a piece of land.

○ In agricultural areas, the main organisation to watch for is the SAFER – *Société d'Aménagement Foncier et d'Établissement Rural* – which exists to ensure that agricultural land, forests and fields are put to appropriate use, and in particular to try to bring small parcels of land under one ownership.

○ The notaire handling the sale is legally obliged to inform SAFER of the impending transfer.

○ Where it appears that there is going to be a change in the use of land, the SAFER can intervene and negotiate with the seller to find a more suitable use for the land, or they can buy the land themselves and sell it on.

○ Where the land is being sold to family members, or co-heirs, the SAFER will not intervene.

Self-Build

There are a number of ways you can go about building your own property. You can either hire an architect to design the building, or design it yourself, if it is fairly small, or go to a builder and ask them to supply you with a ready-made plan. If you choose to take a ready-made plan, then the contract you sign is a *contrat de construction d'une maison individuelle avec fourniture de plan*. The terms of the contract are strictly regulated by law. The builder must have financial guarantees and insurance. Payments are made according to a well-defined schedule:

- ○ 15%   on starting the work
- ○ 25%   on completion of foundations
- ○ 40%   on completion of walls
- ○ 60%   when the roof is put on (*mise hors d'eau*)
- ○ 75%   on completion of walls (*mise hors d'air*)
- ○ 95%   when the heating, plumbing and carpentry are completed
- ○ 100%   at the hand-over

Not many foreigners go for this type of arrangement, since they would rather have a design of their own.

Main Points of Self-Build if Hiring An Architect

- ○ The more usual procedure is to hire an architect to draw the plans.
- ○ The contract evidently needs to include details of estimates of the cost, and stage payments.
- ○ The actual building work is usually handled by a *maître d'œuvre* or master builder, who oversees the whole process, and engages the various specialist tradesmen.
- ○ A maître d'œuvre will not be as highly qualified as an architect, but will have more time to spend on-site.
- ○ Note that the person who engages a maître d'œuvre is called the *maître d'ouvrage*. The contract you sign with him is the *contrat de maîtrise d'œuvre* which is again not regulated by law.
- ○ The notaire handling the sale is legally obliged to inform SAFER of the impending transfer.
- ○ The maître d'œuvre will normally hire tradesmen that he has worked with in the past, or he may give the job to a local co-operative.
- ○ Where the land is being sold to family members, or co-heirs, the SAFER will not intervene.

Leaseback Property

The types of property mentioned above are the most usual for those wanting to retire to France. Unlike the Spanish costas there are few retirement villages built along the coasts as building in coastal areas is normally restricted. Instead France has pioneered *le leaseback*, an arrangement which operates on a type of buy-to-let basis. It is the French government's way of encouraging private investors to fund new tourist accommodation. You buy a new or completely rebuilt property in a tourist complex, and then lease it back to the developer on a contract of nine to twenty years. During this period you get a guaranteed rental income which helps pay off the mortgage on the property. You can also use the property in the off season for a restricted number of weeks. After the contracted period you are the owner of the property. However this type of property is not typically used for retirement even though most leaseback schemes are found in tourist areas, on the coast and in Paris. One of the largest companies in this area is *Pierre et Vacances* which pioneered leaseback.

GLOSSARY OF PROPERTY TERMS

à débattre	negotiable
à rénover	to be renovated
aménageable	can be put to use
un appentis	lean-to
attenant	adjoining
BE/bon état/bien entretenu-	good condition; well-maintained
un/les bien(s)	goods, property, estate, assets
le bornage	boundary marking
les bornes	boundary markers
la buanderie	washhouse
le carrelage	tiling
carrelé	tiled
la cave	cellar
la cazelle	dry-stone shepherd's shelter
le cellier	storeroom, pantry
le chai	wine/spirit storehouse
le chauffage fuel	oil heating
la clôture	fencing, paling, hedge or other enclosure
les combles aménageables	loft conversion possible
CC/commission comprise	estate agent's commission included

le crépi	roughcast
le débarras	junk-room
les dépendances	outhouses
un double séjour	large living room
une écurie	stables
en étage	on the same floor
en exclusivité	only one estate agent is handling the sale
F1	one room + kitchen/bathroom
FAC/frais agence compris	agency's commission included
le galetas	garret; hovel
le grenier	attic
HNC/honoraires agence	agent's commission
non compris	(not included)
HT/hors taxes	not including taxes
un immeuble	apartment block, or commercial property
le madrier	beam
la maison de caractère	dilapidated or unusual
la maison mitoyenne	semi-detached/terrace house
mitoyenne d'un coté	end of terrace/ semi-detached
n.c./non compris	not included
la penderie	wardrobe
le piano	cooking range
le plain pied	one storey
les poutres apparentes	exposed beams
les prestations	features
le ravalement	rendering
refait à neuf	completely renovated
le rez/rez de chaussée/RDC	ground floor
la salle	living room
sans mitoyenneté	no commonly owned boundary walls or structures
sans vis-à-vis	no houses opposite
SdB/salle de bain	bathroom
SdE/salle d'eau	washroom
séj/séjour	living room
le séjour cathédrale	open-plan living room on two floors
le sous-sol	below ground-level
les tommettes	hexagonal floor tiles in Provence
T1	Type 1; same as F1

TBE/très bon état	very good condition
TTC/toutes taxes comprises	all taxes included
le verger	orchard
une vue imprenable	unrestricted view

FEES, CONTRACTS AND CONVEYANCING

Notaires

Notaires have the monopoly on conveyancing in France. The most important thing to understand is that the notaire does not look out for your interests. One of the biggest mistakes that Britons make in France is to imagine that a notaire is the equivalent of a solicitor. A notaire is a state official whose main function, as far as property transfers are concerned, is to ensure that everything is done correctly, and that all taxes on property transactions are paid. If you want impartial legal advice it is best to approach a bilingual lawyer or *avocat*, most likely one based in the UK. Addresses of these can be found on the internet or in the French property magazines mentioned earlier.

Main Points About Notaires

O In order to become a notaire you have to train for 7 years, and then buy a licence (*charge de notaire*) from someone who is giving up the profession.

O Although a notaire may know a great deal about the property being sold, they are not bound to tell you anything more than they have to.

O Since they also act as tax collectors, you should be on your guard about what you tell them.

O Notaires are supervised by the departmental *chambre des notaires* and have professional liability insurance.

O The notaire's main concern is to ensure that they do not make an error and leave themselves open to being sued.

Functions of a Notaire

If you want a deed of sale that is binding on third parties, then the intervention of a notaire is legally necessary at the signing of the acte of sale/*acte de vente*. The notaire will deposit a copy of the *acte* with the deed and mortgage registry (*bureau des hypothèques*) and that is it. As a foreigner buying property in France, it would be foolish not to use a notaire, otherwise you leave yourself at risk of all sorts of unpleasant surprises later on after you have taken possession of your property.

Amongst other things the notaire will:

- Conduct a search in the land registry to see whether any third parties have any claim on the property, or the right to use the land for any purpose.
- Transfer your money via an escrow or blocked account to the seller, while ensuring that all fees and taxes have been paid in full.
- Ensure that any pre-emptive rights on the property are 'purged'.
- Witness the acte de vente or other agreement to sell the property to you.

Pre-Contracts

Once you find a property that you like, the next step is to make an offer. Private sellers will ask for rather more than the property is worth, and you can reasonably offer 5-10% less than the asking price. In the areas where there is a lot of foreign interest and prices are rising, there is less scope for bargaining. Knowing how long a property has been on the market is a useful guide to bidding. The offer is made to the estate agent, or the vendor if it is a private sale. You can make a formal written offer, an *offre d'achat*, or *promesse d'achat* – promise to buy – which the seller can consider. It only becomes legally binding on the seller if he or she accepts it. You are not allowed to make any deposits accompanying an offre d'achat. On the whole, it is simpler to make a verbal offer, and then ask for a preliminary contract to be drawn up.

If your offer is accepted, a preliminary contract – an *avant-contrat*

– will be drawn up. Although there is no legal obligation to have a preliminary contract, it is universally used. There are two main types of contract in France: the *compromis de vente* which is binding on both parties, and the *promesse de vente* (promise to sell), which is binding on the seller, and which gives the buyer the chance to renege on the contract (while forfeiting their deposit). The latter is used north of the River Loire, including in Paris.

Before Signing the Pre-Sale Contract. Because of the binding nature of pre-contracts, it is vital to go through the following points before you sign anything:

○ Are you sure that you can use the property for your intended purpose?
○ Have you obtained preliminary planning permission for any work you want to do?
○ Does the sale include all the outbuildings and attached land, without reservation?
○ Are the boundaries of the property clearly marked out?
○ Are there any rights of way over the land?
○ Do any third parties have any rights relating to the property?
○ Will you share property rights over boundary walls with neighbours?
○ If the property is recent, have you seen the handing-over report: the *procès verbal réception des travaux*?
○ Has planning permission been obtained in the past for any work?
○ Has the contract been checked by a qualified person?

You have the right to obtain an extract from the land registry (*extrait de matrice cadastrale*) from the *mairie* to verify the above points.

The Promesse de Vente

With the 'promise to sell' the seller commits himself to selling within at least one month, or more usually within two to three months. In return the potential buyer will pay an *indemnité d'immobilisation*, a sum that compensates the seller for temporarily taking his property off the market. The usual amount is 10% of the sale price.

The *promesse de vente* can be signed in front of a notaire, or can be signed privately. The seller pays a charge of €300-400 to the notaire. If the promesse is signed privately, it is to be signed in triplicate, and one copy is deposited with the *recette des impôts*. It is in the buyer's interests to sign the promesse in front of a notaire. The notaire will not witness a contract unless they are satisfied that it is free of flaws.

It is strongly recommended that the indemnité d'immobilisation be paid into a blocked account held by a notaire, and not directly to the seller. If you exercise your option to purchase – *lever l'option* – the indemnité will be deducted from the sale price. If the deal falls through, the indemnité will be returned to you if one of the get-out clauses can be invoked within the allotted time; otherwise you will lose it outright.

The Compromis de Vente

The more common type of pre-contract, or *avant-contrat*, also goes under the name of *promesse synallagmatique*, since it binds both seller and buyer. It is usual to pay 5-10% of the sale price as a deposit or indemnité; this is not the same as the indemnité d'immobilisation mentioned above. The deposit should be paid into a blocked account – *compte séquestre* – held by a notaire or by the estate agent.

The nature of the deposit is vitally important. If it is an *arrhes*, then the buyer can withdraw from the agreement but will forfeit the deposit. If the seller decides not to sell, then they are required to pay the buyer twice the amount of the arrhes as compensation. A variation on this type of deposit is a *dédit*, a specified sum that is forfeited if the buyer pulls out of the deal.

The more usual type of deposit, the *acompte* – which can be translated as 'down-payment' or 'instalment' – has more serious implications. In this case the sale is legally enforceable on both buyer and seller. There is no way to prevent the sale from going ahead. The nature of the deposit will be stated explicitly on your *compromis*.

The *compromis de vente* can be signed in front of a notaire, for which there is a charge. You have a week's cooling-off period after receiving the draft compromis de vente by registered post, during which you can decide not to go ahead with the deal. All payments should be made by cheque or bank transfer through the estate agent or notaire's blocked account. It is no longer allowed to pay deposits in cash, and you should not agree to any request to make such a payment.

The Contents of the Compromis de Vente

It is important to understand that signing the compromis de vente virtually makes you the owner of the property you are promising to buy. If you sign a *promesse de vente* the seller remains the owner of the property. Getting out of a compromis de vente will be expensive and difficult, so you must be entirely satisfied that the contract is worded the way that you want. You may be asked to sign a standard printed contract by the estate agent, which will not contain the get-out clauses that you need. While there are no standardised requirements as to the content, the contract should at least contain, or be accompanied by the following:

- The *état civil* (entry in the population register) of the buyer(s) if they are already resident in France.
- Details of passports, birth certificates, marriage certificates, divorce certificates.
- Official declaration as to the marriage regime, or civil partnership contract (PACS).
- A description of the property, including outbuildings.
- The address.
- The surface area of the land.
- The habitable surface area of the property (compulsory in the case of *copropriétés*).
- Proof that the seller is the rightful owner of the property, i.e. an authentic copy of the previous acte de vente.
- The agreed selling price of the property.
- Name of the notaire handling the sale.
- Who is to pay the notary's fees and other costs.
- Who is to pay the estate agent's commission.

O The property's unique number in the *Plan Cadastral* – land
registry.

O Any equipment or fixtures included in the sale: e.g. fitted
kitchens, burglar alarms.

O Results of reports on termites, lead and asbestos.

O Details of guarantees with newer properties.

O Date by which the acte de vente is to be signed.

O Receipt for any deposit.

O Date on which you will have the use of the property.

O Penalties if one of the parties withdraws from the deal.

O Get-out clauses: *conditions suspensives*.

O Who will be responsible for dealing with *vices cachés* or 'latent
defects'.

The last point is very important. Generally there is a clause stating
that the property is sold as seen, on the assumption that the buyer has
had enough time to check the condition of the property. If the vendor
hides a defect in such a way that a reasonably attentive buyer could
not be expected to see it then the vendor can be pursued through the
courts. If the vendor is a property professional then he has to be completely open, and cannot hide behind any clauses about vices cachés.
It is up to the buyer to have a survey done to be entirely certain about
the condition of the property.

Property cannot be sold without the compulsory survey for asbestos,
and for termites and lead, if required. The notaire will not allow the
sale to go through if these surveys have not been done. If the property
is less than 10 years old, it will be covered by a *garantie décennale* – a
10-year insurance policy against major construction defects. Minor
repairs and building work will be covered by a 2-year guarantee against
faulty workmanship. Once a buyer agrees to take responsibility for
hidden defects, then there is no further room for negotiation if any
are found. Another solution is for either the seller or the buyer to take
out an insurance policy against the discovery or appearance of major
faults in the building. The policy will cover you against faults in the
walls and foundations for five years, in the secondary construction
(e.g. roof) for three years, and in the heavy equipment (e.g. lifts and
heating) for one year.

Get-Out Clauses

The negotiation of *conditions suspensives* (popularly called *clauses suspensives*) is an area where expert legal help can be very useful. The most usual one is that the signature of the final deed is dependent on obtaining mortgage finance, the condition suspensive *de prêt*. This get-out clause should not be treated lightly. If you do not make reasonable efforts to obtain mortgage finance, and you are shown to be acting in bad faith, then you could lose your deposit. If you require a loan to complete the purchase, you can benefit from the provisions of the Loi Scrivener as regards get-out clauses: see 'Mortgages' above.

Other clauses can be inserted, e.g. you can make the purchase dependent on being able to sell your existing property. For example, you can put in get-out clauses such as:

- The owner has to carry out necessary repairs.
- There are no works planned by the local government that would interfere with your use of the property.
- Building permits can be obtained.
- A report on the presence of 'termites' has to be produced.
- No one is going to exercise pre-emptive rights on the property.
- The property will have no sitting tenants.
- There are no legal constraints on the owner selling the property.
- The dimensions of the property correspond to what is in the contract.

A variation on the term condition suspensive is a *condition résolutoire:* a clause that nullifies the contract automatically if its conditions are met.

It is easy enough to find out if the local municipality is planning to construct a main road or do some other works near your property in the near future, by asking the local *Division Départementale de l'Équipement,* the town-planning office.

Rights and Obligations/Servitudes

In between the signing of the compromis de vente and the acte de vente, the notaire has some time in which to make enquiries about the status of the property. Between one and three months can elapse between the preliminary and final contract signings; two months is a normal interval. During this time he will be able to obtain clearance from any bodies – such as SAFER – that might have pre-emptive rights over the property that they do not intend to exercise them. SAFER has the right to match the highest offer made for your land/farm so that it can sell it on to another farmer. The notaire should establish that there are no mortgages still applying to the property. In the case of property that has been completed recently the seller will have to supply a *certificat de conformité* from the mairie certifying that all the necessary building permits were obtained when the property was constructed, and no regulations regarding urban planning have been broken. There are cases where properties have been modified or even built without planning permission, so it pays to be on your guard.

The matter of *servitudes,* that is rights and obligations, is particularly important. The most common type of servitude is where a farmer has the right to use part of your land, or allow animals to roam on it, or to draw water from your well. Your neighbour may have obtained the right to make windows in a wall overlooking your property, a *servitude de vue.* The biggest headache can be rights of way – *droits de passage* – which allow hunters to walk over your grounds on their way to a designated hunting area. If you see notices saying *chasse gardée* or *chasse privée* you know that there will be hunters in the vicinity. It is quite likely that your notaire will ask neighbours to sign a document agreeing that they have no right of way over your land.

If you are worried about servitudes and other claims by third parties, it is possible to take out an insurance policy guaranteeing good title to the property for a small sum. The French insurers, *Axa Courtage,* offer title insurance, known as *Assur'Titre*; this can be obtained via London & European Title Insurance Services: see www.europeantitle.com.

The Acte Final

After a period stated in the preliminary contract the parties will proceed to signing the final deed of sale, known as the *acte authentique de vente.* Only actes witnessed by a notaire are considered actes authentiques, legally binding on third parties. The acte de vente is signed by the buyer, the seller and one notaire. If there are two notaires involved, one acting for the buyer and one for the seller, only one of them will witness the acte de vente. Which one depends on local custom.

You will be sent a *projet de l'acte* – a draft of the acte de vente – well in advance; a month is normal. This will contain much the same information as the original compromis de vente. You will be asked to produce originals of your birth/marriage/divorce certificates, and they may have to be translated and notarised; ask well in advance. At this point you should have made arrangements for payment of all the sums involved in the purchase, including the taxes and notary's fees. The notaire will in any case require advance payments to cover his expenses. If a mortgage is involved, the notaire will draw down the money from your bank account.

There must be an interpreter present if the person signing the acte de vente is not of French nationality. There is no legal requirement to supply an English translation; many *immobiliers* have a translation of the compromis de vente available, if not the *acte* itself. An English translation has no legal force in any case. The presence of an interpreter makes it impossible for the buyer to claim that they did not understand what they were signing, and thus protects the notaire from being sued. The cost of an interpreter is steep – as much as €300 – because they need to be approved by the *préfecture*. The notaire will most likely say nothing in English during the signing, for fear of misleading the English buyer, even though he will speak in English before and after.

Power of Attorney

A date will be fixed for the signing. Very often there are last-minute hitches and the date may be put off. For this reason it is highly desirable to arrange to give a trusted person a power of attorney – a *mandat* – to act on your behalf if you are unable to attend the actual signing. The signing must take place on French soil. For practical reasons, the power of attorney is best made up in the French form. It should be witnessed by a notary, or at a French consulate. If it is witnessed by a

British notary public, it will have to be legalised by the Foreign and Commonwealth Office (www.fco.gov.uk) to make it valid in France. The document should state what powers you are giving to your representative. The power of attorney allows your representative to do virtually anything you wish, and should only be given to a reliable person; preferably a close relative.

The Actual Signing

Assuming that all the loose ends are tied up, you will be invited to the signing of the acte de vente. This will be an interesting experience, or perhaps nerve-racking if there are last-minute hitches. Apart from yourself, the seller and the notaire, and their clerk, there may be other interested parties present. By this point, all the necessary funds should have been transferred to your notaire's blocked bank account. There are various taxes and fees to be paid at the last minute, and you should be prepared for this. It is highly embarrassing to find that the sale cannot go ahead because you haven't left any money in your French bank account. You should also have paid the first insurance premium on the property, *before* signing the acte de vente. Subsequent payment dates are based on the date of the signing.

Certain items will often be mentioned in or attached to the acte de vente that will not have appeared in the compromis de vente, such as:

○ Details of mortgage loans.
○ Full description of the property, with details of previous sales.
○ Details of the insurance policy on the property.
○ The amount of Capital Gains Tax payable by the seller; or exemption.
○ Reports on the presence of termites/lead/asbestos.
○ Statement that the buyer accepts the property in the condition it is sold.

You will be asked to confirm that all the information you have given is truthful: the *affirmation de sincerité*.

Firms Dealing with French Property

Ideally, when acquiring a new home in France, you will want to use the services of a UK law firm, with lawyers qualified in both UK and French law. Some firms have French lawyers working for them in the UK, or have offices in France. Such lawyers can advise one on whose name to put the property in, and what measures to take to minimise inheritance taxes. The acte de vente still has to be signed in front of a French notary and registered in France.

Useful Addresses

A Home in France: The Old Granary, Low Lane, Cuddington, Bucks HP18 0AA; ☎0870-748 6161; www.ahomeinfrance.com. Run by Danielle Seabrook, this company offers complete bilingual legal assistance to British residents to manage their risk in buying in a foreign jurisdiction. Also has an office in Chinon, Indre-et-Loire.

Bennett & Co Solicitors: Fulshaw Hall, Alderlley Road, Wilmslow, Cheshire SK9 1RL; ☎0870-428 6177; www.bennett-and-co.com. International property lawyers.

Blake Lapthorn Linnell: Holbrook House, 14 Great Queen St, London WC2B 5DG; ☎020-7430 1709; fax 020-7831 4441; e-mail info@bllow.co.uk; www.bllaw.co.uk. Has an in-house team of three French lawyers. Offices in Oxford, Fareham, Southampton and Portsmouth.

Fox Hayes Solicitors: Bank House, 150 Roundhay Rd, Leeds LS8 5LD; ☎01132-496 496; fax 01132-480 466; www.foxhayes.co.uk. Contact Graham Platt: qualified both in Britain as a solicitor, and admitted to practise as an Avocat in France. Deals with property, company, litigation and probate.

French Lawyer: Isabelle Cès, 26 Cassland Rd, London E9 7AN; ☎0845-644 3061; fax 0845-644 3062; e-mail info@french-lawyer.com; www.french-lawyer.com.

John Howell & Co: The Old Glass Works, 22 Endell Street, Covent Garden, London WC2H 9AD; ☎020-7420 0400; fax 020-7836 3626; e-mail info@europelaw.com; www.europelaw.com. John Howell have been specialising in the law of other countries for over 20 years. From their London offices their 40+ strong staff pride themselves on finding cost effective solutions to their clients' international legal problems.

Howard Kennedy Solicitors: ☎020-7636 1616; www.howard-kennedy.com. Large London firm dealing with the top end of the market.

Kingsfords Solicitors: 2 Elwick Rd, Ashford, Kent TN23 1PD; ☎01233-624544; fax 01233-610011; e-mail enquiries@kingsfords.net; www.kingsfords-solicitors.com. British lawyers with expertise in French conveyancing. Fixed-price property buyer's package and other services.

The International Property Law Centre: Suffolk House, 21 Silver Street, Hull HU1 1JG; ☎0870 800 4565; fax 0870 800 4567; e-mail; internationalproperty@maxgold.com; www.internationalpropertylaw.com. Specialists in the purchase and sale of property and businesses in France, with in-house foreign lawyers. Fixed quote and no VAT payable. Contact Stefano Lucatello, Senior Partner ☎0870 800 4565, e-mail stefanol@maxgold.com).

Liliane Levasseur-Hills: 69 Pullman Lane, Godalming, Surrey GU7 1YB; ☎01483-424303. Fully qualified French notaire offering assistance with buying and selling French property, French inheritance law, and French wills.

Pannone & Partners: 123 Deansgate, Manchester M3 2BU; ☎0161-909 1553; fax 0161-909 4444; e-mail lindsay.kinnealy@pannone.co.uk; www.pannone.com. Contact: Lindsay Kinnealy.

Penningtons Solicitors: Bucklersbury House, 83 Cannon St, London EC4N 8PE; ☎020-7457 3000; fax 020-7457 3240; www.penningtons.co.uk. Paris office: 23 rue d'Anjou, 75008 Paris; ☎01 44 51 59 70; fax 01 44 51 59 71.

Prettys Solicitors: Elm House, 25 Elm Street, Ipswich, Suffolk IP1 2AD; ☎01473-232121; fax 01473-230002; e-mail france@prettys.co.uk; www.prettys.co.uk. Prettys' French Property Group are bilingual and assist clients in the whole process of buying and selling a property in France including matters relating to estate planning, inheritance tax, wealth tax and capital gains tax.

Riddell Croft & Co Solicitors: 27 St Helen's St, Ipswich, Suffolk IP14 1HH; ☎01473-384870; fax 01473-384878; www.riddellcroft.com. Experienced, bilingual practitioners offer help with buying and selling property in France, rentals, tax and estate planning and wills. Can also help with property search. Contact: sue.busby@riddellcroft.com.

Russell-Cooke: 2 Putney Hill, Putney, London SW15 6AB; ☎020-8789 9111; fax 020-8780 1679; e-mail Aldersond@russell-cooke.co.uk; www.russell-cooke.co.uk. Large firm with French law and property department, headed by Dawn Alderson, qualified in both English and French law and member of the Bordeaux bar. Bordeaux office: 42 place Gambetta, 33000 Bordeaux; 05 56 90 83 10; fax 05 56 90 83 11.

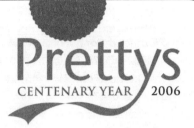

CENTENARY YEAR 2006

Quality legal advice on French property and inheritance law

Prettys' French Property department has recently been quoted in the Legal 500 as having 'a longstanding specialism in French wills and property'.

Head of department Matthew Cameron has a recognised reputation in handling high value, luxury properties, historic chateaux and estates. Matthew's team provides a full range of legal services ensuring that your concerns are taken care of, including: inheritance tax, wealth tax, capital gains tax, and general property matters.

Elm House, 25 Elm Street
Ipswich, IP1 2AD

01473 232121
france@prettys.co.uk

www.frenchpropertylawyers.com

Prettys is regulated by the Law Society and is authorised and regulated by the Financial Services Authority

Sean O'Connor & Co: Bilingual Solicitors, 2 River Walk, Tonbridge, Kent TN9 1DT; ☎01732-365378; fax 01732-360144; e-mail seanoconnorco@aol.com.
Stephen Smith (France) Ltd: 161 Cemetery Rd, Ipswich, Suffolk IP4 2HL; ☎01473-437186; fax 01473-436573; e-mail stephen@stephensmithfranceltd.com; www.stephensmithfranceltd.com. One of the leading UK specialists on French property law and tax, with over 20 years experience covering all aspects of buying and selling residential and commercial property in France. Also frequently writes and broadcasts on French law and tax.
Taylors Solicitors and Notaries Public: The Red Brick House, 28-32 Trippet Lane, Sheffield S1 4EL; ☎0114-276 67 67; fax 0114-273 1287; www.taylorssolicitors.co.uk.
Turner and Co Solicitors: 59 Charlotte St, Birmingham B3 1PX; 0121-200 1612; fax 0121-200 1613; e-mail turneranco@aol.com; www.french-property-news.com/turnerandco.htm.
Thrings and Townsend Solicitors: Midland Bridge, Bath BA1 2HQ; ☎01225-340000; fax 01225-319735; solicitors@ttuk.com; www.ttuk.com. French property purchase, setting up a French business. Offices in Newbury, Swindon and Frome.

COSTS ASSOCIATED WITH PROPERTY PURCHASE LAW

The high level of costs involved with property purchase is one of the main reasons that property prices do not go up very fast in France. The fees and taxes that have to be paid to the notaire and to the state are inaccurately referred to as *frais de notaire*, when only a part of them go to the notaire. The notaire's own emoluments are based on a sliding scale between 5% and 0.825% + TVA at 19.6%, depending on the value of the property. Some properties, so-called Group 2 and Group 3, attract smaller notaire fees, but most fall into Group 1. The notaire's fees are fixed by the state, and are not negotiable. It is normal practice for the notaire to ask in advance for more than the final bill, to cover for all eventualities, so you will probably receive a small repayment.

NOTARY'S FEES

up to €3,049	5%
€3,049-€6,098	3.3%
€6,098-16,769	1.65%
€16,769 and above	0.825%

It follows from the above, that the notaire's fees will come to about 1% of the sale price, except for very cheap properties, where they will be slightly higher.

In addition there are the *droits de mutation* – transfer taxes – adding up to 4.89% on old property, made up of:

Taxe départementale	3.60%
Frais de recouvrement	0.09% (2.5% of the above)
Taxe communale	1.20%
	4.89%

The *frais de recouvrement* are the expenses involved in collecting the *taxe départementale.* TVA (Valued Added Tax) is levied at 19.6% on new properties. The same rate is applied to extensions, garages and outbuildings added on by the seller in the last 10 years, which could come to a substantial amount.

There are some other fees to be paid, namely

○ The salary of the keeper of the land registry: 0.10% of the sale price.
○ Costs of registering a mortgage, at about 2%
○ Costs of paper, official forms, stamps, extracts from the land register, etc. paid by the notaire.

Finally, there is the commission payable to the estate agent or immobilier, which can range from 3% to 10% or even more with very cheap properties.

Before signing the acte de vente, it is advisable for you or your representative to check again on what is included in the sale price. The contract will state whether you will have vacant possession – *possession libre* – or if there are any tenants present. In the UK it is assumed that once the final contract is signed the property is available to move

into, but this does not always happen in France. If the sellers wish to
remain for a few weeks, you can expect them to pay you something as
compensation. The date by which the property is ready to move into
should be stated in the *acte de vente.*

After the Sale

Once the acte de vente has been signed, the notaire has to pay all the
taxes and commissions (unless you are paying the immobilier directly)
out of the sums that you have passed over to him. The title is registered
with the *bureau des hypothèques* – the register of deeds and mortgages,
as well as the mortgage, if any. Eventually you will receive a certificate
informing you that the title has been registered. The whole process will
take some months. The original title deed remains with the notaire.
He is authorised to make authentic copies if necessary.

Under-Declaring the Sale Price

It was once common practice to under-declare the sale price so as to save on
taxes and fees, while paying a part 'under the table', or *sous la table*. There
is no advantage in the long run to the buyer, since they will be penalised with
higher Capital Gains Tax in the future when they resell. The penalties for under-
declaring are serious. The one way around this is for the seller to leave some
furniture or other moveable goods in the property, which can be given a slightly
inflated value, thus reducing the taxes payable.

Notaires as Estate Agents

It might come as a surprise to Brits that notaires also act as estate
agents, especially in western France and in country areas. Many French
people wouldn't dream of using an *agent immobilier* to find property.
Notaires keep lists of properties; they often have the best deals around.
They make very good estate agents: they have the best database on
property prices, they are keen to make a quick sale to get their clients
out of difficulty, and they are more likely to give an honest description
of the property, compared with an immobilier, who will try to embel-
lish on its merits. The notaire will require a commission on the sale,
but not as much as an immobilier; the commission is on a sliding of

scale of 5% on the first €50,000 and then 2.5% above, plus TVA. One can reckon on paying 3% of the sale price.

Some properties held by notaires have 'problems' associated with them. This mainly happens when legatees find themselves in a situation known as *indivision* after someone has died, when two or more people have rights to the proceeds of a sale, and neither can sell without the other's agreement. There are also properties which have servitudes or obligations attached to them, e.g. someone has the right to live in the property for the rest of their life, or someone has a right to use the land or rights of way.

RENOVATING A PROPERTY

Main Points About Builders

○ Most French builders are good at their job; but they are also in demand and booked months in advance.

○ Many French tradesmen are used to a two-hour plus lunch break and a bottle of wine.

○ There is a strong temptation to bring over your own builders from Britain or Ireland but there are drawbacks.

○ Not using local tradesmen can cause resentment and put you on bad terms with the village.

○ British builders may be quite unqualified to make repairs to traditional French buildings, and their work will have no legal guarantees in France.

○ Work done by builders registered in France has to be insured for 10 years – the *garantie décennale.*

○ Registered French builders have gone through a long apprenticeship.

○ You should beware of using unregistered British builders, unless you know them well, because of the insurance implications. You are 100% liable if the builder is injured.

○ Using foreign tradesmen means you will not qualify for grants towards doing the work and the cost will not be taken into account in reducing Capital Gains tax liability.

○ If you have obtained a loan to do renovation work on your house from a French mortgage lender, it is a condition that you use registered French tradesmen.

Finding A Builder

All tradesmen in France should be registered with the local *chambre des métiers* and have an official business number: the SIRET. This is shown on advertisements. One will find numerous British and other English-speaking tradesmen advertising in French property magazines, such as *French Property News, France* and *Living France*; many of them have a SIRET number, the others in the process of applying for one: SIRET *en cours*. The normal procedure is to ask for an estimate – a *devis* – from several tradesmen; the *devis* is then binding. It is essential to obtain references from builders, and ask to see photos of their previous work if possible. TVA is levied at only 5.5% on building materials and work done to restore or maintain properties more than two years old. If you use an unregistered tradesman you will pay the full rate of 19.6% on building materials. It is illegal to pay for any services in cash above €2,000.

If you are having a substantial job done, involving several tradesmen, you may wish to appoint a *maître d'œuvre* to supervise the whole operation. You will need to draw up a written contract with the maître d'œuvre. For more information see *Buying Property* in the chapter: *Your New Home in France.*

Before building work begins, you can draw up an *état des lieux*, a description of the property, in the presence of the builder so that you have some evidence if they damage trees or verges. They may not, of course, agree to this. Every foreign property-owner who has had work done by French tradesmen will tell you that they need to be supervised. They are generally very honest, but they may have assistants who are not.

Restoring A Property

For some foreigners, the whole point of buying in France is to find a derelict building and turn it into a bijou residence they can retire to. Some properties in remoter areas are put on the market by the French in the full knowledge that only a foreigner would buy them. One should be wary of getting sucked into a project which could eat up huge sums of money for little return. Doing up a derelict property can cost as much as building a house from scratch.

Think local

Tim Weir bought a traditional farmhouse in Deux-Sèvres in 2002 with the intention of renovating and starting *gîtes*. His website is www.leshiboux. com.

If you are lucky enough to find the 'ideal' property for restoration, I think the project is at least one year away from the real start. All sorts of rules and regulations need to be adhered to, e.g. architects plans are obligatory if the build size is greater than 170 sq.m. Engaging an architect is a good idea. He will either charge a set fee for the drawings – including submission to the local mairie – or he will act as a project manager and charge a percentage of the final build. Either way a good architect is a valuable friend and best found by recommendation (the local mairie is a good starting point!)

Having got your permis de construire, *you then have to look for artisans. You can start the search before you have permission, but if you need to revise the plans you will have inconvenienced many of your potential employees. Again we found that recommendations are the best route and a trip back to the local mairie is essential. It is quite usual to obtain at least 3 devis (estimates) for all jobs and to take your pick. Keeping a good flow of artisans along with all their materials is a juggling act, as it would be in the UK. We have found that it is almost impossible to find a 'Jack of all Trades' and artisans are usually unprepared to do another artisan's work, i.e. a plumber will be unwilling to cut wood. Perhaps this originates from the 10-year guarantee supplied on all work carried out by registered artisans and therefore they don't wish to be held responsible for work outside their own trade. We have found that any artisan worth his salt will have at least a three-month work list and this is the minimum time that should be allotted prior to commencing work. But once you start getting to know the locals, and in particular artisans, two things seem to happen: They are very often prepared to do 'Saturday' work for cash with almost no delay, or the time period of availability is reduced in proportion to the length of time you've known an artisan – perhaps they deliberately leave spaces in their work diaries to help out mates in need?*

Water was already present at the main house and premier gîte so they required 'tapping off', as were the electrics but these required upgrading and on the advice of the chap from the local electricity board we had all main incoming wires put underground to improve the 'vista' and avoid loads of ugly wires running through our picturesque courtyard. We had the electrical supply to the house split three ways to include the two new builds. The advantage is that all new supplies are subject to rigorous and costly inspection but this also triples your annual line rental charges.

We were lucky enough to find a fantastic local bloke with a digger who helped with digging out the barns ready for internal foundations and putting in the trampoline pit whilst digging trenches for the above cables. A lot of the other 'big' works, e.g. laying of concrete slabs and building limestone external walls, were carried out by a local building company, with the remaining works e.g. building internal walls and insulation, carried out by ourselves, often with guidance from friends and local artisans.

It is advisable to spend time doing some background research on tradesmen. Unfortunately there are increasing numbers of unscrupulous unregistered English tradesmen who are prepared to work in your own language, but often at a cost to you financially and otherwise later on. They may say: 'Aaarrh, you don't wanna do it like that mate, that ain't how we done it in England. I know a much betta way, guv.' Local regulations are very different from those in the UK, and there are also practical considerations, for example, local stone has been used for hundreds of years to keep out the heat in the summer and keep it in during the winter, so carry on using it, because usually it's cheaper, more readily available and your London brick house will look out of place amongst the local Charantaise limestone!

The details of property renovation are beyond the scope of this book. There are several books on the market that deal with renovation; the best is David Everett's *Buying and Restoring Old Property in France*, which is mainly concerned with restoring rather than buying. If you read French, it is worth getting *Architecture Rurale et Bourgeoise en France*, by Georges Doyon and Robert Hubrecht, a fascinating survey of traditional building techniques and terminology covering the whole of France, through www.amazon.fr. This also gives advice on how to restore properties in an authentic style.

Grants

It is worth enquiring about grants – *subventions* – for restoration. The ANAH – *Association Nationale pour l'Amélioration de l'Habitat* – has offices in every DDE – *Division Départementale de l'Équipement*. There are more generous grants available for listed buildings and buildings considered to be noteworthy because some famous person lived there. See the website: www.anah.fr. There are more possibilities if you are planning to start a business or run *gîtes*. Some *communes* may offer grants towards the cost of being connected up to the electricity or water supply. The mairie will let you know what is available.

Glossaries of French Building Terms

Building has its own terminology which is generally ignored in the big French-English dictionaries. Unfortunately, there is no readily available French-English glossary of building terms on the internet. The more basic terminology is explained in the Canadian *Grande Dictionnaire de Terminologie,* available free on www.granddictionnaire.com. The best, and very extensive, work is Don Montague's *Dictionary of Building and Civil Engineering,* published by Spon, which is both French-English and English-French. Hadley Pager Info (P.O.Box 249, Leatherhead, Surrey KT23 3WX; ☎01372-458550) publish a range of French/ English technical glossaries, including *Glossary of House Purchase and Renovation Terms* (56 pages), and *Concise Dictionary of House Building, Arranged by Trades* (256 pages). There is also J. Kater Pollock's *Dictionary of Building, Property and Gardening,* which can be obtained through French property magazines, such as www.french-property-news.com.

Building Permits

Planning permission – the *permis de construire* – is needed for most alterations to property; even if you do not require a PC, you will need to enter a declaration that you are exempt. To be on the safe side you may wish to obtain outline planning permission first, a *certificat d'urbanisme,* which is treated below.

The first rule to remember is that if your restorations or building work cover more than 170 square metres – this is the total floor area, whether one or more storeys – you have to have architect's plans drawn up. The second rule is that you cannot build anything within 3 metres (10 feet) of a neighbouring property, or half the height of a neighbouring wall if it exceeds 6 metres.

It is not necessary to enter the application for the PC yourself; your architect or maître d'œuvre or your representative (*mandataire*) can do this for you, but you are ultimately responsible if the right PC has not been acquired first. The forms you need are held by the *mairie;* they are exactly the same throughout France.

It is not always necessary to get a PC for minor work to the house, nor for some smaller external constructions, but it is necessary to enter a *déclaration de travaux exemptés de permis* for any building work that is exempt from a PC. The request for the PC is sent to the *mairie* by registered letter (*recommandée avec demande d'avis de réception* (or *accusé de réception*), or it can be delivered by hand; you will be given a receipt (*décharge*). The authorities have 15 days to send you a *lettre de notification* with the number of your PC registration, and the length of time it will take them to deal with your PC, which is usually 2 or 3 months from the date on your *avis de réception* or *décharge*, a period known as the *delai d'instruction,* unless the authorities get a court order giving them more time. If the authorities fail to give a decision within the stated time then it is assumed that the PC has been granted automatically, a PC *tacite*. A PC is valid for 2 years.

Planning permission rules are complex, and it is advisable always to ask the mairie before carrying out any building work, however minor. It is important to understand that a permis de construire never allows you to demolish an existing building. For this you need a *permis de démolir.*

Richard Coman on troubles with the *tout à l'égout*

For about 10 years we were fine with our fosse septique *but then we were told by the commune that we had to be on the main drainage system, the* tout à l'égout. *The contractors had to use dynamite because the ground was solid granite under three inches of soil. Then the next-door neighbour found cracks in his walls and accused us of having planted trees too close to his house. I had got a pépiniériste (nurseryman) to plant some trees along our boundary 14 years earlier, but he had failed to observe the regulation that says you can't plant trees within three metres of an adjoining property, so I had to ask him to come and dig the trees up. On top of that the contractors who dug the sewage trenches left a huge mound of granite chippings on my land. I went to see the maire and got a London firm of translators to write a business letter in French, at great expense, but to no effect. Finally I had the notaire threaten legal action, which did the trick, but of course I had to pay the legal fees.*

Special rules apply if you are carrying out work on or next to or within view of a listed building or site. The authorities have four months after acknowledging receipt of your application to consider the case. You should never assume that you have tacit approval where listed buildings are concerned, even if you hear nothing from the authorities. If the application is passed to the national ministry of public works they are not necessarily required to give you any response. If you are working within 500 metres of a listed site, you may be told to use only certain kinds of building material, which can make the work far more expensive.

Certificat d'Urbanisme. Prior to applying for a PC, you may want to obtain outline planning permission, or a *certificat d'urbanisme* (CU). Anyone can apply for a CU, even before they have bought a property or piece of land. The application for the CU – *demande de certificat d'urbanisme* – requires plans and maps of the property, in four copies, and a description and drawings or photos of the work you propose to do. A CU will only be granted for land that is *viabilisé* – namely, where there are adequate roads and utilities, a pre-condition for it becoming *constructible*. The CU is delivered within two months of the application, if it is not turned down. You then have one year during which you are more or less guaranteed a PC. Buyers are sometimes told that a CU has been obtained, when it has in fact already lapsed.

A recent property will have a CU: you couldn't build it without one. Older properties will not have a CU necessarily, unless someone applied for one, but there should have been a PC. There is the outside risk that a property was built without planning permission in the past. Once it has been standing for 30 years then the authorities cannot make you demolish it.

SWIMMING POOLS

A swimming pool (*piscine*) is a luxury that you may want to add to your new home in France. It is important to bear in mind that a swimming pool entails substantial running costs; £1,500 annually for a minimum £15,000 pool is a fair average.

Deciding on what kind of swimming pool to install is not an easy decision. The three main possibilities are the pre-fabricated fibre-glass pool, a galvanised steel construction with a vinyl liner, or reinforced concrete. A concrete construction consists of a double layer of blocks with steel reinforced concrete inside. Another possibility is a prefabricated fibre-glass pool which is then back-filled with pea-shingle. There is also the possibility of a smaller plastic pool of which there are plenty available in France.

France has numerous swimming pool companies; it is a matter of whether you feel comfortable dealing with French contractors, or would rather deal with an English-speaking company. It is best to avoid national franchises; rather go for local companies. If you want to know more about French pools, there is a dedicated magazine: *Techniques Piscines* (www.techniques-piscines.fr).

Construction of swimming pools up to 20 sq.m. does not require *a* permis de construire but you must apply for an exemption from the PC, on form PC156. An experienced swimming pool contractor will be able to advise you on the procedures. You are not allowed to build a swimming pool within view of a road, as the sight of scantily clad swimmers could cause a traffic accident. There is also a rule that you cannot build anything closer than 3 metres to someone else's property or boundary, or half the height of the adjoining wall if this exceeds 6 metres.

Strict new regulations came into force in May 2004, making it compulsory for safety devices to be installed to prevent young children from drowning. One solution is to install a cover, either electrically or manually operated, which cannot be removed by a child under five. There is a €45,000 fine for failing to install safety devices. Insurers will make it obligatory for you to comply with the law. These four solutions must meet AFNOR standards NF P90 306, 307, 308 and 309.

THE RENTAL SCENE

Renting rather than buying was until recently the preferred choice of many French people. With some steep rises in the price of property, and plenty of cheap loans, the idea of buying is now becoming more popular, and there are almost as many owner-occupiers as in the UK. The most significant feature of the French rental scene is that while there are more properties for rent than in the UK, the percentage of social housing is smaller.

Foreigners looking for property to buy are not going to remain in France long enough to qualify for subsidised rentals and are forced to look on the open market. Rents vary enormously around the country. The highest prices are in Paris, Strasbourg, Lyon, western coastal resorts, and the Riviera. The lowest can be found in the economically depressed areas of the northwest, central and eastern France. The typical rental property is an unfurnished apartment, often in a *copropriété*. Large apartment blocks are often owned by banks or insurance companies. The main thing to look for is a *digicode* – a digital entry system – or *vidéophone*. The presence of a *concierge* or *gardien* is a great advantage. The kinds of problems found in large apartment blocks in the UK also exist on certain estates in France – the HLM. Apart from these estates with social problems, privately-run apartment blocks are acceptable places to live. In addition to paying rent, one has to expect to pay one's share of the communal *charges*. Whether you rent an apartment or a house, you will be required to take out a minimum insurance policy: the *assurance multirisques habitation*.

For legal reasons property must be either fully furnished or not at all. A property that lacks essential equipment such as a cooker or refrigerator is not considered furnished. It is also illegal to rent out an apartment where the principal room has a surface area of less than 9 square metres. There are plenty of studios or *studettes* with 10 sq.m. living rooms. There should also be cooking facilities and running water. The lessor will require evidence that you can pay the rent, such as recent pay slips and bank statements. They may not agree to rent a property to you if the rent exceeds one-third of your monthly income. The lessor will have a standard rental agreement for you to sign. There is a deposit to pay – the *dépôt de garantie*.

Rental Deposit (Dépôt de Garantie)

The deposit is often referred to by the French as *la caution*, but the official term is *dépôt de garantie*. The amount of the rental deposit can vary: when a property is rented out by the month, the maximum is two months' rent, when rented out by the year, the maximum is three months. For some dwellings, known as *logements conventionnés*, the maximum is one month's rent. Owners are required to refund the deposit within two months of the tenant leaving the property, minus any deductions for damage. Where the owner fails to restore the deposit in time, the tenant can obtain a summary judgment from a lower court obliging the owner to pay up, by filling in a simple form called a *déclaration au greffe*; should the sum be over €3,800 a hearing has to take place before a *juge d'instance* (civil magistrate). If the tenant is aware that they owe money to the owner, then they can have this taken into account by the court.

Unlike in some countries, the owner can invest the deposit as they please; the tenant does not receive any interest on this.

> **Eric Smith rented several apartments in Antibes before buying his current property.**
>
> *There were particular problems with one apartment; it was on the top of a 5-storey building, and all charges were included. But the heating didn't work. When we moved out after a year we received a bill for €1,400 for the heating. We made a mistake because we had only informed the landlady and the syndic (manager) of the* copropriété *verbally that there was a problem. We were then taken to court for non-payment, and eventually had to pay half. This made us realise that you absolutely must send any complaints by* lettre recommandée *(registered letter), otherwise you have no recourse. Because we were on such good terms with the owner, the agent and the manager we never imagined that they would do this to us.*
>
> *Practices on the south coast seem to be generally rather relaxed. We gave the estate agent a cheque as a deposit, and he simply held on to it and never cashed it, so we got the cash back when we moved out and it had no bearing on the court case about the central heating. This seems to be a standard practice down here. Also we have never actually seen an* état des lieux *(inspection report) on a rented property. We made a list ourselves of anything that looked damaged, and there were no problems when we moved out, but strictly speaking you could get into trouble without having an official report made up when you move in. Again it seems that no one bothers around here. Our contract was for one year, because it the owner's second home.*
>
> *My only suggestion is not to do everything by word of mouth, but it is difficult to go against local practices.*

Advertising

The basic term for rental is *location:* every local newspaper has a section. If you are simply looking around shops or houses, you will come across adverts *A Louer* (For Rent). Some advertisements are put up by professional agents, called *marchands de listes,* who look for tenants on behalf of owners. They are subject to the same regulations as agents immobiliers, who also have rental property. The property websites that are given below have rental sections and should prove useful for anyone looking to rent a house or apartment.

Useful Websites	
www.alouer.fr	www.appelimmo.fr
www.bonjour.fr	www.colocataire.fr
www.entreparticuliers.fr	www.foncia.fr
www.journaldesparticuliers.fr	www.kitrouve.com
www.lacentrale.fr	www.lesiteimmobilier.com
www.locat.com	www.pap.fr

Places to Stay While House-Hunting

Fortunately, France has plentiful and cheap hotel accommodation which puts the UK to shame. Starting at the top end, you could check out the website www.chateauhotels.com, or order their brochure. Naturally, the prices are fairly steep, but the locations are superb. The next step down is the organisation *Logis de France* (www.logis-de-france.fr), which covers hotel-restaurants in the two- to four-star category; many Anglos swear by it.

If you are looking for *chambres d'hôtes* or *gîtes,* Gîtes de France dominates the market: their annual catalogue will give you places to stay anywhere in the country; see www.gitesdefrance.com. You can get in touch with owners for longer-term rentals through www.cheznous.com or www.abritel.fr (in French). Because of the difficulties that gîte owners are currently experiencing in finding tenants, you can expect to find a good deal. For Paris try the very useful website www.paris-exchange.com. If you want to be guaranteed a personal and welcoming service, the best book is Alastair Sawday's *Special Places to Stay in France.*

Longer stays in France can be more difficult to arrange than holiday lets. Because the French tend to stay put for years thanks to the letting regulations, it is less common to rent a place for three or six months than it would be in the UK. One way around this is to advertise on a website such as www.french-property-news.com or www.french-news.com to see if another foreign property owner will rent you their property (usually out of season) for a lengthy period, or you could offer to be a caretaker and live rent-free. You can also look around in your favoured location for a French owner who is willing to rent out for a few months.

Formalities Of Renting

Househunters will be looking for short-term rented accommodation, but not at an exorbitant price. While long-term unfurnished rentals are covered by the 1989 laws, which give tenants wide-ranging rights and make eviction very difficult, furnished seasonal rentals, holiday homes and sub-lets are governed only by the *Code Civil,* the basic civil law. Such rentals are termed *location libre.* The landlord (*bailleur*) and tenant (*locataire*) can come to any agreement they wish – unless it is illegal – regarding the length of the tenancy and the conditions of payment. This can be a verbal or written agreement. The duration of the rental agreement can be fixed or indeterminate.

Tenants are liable for some repairs – the *réparations locatives.* Anything that is not a réparation locative is the responsibility of the landlord. One also needs to be aware of the *charges récupérables* – the costs the landlord can require the tenant to pay. These are fixed by law. These items are listed in great detail in *Propriétaires et Locataires: Qui Paie Quoi?* published by PRAT.

L'État des Lieux

Drawing up a description of 'the state of the premises' is an important step to be undertaken before actually moving into a new home. It is meant to safeguard the tenant from being accused of damage that is not of their doing, and thus unfairly being made to pay for repairs before they can recover their rental deposit (*dépôt de garantie*). It also protects the owner from having to pay for damage caused by the tenant.

Model forms for *états des lieux* can be found at town halls. The whole business of the état des lieux may seem an unnecessary bother, but it does have advantages for both parties. Without this description of the premises, it is assumed that they were in good condition when the tenant moved in. The tenant will not then easily be able to contest the owner's demand that the premises be restored to their original condition (*remise en état*). By and large, the law favours the tenant in such situations.

Rental Contracts

Standard contracts are sold in bookshops. A letting contract is a lengthy document. It will always state the type of lease that is involved, whether short-term (*saisonnière*) or the standard unfurnished lease under the 1989 law. Tenants are always entitled to request a written lease if the premises are let under the 1989 law. The owner is not permitted to insert clauses that prevent the tenant from working from home (with certain restrictions), or from keeping a pet. The tenant is free to pay the owner by the method that he chooses. He or she cannot be compelled to pay by standing order or by cheque.

A lease is either for 3 years if the owner is a private individual, or 6 years if the owner is a company. The tenant can give notice at any time of 3 months, which is reduced to 1 month if the tenant is compelled to leave because of job relocation, a fall in income or their state of health (but only if he or she is over 60). There are strict rules about rent increases. The owner can give the tenant notice to quit if the landlord wishes to occupy the premises or where the tenant has committed a serious breach of the contract.

The following is an example of a letter from a tenant giving notice (unfurnished premises):

Monsieur (ou Madame)

J'ai l'honneur de vous donner congé pour le ..... de l'appartement que j'occupe et qui m'a été loué suivant bail sous seing privé en date du ...., conformément

aux dispositions des articles 12 et 15-1, al.2, du 6 juillet 1989.
I hereby wish to give notice from the ..... for the apartment that I currently occupy and which is let to me according to the rental contract dated ....., in accordance with the provisions of the law of 6 July 1989, articles 12 and 15-1, para.2.

Je me tiens à votre disposition pour établir un état des lieux si vous le souhaitez, à l'occasion de la remise des clés.

I am available to draw up an inspection report if you so wish at the time of returning the keys.

Je me permets de vous rappeler que vous devez me restituer, conformément à l'article 22 de la loi du 6 juillet 1989, dans un délai maximal de deux mois après mon départ la somme de ..... euros qu je vous ai versée en dépôt de garantie et vous remercie de bien vouloir prendre vos dispositions pour le faire.

I take this opportunity to remind you that you are required to return to me the sum of .... euros being the deposit I paid to you, within at the most two months, in accordance with article 22 of the law of 6 July, and would be grateful if you would take the necessary steps to do so.

Veuillez agréer, Monsieur (ou Madame), l'assurance de mes salutations distinguées.
Yours sincerely,

(Adapted from *300 modèles de lettres et de contrats*, published by PRAT).

UTILITIES

Electricity and gas are supplied by the state monopoly organisation EDF/GDF. In most of France there is no mains gas (*gaz de ville*), so you have the option of installing a large *citerne* (2 cubic metre tank) and having liquefied gas delivered, or using bottled gas. For more information see www.gazdefrance.com.

Electricity

Many foreign property-buyers take little notice of the state of the wiring in the property that they are thinking of buying, something that can prove to be an expensive mistake. Almost all pre-1970s houses have potentially hazardous wiring, unless they have been rewired. The main problems are lack of, or insufficient earthing, corroded wiring and unsuitable circuit-breakers. In older properties you can still find WWI-style cotton-covered wiring. Apart from any risk of electrocution, if you are taking over an older property it is essential to find out whether the wiring can handle heavy-amperage equipment such as washing machines and electric cookers. If you need to run electric heating at the same time as other heavy equipment such as an electric cooker, water heater, washing machine etc., then you will require a supply of at least 12 KvA (kilovolt amperes or kilowatts), for which heavier wiring is needed to the electricity meter. Where you are planning a business that involves using heavy equipment, then you need to consider whether your supply is going to be adequate.

If the power supply to your property has been cut off before you buy it then you will require a *certificat de conformité* or CC from the electricity safety organisation Consuel to certify that the system is safe before EDF will reconnect your supply. Consuel does not inspect an electrician's work unless there is a good reason, neither does it certify that your system conforms to a certain level. They will only test the earths and the consumer unit (*tableau principal*). If you buy a house without an electricity supply, the French state monopoly, *Électricité de France* (EDF), will connect you to the grid. There is a basic charge of €600 for a new connection, plus €1,500 for every new electricity pole that has to be erected. If you cannot see an electricity pylon nearby then your connection could cost more than the property itself.

If you are intending to buy a property in France, it is in your interest to ask the seller to allow a *Diagnostic Confiance Sécurité* to be carried out. This is a 40-minute inspection covering a list of 53 points resulting in an objective assessment of the state of the wiring of your house. Once the inspection has been carried out, you can call in an electrician to give an estimate (*devis*) of the cost of any work needed. The DCS only costs €80 including taxes. Needless to say, if your prospective seller refuses to allow a DCS then you should be suspicious. Do not under any circumstances take the seller's word for it that everything is fine with the wiring. A DCS can be arranged by calling an EDF advisor on ☎0801 126 126, or through Promotelec who carry out the DCS, on ☎0825 046 770 or through their website www.promotelec.com. Information about different tariffs can be found on EDF's websites: http://monagence. edf.fr and www.mamaison.edf.fr.

Water

The mains water supply is safe to drink, if not always that tasty. The French consume a lot of bottled mineral water, on average 100 litres per person per year.

Mains water is supplied by *Générale des Eaux* and other local companies around France. *Lyonnaise des Eaux* is well-known and owns some UK water suppliers. There have been water shortages in central and southern France in recent years during hot weather. The water supply is metered and can cost twice as much as in the UK. There will be a meter outside the property. It is essential to check the reliability of the supply if you are buying property. Water leaks should be reported quickly.

If there is no water supply to a property, one can either arrange for a connection to be made, or try to sink a well – *puits* – on the land, or tap into an underground spring. The quality of the water has to be analysed first before you can use it. Water with a high nitrate content – where there is intensive agriculture – presents a real health risk.

On average, mains water costs €2.8 per cubic metre. The average person in the north of France uses 43 cubic metres a year, while on the Côte d'Azur the figure is 74 cubic metres. In Paris it is 66 cubic metres. Evidently, it is worth investing in water saving measures if possible. To find out the local price of water, and the nearest supplier, look at the website www.generale-des-eaux.com.

For large-scale use of the water supply for activities such as brewing your system will have to be inspected by the *Police d'Eau* (water police). If you generate large amounts of waste water you will need to build natural filtration tanks – *lagunage* – and have your facilities approved.

Septic Tanks/Fosses Septiques

The state of one's septic tank is a favourite subject of conversation with foreign residents in France. Septic tanks exist in the UK, but they are more common in France, where many properties are far from the main sewage system. There is a trend in France to connect more properties to the main sewage system, known as *tout à l'égout*. Cesspits – *puisards* – where all the waste simply goes into a hole in the ground, are being phased out, and it is no longer legal to build one. All *fosses septiques* are subject to a new government standard introduced in 2005.

If you are looking at country properties, make sure to find out whether there is a fosse septique. If there is none you will be required to install one. Since the whole contraption extends at least 70 feet from the house, it is essential to have enough land to build one. The larger your fosse septique the less trouble it will give you. You cannot construct anything over the fosse septique, and there should be a minimum of trees around it. You should also look at the slope of the land, and make sure that the water table is not too close to the surface. Generally, fosses septiques work better in hotter climates, which favour the breakdown of the wastes. The price of new fosses septiques is going up rapidly because of ever more stringent regulations. A new one, including the cost of installation, can cost €5,000. For suppliers look at French property magazines, or the website www.profosse.com.

Telephones And Internet

The telephony scene in France is in something of a flux. In most places *France Télécom* is the only company that can install your first phone-line and all calls go through them, but in some cities it is now possible to have a phone line installed by *Cegetel* or *Free Telecom*, such as Paris, Lyon and Bordeaux, and to pay your line rental to these companies. Very soon the fixed telephony scene will be revolutionized by the use of VoIP, or calling via the internet. For more details of communications see *Keeping in Touch*.

France Télécom has been gradually privatized; by June 2005 the state held only 34.9% of the shares. It now has the distinction of being the world's most heavily indebted company. The website www.francetelecom. fr has a lot of information (if you can find it) and this may not be entirely positive, especially if you live in a country area. Up until now there has been no difference in the price of having a new phone line installed in a city, or in the remotest parts of the hinterland. Sooner or later, France Télécom will decide it cannot spend 1,000s of euros on connecting rural customers to the nearest exchange. You can use other telephone services providers, e.g. Onetel and 9 Télécom. The comparison of the prices can be found on the website www.comparatel.com.

British handsets need an adaptor to work in France; the British variety has three wires, while the French ones have only two. The keys on French telephones are much the same as on British ones. The only point to note is that the hash symbol is called *dièse* – the same as a 'sharp' in music – needed for cheap-rate telephone cards. Both business and private phone numbers are on the internet. The Yellow Pages are on www.pagesjaunes.fr and private subscribers on www.annuaire.com or www.annu.fr. There is also Minitel, which is expensive but can be used free in post offices. There is always Directory Enquiries: dial 12.

Mobile Phones

Mobile phone contracts are a subject of some controversy in France. Unless you are prepared to stay with one company for a certain time, you will not be able to keep the same phone number or list of numbers if you buy another phone. If you spend any amount of time in France you will want to rent or buy a mobile phone there, but before you sign a contract it is worth considering the small print. You can try to have the SIM card in your phone replaced with a French one, so you can carry on using the same phone. If your phone is 'SIM-locked', i.e. the card cannot be changed, then you need a French mobile. Unless you are officially resident in France, French mobile phone companies will only let you use a phone with a pre-paid card, on production of your passport. The well-known deals are *Orange La Mobicarte, SFR La Carte*, and *Bouygues Carte Nomad*.

To buy a phone you need a proof of identity and a proof of address. You also have to produce an RIB – a bank account number – which is in any case unavoidable if you pay by direct debit. You will also be asked to produce a cheque written out to you that has gone through your account, or a French credit card.

As France is relatively thinly populated in comparison to the UK, mobile phone coverage is not guaranteed, and there are areas in the countryside where you will not have any reception. Out of the three main phone companies, Orange and SFR are supposed to have better coverage than Bouygues Télécom in country areas. All three claim to cover 98% of the population and 87% of the land area.

The mobile phone market is competitive and rapidly changing. For a clear overview of the different deals on offer, look at the website www.comparatel.com. From this it is evident that there is not that much to choose between the three main operators, although Bouygues comes out slightly better if you are a light user. For the three main companies see: www.orange.fr, www.sfr.fr and www.bouyguestelecom.fr.

Internet

The French government has had the bright idea of installing internet terminals in 1,000 post offices. Unfortunately, many of these terminals do not work properly, and you can only use the post office's own web-mail, www.laposte.net in any case.

The French are still trying to decide on a word for 'e-mail'. The *Académie Française* favours *courriel*, an abbreviation of *courrier électronique*, but almost no one has taken this up. Most people prefer the ugly-sounding *mél*; a lot of companies use the word *e-mail*, but it is not likely to become the standard written form of the word in French.

A light user may do well with *Wanadoo.fr* or *Club-internet.fr*. Wanadoo (owned by France Télécom), *Club-internet, Tiscali, Free* and *Freesurf* also offer 'free' packages where you only pay for the telephone call. If you are connected to cable, you can get good deals with *Noos*. For the moment you will only be able to have ADSL (high-speed connections) in certain areas. Even if your modem speed is 56kbps it may effectively be only 10kbps or less. The French government is committed to providing ADSL all over the country, which may mean having small aeroplanes flying overhead in remote districts 24 hours a day. For more information about different ISP charges, look at the website www.comparatel.com or some back issues of the French consumer magazine *Le Particulier*. For more information on telephoning using the internet see *Keeping in Touch* in the chapter *Quality of Life*.

Foreign Exchange… How to get the most from your money

When you start to plan your retirement to France there are lots of things that you need to consider to make sure that your new life is a happy one. Currencies Direct explain how one of the most important things that you need to consider, and often one of the most overlooked, is foreign exchange.

If you're retiring to France you will no doubt have to change your hard earned money from sterling into euros. Whether it's to buy a new house or simply to transfer your savings to live off, foreign exchange can't be ignored. Unfortunately, no one can predict the exchange rate as many economic and political factors constantly affect the strength of the pound. Exchange rates are constantly moving and there is no guarantee that they will be in your favour when you need your money, so it is vital that you protect yourself against these movements. A lack of proper forward planning could potentially cost you thousands of pounds and reduce your spending power abroad.

For example, the affect the exchange rate can have on the cost of a new house can be seen if you look at what happened to the euro during 2005. Sterling against the euro was as high as 1.5124 and as low as 1.4086. This means that if you were buying a house worth €200,000 it could have cost you as little as £132,240 or as much as £141,984, a difference of almost £10,000.

However, it is possible to avoid this pitfall by buying and fixing a rate for your currency ahead of time through a **forward contract**. This is the *Buy now, Pay later* option and is ideal if you still have some time to wait before your money is due in France or if you are waiting for the proceeds from the sale of your UK property. Usually a small deposit will secure you a rate for anywhere up to 2 years in advance and by doing so you will have the security of having the currency you need at a guaranteed cost and knowing exactly how much money you are taking with you.

Another option available to you if you have time on your side is a **limit** order. This is used when you want to achieve a rate that is currently not available. You set the rate that you want and the market is then monitored. As soon as that rate is achieved the currency is purchased for you. You can also set a 'lower' level or 'stop' to protect yourself should the rate drastically fall. This is ideal for when you don't have to make an immediate payment and you have a specific budget available.

If however you need to act swiftly and your capital is readily available then it is most likely that you will use a **spot transaction**. This is the *Buy now, Pay now* option where you get the most competitive rate on the day.

It is however fair to admit that many of us do not have the time or sufficient knowledge of these options to be in a position to confidently gauge when the foreign currency rates are at their most favourable, and this is where a foreign exchange specialist can help. As an alternative to your bank, foreign exchange specialists are able to offer you extremely competitive exchange rates, no commission charges and lower transfer fees. This can mean considerable savings on your transfer when compared to using a bank.

It is also very easy to use a foreign exchange specialist. The first thing you will need to do is register with them as a client. This is usually very straightforward and requires you to complete a registration form and provide two forms of identification, usually a copy of your passport and a recent utility bill. Once you are registered you are then able to trade. Your dealer will talk you through the different options that are available to you and help you to decide which one is right for you depending on your timing, circumstances and foreign currency needs. Once you have decided which option is best for you and agreed a rate you will then need to send your money. With clearance times at each end some companies can complete the transfer for you in as little as a week.

Even once you have retired to France you may find yourself in the position where you need to regularly transfer funds from your UK bank account to France. This may be because you are still receiving a pension in the UK or perhaps you have decided to rent out your house until you settle and so are receiving rental income. If this is the case using a reputable foreign exchange specialist to do the transfers for you can make sure that you get more of your money each time, even on small amounts. This is because unlike your bank they will offer you competitive exchange rates on these smaller amounts plus they won't charge you commission and transfers are often free.

Currencies Direct is a leading commercial foreign exchange company; offering superior rates of exchange and a personalised service they meet the needs of thousands of private and corporate clients every year.

With offices in the UK, Spain, Australia, South Africa and India Currencies Direct is always on hand to help you. For more information about their services, please contact one of their dealers who will be happy to discuss your currency requirements with you.

UK Head Office: 0845 389 0906
Email: info@currenciesdirect.com
Web: www.currenciesdirect.com

Housing Finance

CHAPTER SUMMARY

○ One of the most important decisions is probably going to be the way you utilise your UK assets, in particular your home, to fund retiring to France.

○ With a French mortgage monthly repayments may not exceed a third of your income, and mortgages may be up to 85% of the property value.

○ Real Estate taxes in France are considerably lower than Britain's Council Tax, but there are many other taxes in France including VAT which is levied on more items than in Britain.

○ Capital gains taxes in France discourage property speculation so you should spend time finding the right property for your retirement as a mistake could be financially punitive.

○ As France's inheritance laws are vastly different to the UK's you need professional advice before you sign a contract to buy a property.

○ You can save thousands of pounds by using the services of a currency dealer to pay for your property, rather than using a high street bank.

○ Pensioners (those over 60) are exempt from *Taxe d'habitation*, one of the main principal French property taxes.

○ *Taxe Professionelle* is levied on properties used for business purposes, but those renting rooms in their principal residence or running *gîtes* and *chambres d'hôtes* are exempt.

○ If you rent a property for a long period, the owner will ask you to take out insurance for the building and contents. This is also usually a clause in the tenancy agreement.

AFFORDING THE MOVE

Using Your UK Home As Funding

Before departing for France deciding what you are going to do with your UK home is a paramount consideration. The decision will vary depending on individual financial situations. Many people sell their UK home and use the funds to buy a property in France and provide enough additional funds to live on for their retirement in France. Currently, the UK housing market is slowing down, which is a cloud with a silver lining for those wanting to sell up and retire in France. The cloud part is that it may take you longer to sell your UK property than you expect and so you should not sign any documents committing you to buy a property in France unless you have exchanged contracts in the UK; this is assuming that your UK property is your only source of funding. While you are waiting for a buyer you could consider letting the UK property to fund renting in France while you look at French properties. The silver lining is that as Britons are the main market for many French property agents, they will have to persuade their clients to accept a lower sum for their property.

Below are some of the options for dealing with your UK home. Rather than sell outright, you can progress through some alternatives first before deciding what will suit you best in the long-term.

Deciding What to do With Your UK Home

○ Sell it to have funds for purchasing a French property outright and fund your retirement in France with the excess. (If you sell it you will have nowhere to return to if things do not work out in France).

○ Not sell it for the time being, but instead remortgage it to pay for a French property. (This could put your UK home at risk as it will be used as collateral if things go awry financially with your property in France).

○ Rent it out to fund rental of a French property for your trial period.

○ Rent it out to help fund a mortgage on a French property.

○ Rent it out to cover its upkeep and maintenance costs while you decide whether or not to sell it or while you are trying to sell it.

○ Rent it out as a private landlord to avoid paying management fees.

○ Rent it out through a letting and property management agency. and pay fairly hefty charges for a full management service.

○ Leave it empty and arrange for someone you trust to keep a regular eye on it.

○ Employ a housesitter through an agency.

○ Inform your insurance company of any changes and discuss any necessary changes to your policy. (Insurance companies usually raise premiums on empty houses).

MORTGAGES

French Mortgages

French mortgages – *hypothèques* – work in a rather different way from those in the UK, even if they appear similar at first sight. Fixed-rate mortgages are by far the most common; it is also possible to mix fixed and variable rates, or to adjust the number of years you need to pay off your mortgage. The variable rate mortgage is the most flexible. Lump sums can be paid off and the mortgage redeemed early without any financial penalties. You can also move to a fixed rate without any charge. There can be hefty financial penalties for early redemption of a fixed rate mortgage. The maximum mortgage is 85% of the property value.

There is also a basic difference in concept: the mortgage lender does not hold the deeds to your property as security; these remain with the notaire. All property and land is registered with the *cadastre* – the French land registry – and given its own unique number. This is stated in the acte de vente, which remains with the notaire, while you have a copy. Your mortgage is registered with the local *bureau des hypothèques*, and there is a fee to have the mortgage removed once you have paid it off. When you take out a loan (*prêt*) you give the lender a *hypothèque* or charge on the property, which allows them to auction it off if you default on the loan.

French versus UK Mortgage

There are two possibilities: one is to remortgage your UK property, the other is to take out a mortgage with a French bank using a French property as security. UK-based banks will not lend money on foreign properties; French branches of UK banks operating in this field, as well as one or two specialised UK lenders will. All banks and mortgage providers, even those with a British name, are registered in France. They all operate under French banking regulations and only offer euro mortgages.

Remortgaging in the UK is easier in some ways: banks lend cash more readily than in France, but you could end up putting your UK home at risk for the sake of buying property in France. Interest rates are less stable in the UK than in France, and likely to remain higher. The French mortgage interest rate is generally about 1.4% higher than the European Interbank Rate, which was about 2.2% in 2005. Some mortgage lenders can offer a rate of as low as 3% on a 70% mortgage. On the other hand, the charges involved with setting up a French mortgage (*frais d'hypothèque*) are high and have to be paid upfront. Lower interest rates, however, make the French mortgage more attractive at the end of the day.

Mortgage Providers & Brokers

Barclays: ☎0845 675 5544; www.Barclays.fr.

Barclays France Solutions: ☎0810 06 06 60.

Credit Agricole Britline: ☎02 31 55 67 89; www.britline.com.

UCB BNP Paribas: ☎0800 169 8470; www.ucb-french-mortgage.com.

Templeton Associates: ☎ 01225-422282; www.templeton-france.com.

PROPERTY TAXES

Most local taxes are real estate taxes. There are some minor taxes that are not dealt with here in detail, namely, regional development tax, the tax to finance local chambers of commerce, and the refuse collection tax. The main real estate taxes come under three headings:

○ *Taxe d'habitation*
○ *Taxes foncières*
○ *Taxe professionnelle*

These are local taxes raised for the benefit of local *communes, départements* and *régions*. The rates of tax are set by the local administrative collectivities, up to specific limits set by the national government. The rate for your area can be found in the annual publication *Impôts Locaux*, published at the start of November. See www.guideducontribuable.com.

Taxe d'Habitation

The *taxe d'habitation* is payable by anyone who has premises at his or her exclusive disposal subject to the tax. This includes principal residences as well as any secondary homes that are available for your use. Whether you rent or own the property, if you occupy the property on 1 January you are liable for the entire year's tax. It follows that if you move house during the year, the person whose dwelling you are taking over pays the tax for the year.

Any type of premises that are furnished so as to be habitable, as well as garages, parking spaces, gardens, staff accommodation and other outhouses within one kilometre of the main building are assessed for the taxe d'habitation. Business and farm buildings are exempt from taxe d'habitation.

Main Points of the Taxe d'Habitation

o The tax is calculated by the local authorities on the basis of the cadastral value on 1 January, cadastral value being the nominal rental value of the property.

o If you own an empty habitable rental property, then you pay the taxe d'habitation, otherwise the tenant pays.

o If the owner can prove that the property is uninhabitable, i.e. has no furniture in it, or is being renovated, then he or she can qualify for a temporary exemption. This should be negotiated with the *Trésor Public*.

o A person who rents a property short-term cannot be made to pay the taxe d'habitation. Otherwise, the tenant pays the taxe d'habitation.

o Unoccupied, but habitable, holiday homes are liable for *taxe d'habitation*.

Exemptions. Those on very low incomes are exempt. Also exempt is anyone who is over 60, widowed, or disabled and unable to work.

The television licence fee, or *redevance,* is now levied as part of the taxe d'habitation. It is necessary to opt out of paying it, either because you do not have a television or because you are exempt for being over 65 or for other reasons.

Taxes Foncières

There are two land taxes, or *taxes foncières:*

o Tax on unbuilt land
o Tax on built-up land

Unbuilt Land

Agricultural land is subject to the element of the tax that goes to the commune, but not those parts that go to the département and région. There are exemptions for certain kinds of forests and tree plantations for fixed periods of time.

Built-up Land

Types of buildings and constructions subject to the taxe foncière include anything that has the character of a permanent construction, private roads, hard standings and boats with permanent moorings.

The owner of the property pays the taxe foncière. If the property remains empty through circumstances outside your control for more than three months, you may obtain a rebate of the tax proportional to the time it has stood empty. If you buy a property you can agree to divide the taxe foncière for the year pro rata temporis with the vendor, unlike the taxe d'habitation.

Built-up land is assessed on the basis of 50% of the nominal rental value, the *valeur locative cadastrale.* Un-built land is assessed at 80% of the cadastral value. There are exemptions for the over-75s and the disabled, subject to certain conditions.

Taxe Professionnelle

The *taxe professionnelle* is by far the most lucrative for the local authorities, and accounts for about half their income. The tax is levied on individuals (*personnes physiques*) and companies (*personnes morales*) that regularly carry on a non-salaried business. Members of partnerships and so-called fiscally transparent companies (whose members are assessed individually for income tax), are assessed in their own names.

There is a long list of persons exempt from the tax of which a few are relevant to foreign residents:

○ Writers, artists, and teachers.
○ Recognised private schools.
○ Artisans working alone, or in a co-operative.
○ Correspondents on local newspapers.

The most significant exemptions (if they are granted) are for people who rent out chambres d'hôtes and gîtes, who fall under the category of *loueur en meublés*. Rooms rented out in your principal dwelling to another person who uses them as their own principal dwelling are always exempt from the taxe professionnelle. The tax is calculated on the basis of the cadastral rental value of the premises.

Non-Residents and Local Taxes

Non-residents who own property in France are liable for the taxe d'habitation and taxe foncière unless they qualify for an exemption. They would not normally have to pay the taxe professionnelle. There are several other local taxes but they will mostly not concern people retiring to France.

CAPITAL GAINS TAX OR CGT

In French CGT is known as *Impôt sur les Plus Values* or IPV. The tax is levied on the sale of:

○ Buildings
○ Land

○ Shares
○ Furniture and other movable goods
○ Antiques and works of art
○ Precious stones and precious metals

A distinction is made between short-term gains – *plus values à court terme* – made within two years of acquiring the assets, and long-term gains – *plus values à long terme*. In the following only the taxation of land and buildings will be dealt with. Companies 50% or more of whose assets consist of property are treated as properties.

Method of Calculation

If you sell your French property within 15 years of having acquired it, then you will be liable to pay French Capital Gains Tax or *Impôts sur les Plus Values* (IPV) on a graduated scale. If you are selling your principal residence then there is no liability for IPV. A non-resident who owns a second home in France will be liable for IPV (see below). The *plus value* on your property sale is worked out by deducting the original purchase price – *prix d'achat* – from the selling price – *prix de cession*.

Your capital gain is taxed as income at 16%, with a further 11.1% in social security taxes also payable. If you sell the property within 5 years of acquiring it, or it is repossessed, the gain from the sale of the property is added directly to your income tax liability, and the tax has to be paid immediately. Since 2004, where there is a long-term gain, the capital gains tax is payable at the time of signing the final deed of transfer (acte de vente). The notaire will take the amount of IPV out of the sale proceeds. Sellers are not required to enter a special declaration for IPV. The tax cannot be deferred.

There are two main methods of reducing IPV. In the first place, the gain is reduced by 10% for every full year after 5 years since the purchase of the property. Thus after 15 years there is no more IPV to pay. Secondly, there is a flat rate deduction of €1,000 from your gross capital gain (but only on one transaction per year). There are also deductions for holiday homes that have been owned for more than five years, which you have always had at your disposal.

Residents of other EU countries who are not tax resident in France are exempted from the social security tax element of 11%. Those who are neither residents in France or another EU country will pay IPV at 33.3%. If a non-resident is considered to have been trading in property then IPV is payable at 50% on the capital gain. The provisions of France's Double Taxation Agreement with your country may apply.

It is advisable to make enquiries about possible ways of avoiding IPV, or whether you are even liable, before you try to sell the property. If you can show that the sale of the property was forced on you by family circumstances or because you had to move to another part of the country, you can claim exemption. No IPV is payable if you receive the property as an inheritance, as a gift, or through a divorce settlement. If you originally received the property free of charge, the fair market value at the time you acquired it is taken as the purchase price; there are no deductions for any taxes paid at the time on the transfer of the property.

TRANSFERRING MONEY

There will be situations where you need to send money to someone in France or vice versa. A transfer of money to or from France is a *transfert* in French, rather than a *virement,* a transfer within France. Telegraphic Transfer, via Western Union or American Express is the most expensive way, but may be unavoidable if you want to send money to the USA. The most usual system between banks is SWIFT, which takes a day or two, and costs from €25 upwards. A more cost-effective method is to open a post office account in France and a Girobank account in the UK. Transfers between post offices take three to 10 days, and there is only a fixed charge to pay however much money you transfer. The least effective way of transferring money is to send a cheque drawn on a foreign bank account; it could take a month to clear and the charges will be very high. For small amounts it would be simpler to send cash with an International Registered Letter.

There is another possibility for making payments to French companies, which is to use a postal order, or *mandat cash,* obtainable in a post office. You pay a small charge in addition to the actual amount. The mandat is made out to a specific beneficiary; if for some reason you don't use the mandat or the beneficiary doesn't cash it, you will receive a notification from the post office so you can get a refund. If you lose the receipt then you have to go back to the post office where you originally bought the mandat, otherwise it is refundable at any post office in France.

To transfer large sums, i.e. for your house purchase, the best method is to use a specialised company see *Importing Currency For House Purchase* below.

Importing Currency for the House Purchase

When buying property in France, you will, under normal circumstances have to pay in euros, the local currency. In the days of foreign exchange controls, before 1974, it was usual to take a suitcase full of pound notes over to France to pay for your property. Thanks to the Single Market, you can take as much cash as you like with you, but there is no advantage in doing so, and it is certainly risky. If you take more than €8,000 in cash with you into France you are required to declare it. Taking a large amount of cash is not only risky; you could be suspected of being a drugs dealer or terrorist by the French customs if they find out.

Currency is nowadays normally sent using electronic transfer; the SWIFT system is the best known. There are charges involved at both ends so you need to know who is paying for them, and how much the receiving bank in France is likely to charge. The receiving bank should charge very little. The use of banker's drafts is not recommended as they are far too slow, and there is the risk of losing the draft. If you are transferring to a French bank, it is useful to know the IBAN (International Banking Number). The French have been slow to take up the IBAN system, which is gradually becoming compulsory all over the EU.

Since the UK is not part of Euroland, anyone buying property abroad is confronted with the painful possibility that a percentage of their money is going to disappear into the pockets of a high street bank. A report in the Sunday Times in February 2006 highlighted this fact: 'Britons buying property abroad could have lost up to 1.8 billion because high street banks offer such a poor deal on foreign exchange.' Fortunately, this need not be the case, since a number of specialist foreign exchange companies offer commercial exchange rates that lessen the losses on such transactions.

A specialised foreign exchange company such as Currencies Direct (www.currenciesdirect.com) and others that advertise in magazines about foreign property, can help in a number of ways, by offering better exchange rates than banks, without charging commission, and giving you the possibility of 'forward buying' – agreeing on the rate that you will pay at a fixed date in the future – or with a limit order – waiting until the rate you want is reached. For those who prefer to know exactly how much money they have available for their property purchase, forward buying is the best solution, since you no longer have to worry about the movement of the pound against the euro working to your detriment. Payments can be made in one lump sum or on a regular basis. It is usual when building new property to pay in instalments.

There is a further possibility, which is to use the services of a law firm in the UK to transfer the money. They can hold the money for you until the exact time that you need it; they will use the services of a currency dealer themselves.

INSURANCE (ASSURANCES)

House and Contents Insurance

The basic house and contents insurance is the *assurance multirisques habitation,* also often called *assurance multirisques vie privée* or *la multirisque.* This will include cover against natural disasters as a matter of course. Civil liability insurance – *responsabilité civile propriétaire* – is essential, in case an event on your property affects your neighbours. Your possessions also need to be insured. This kind of policy does not insure you against personal accidents, unless you ask for it. There are numerous formulas for the assurance multirisques, depending on your requirements.

If you are planning to build on a piece of land, an *assurance dommages-ouvrage* is legally compulsory, although you can get around this if the building is to be your family's principal residence.

It is possible to take over the existing insurance from the previous owner of the property you are buying; if you say nothing then it is assumed. If you do not wish to continue the same insurance policy – generally the wisest course of action for foreign buyers – you are required to present another policy to the notaire before you can sign the final acte de vente.

It is normal to insure the contents of your property as well. The current market value or *valeur vénale* of the items is used to work out the amount of cover; depreciation is taken into account. The insurers can insist on shutters being fitted to windows and bars on doors, and other security measures. You need to keep receipts, guarantees, photographs etc. of your possessions in a safe place for any claims. Read the small print in the policy, and watch out that you are not underinsured.

If there is nothing of value in your property you can take out basic insurance against damage from natural causes, vandalism, terrorist acts, etc., known as an *assurance multirisques d'immeuble*. This is used by condominiums (*copropriétés*) and some owners of blocks of flats. This will be calculated by the square metre. There should be a clause in which the insurer agrees to rebuild or restore the property to its original state within two years in the same style.

Insurance and Tenants

If you rent a property for a long period the owner will ask you to take out an *assurance multirisques habitation* to cover the building and any risks that could affect neighbours, e.g. floods, fire, explosions. According to the laws governing tenancy, the Loi Quillot and Loi Méhaignerie, the proprietor can insert a clause in the tenancy agreement allowing him or her to cancel your tenancy immediately if you don't have adequate insurance. You should ask the owner whether you need insurance well before you sign a tenancy agreement. You are free to choose any insurance company you want.

In the case of a copropriété the building insurance will be taken care of by the manager of the property, and your share of the premiums will appear on the monthly charges. You are responsible for insuring your own possessions, and third party insurance for anyone visiting your premises.

Holiday Homes

Burglaries of holiday homes are common, especially on the Riviera, or in any isolated area. An insurance policy for a principal residence is not suitable for a holiday home; there are usually clauses making the policy void if the house is left empty for more than 30 days. In order to get insurance cover, you will be expected to put in additional locks, shutters, burglar alarms and grills. Some owners go so far as to install webcams so they can watch their property being broken into. The longer you are away from the property, the higher your premiums will be, and the less likely the insurers are to cover valuables. Your premiums will be reduced if you install burglar alarms, electronic surveillance systems, and so on. Premiums vary widely around the country; they are highest in the southeast where there are more fires than in the rest of France. To give a rough idea: a €150,000 property in the Landes could cost €700 per year to insure, while in Aix-en-Provence it would be €1,400. The website www.intasure.com has a very useful calculator to help you work out how much insurance will cost in different parts of France. Mike Farley of Intasure says: 'In today's market, flexibility is central to the cover. A comprehensive buildings and contents insurance policy should allow you to live in, leave your property unoccupied or let it, whether short or long term, to be of any real use to the policy holder.'

There is a particular risk of blocked or frozen pipes causing flooding, and every possible measure has to be taken to prevent this. You need to take sensible precautions: there has recently been a high-profile case of a woman who kept containers of kerosene in her flat, and received nothing when the place burned down. Insurers will take into account the condition of the property when they pay for repairs. If the original plaster or roofing was not that good then they will pay proportionately less to have it replaced.

Terms and Conditions

Thefts. It is a condition of insurance policies that you report thefts within 24 hours to the police, or as soon as possible, if you want your claim to be taken seriously. The police will give you a form

– *déclaration de vol* – with the details of what you have lost. You need to inform the insurers within two working days of the theft and send the receipt of the déclaration by registered post (*recommandée*), with an *avis de réception* (AR) or receipt. It is advisable to telephone the insurer immediately and they will send you a confirmation. You then draw up a list of the stolen goods and send it by registered post.

Natural Disasters. There is a whole raft of regulations about which natural events count as disasters or *catastrophes naturelles*. The amount of time you have to report a disaster ranges from four days for hail to 10 days after a storm, if this has been declared a catastrophe naturelle in the official journal. Your house insurance should cover not only catastrophes naturelles but all kinds of other natural risks. You do not have to pay for cover against snow, unless you think it is necessary. Check that the policy covers damage to electrical items as well.

Checking the Small Print. Look carefully at the small print in the policy to see what conditions are set for reporting damage, thefts, etc., and any exclusions. Check for the *franchise* or excess, i.e. the first part of the claim that is not paid. Taking videos and photos of property is an eminently sensible precaution to make sure you are paid in full. You can use a court bailiff – *huissier* – or an insurance expert, to prepare a report on damage to your property (for a fee). The insurance company will normally send their own expert to draw up a report on your loss.

Policies are renewed automatically (*tacite reconduction*); you are given a period of time before the renewal date when you can cancel the policy. Once the date has passed it is too late to cancel. Premiums should be paid by standing order, within 10 days of the set date. You will receive a warning (*mise en demeure*) from the insurer. If you haven't paid within 30 days your policy will be cancelled, but you will still be liable for the outstanding amount and the insurer's costs.

Insurers may not take you on if your insurance has been cancelled for non-payment. Recent claims for damage through floods, avalanches and other major disasters make it difficult to get insurance.

Where to Find Insurance

Insurance companies are listed in the French yellow pages under *assurances;* some agents advertise in the French property magazines, such as *French Property News.*

Part three

A New Life
in France

Adapting to Your New life
Quality of Life
Personal Finance
Healthcare
Crime, Security & the Police
Returning Home

Adapting to Your New Life

CHAPTER SUMMARY

- Open air markets (*marchés découverts*) held in streets and squares throughout France are still very much part of French life and the best place to buy the freshest, most desirable local produce.
- Your TV licence fee (*redevance audiovisuelle*) is automatically added to your income tax bill. If you do not have a television it is up to you to tick the opt out box on your income tax form. Anyone over 65 is exempt.
- French roads are considered dangerous by European standards due to the anarchic French driving style, which persists in spite of rigorous driving regulations and seemingly unlimited police powers.
- It makes for safer overtaking to have a left-hand drive car in France, but new cars are more expensive to buy in France than in other EU countries.
- The French equivalent of an MOT for a new car is only necessary after four years, and then every two years after that.
- France is divided into 96 departments each of which has a double-digit number used for postcodes and on car licence plates.
- The level of local government that everyone comes into contact with is the commune, of which there are about 36,700 at the last count.
- You can vote in UK national and European elections from abroad by registering to be an overseas voter with the British consulate or embassy.

SHOPPING

Markets

Open air markets (*marchés découverts*) held in streets and squares throughout France are still very much a part of French life and are not likely to lose their popularity. There are food and produce markets, antique and flea markets and mixed markets. They are usually held once or twice a week. Markets begin very early in the morning and some markets in the south go on into the night during hot weather.

The open-air food markets are a wonderful source of the freshest and most desirable local produce including fruits and vegetables, cheeses, bread, honey and many homemade products. You have to shop there in the mornings as most are already packing up by lunch-time. The other great markets for produce are the permanent covered markets (*marchés couverts/les halles*), which open daily. There is usually at least one covered market in every largish town or city. For big shopping trips there are the mammoth hypermarchés with brand names *Auchan, Leclerc, Intermarché* where prices tend to be much lower than in local shops. Like their UK equivalents of Tesco and Sainsbury's, they are situated in the outskirts of towns and cities and you need a car to reach them. There is less organic produce on sale in France than in Britain, but most crops are farmed with fewer chemicals than in other countries.

Brocantes is a generic term used for flea, antique and bric-a-brac markets. Since the French tend to prefer new designs and products these markets can be heaven for Anglos and other émigrés who are doing up an old house and want to find things to decorate and furnish it with. Larger objects so desirable to Brits such as cast iron baths with claw feet, period mirrors, cupboards, as well as smaller items are chucked out by the French in profusion and can be bargained for with zeal. French magazines *Antiquités* and *Aladin* and available from newsagents and hypermarkets publish monthly listings of markets for every département. An impromptu market is a *vide-grenier* (empty attic), the French equivalent of a car boot sale and they are held not in fields, but anywhere from village squares to the grounds of a local château.

Wines and Spirits

As one might expect from a major wine-producing country, wines of all types and qualities seem amazingly cheap, and even the most modest French home usually has a cellar to accommodate them. One of the pleasures of being an expatriate in France is being able to enjoy the local wines and to buy direct from the local producers along with other consumables to enjoy with them, particularly cheeses. There is no room here to do justice to the vast subject of French wines but you can make a start with websites including www.onivins.fr, the website of the *Office National Interprofessionel des Vins* or www.terroir-france.com, primarily a buying site but with lots of useful information. Also look up www.oenologie.fr and perso.wanadoo.fr/etiqvin.

Stronger alcoholic drinks produced in France are about the same price as in many other countries, but you are likely to find better quality and more choice than you do in your own country. Popular brands include Noilly Prat (vermouth), Ricard, Pastis and Pernod (aperitifs) and Marie Brizard (digestif).

Local Shops

Other food shopping revolves around small specialist shops. For example, a *boulangerie* sells bread (and sometimes biscuits) while a *pâtisserie* sells cakes and pastries and may also be a café. Similarly, the general butcher is a *boucherie*, but for pork one must visit a *charcuterie*. Sometimes the charcuterie will also sell a range of cooked meats, not just pork. A *boucherie chevaline* is a butcher which sells horsemeat. Fresh fruit and vegetables are best bought in the open-air markets, but most towns have a greengrocer, usually as part of a shop selling *alimentation* (general provisions). *Primeurs* are early fruit and vegetables but can also mean greengrocers.

Dépôts Vente & Magasins d'Occasion

Dépôts Vente are second-hand emporiums where citizens can dispose of their unwanted furniture and appliances. There is usually a mixed bag of items which can include antiques but battered sofas and fifties furniture are more usual. The joy of them is that anyone can sell their unwanted stuff there on a commission basis; the result is that a lot of it is rubbish. A more promising alternative is usually the second-hand (*d'occasion*) shops where chic French clothes and accessories can often be found at bargain prices.

Factory Shops and E- Shopping

You can also find bargains in factory shops (*les magazines d'usine*). The website www.marquesavenue.com details surplus designer stock available at its outlets. The American guide *Born to Shop in France* by Suzy Gershmann (available on Amazon), gives useful details of factory shops. The French guide to factory shops is *Guide des Magasins d'Usine* by Marie-Paule Dousset.

Internet shopping, known in France as *E-achats*, is not the kind you would normally associate with France but it has taken off. The website www.leguide.com compares the prices of online retailers for every kind of item while the site www.frenchshoppingonline. com brings together a portfolio of online discount stores. To satisfy expatriate cravings for the comfort of 'traditional' British food products including Ambrosia Creamed Rice, Cadbury's Creme Eggs and Chocolate Fingers, Jaffa Cakes, English Mustard, Monster Munch, Marmite, Marks and Spencer foodstuffs, Heinz Beans, Christmas Puddings and many more, there is the possibility of ordering them on the internet from www.xpatshop.co.uk; www. expatdirect.co.uk, www.britishmailorder.com; www.expatshopping. com, www.britishcornershop.co.uk, expatshopping.com and www. expatessentials.co.uk amongst others. The website www.aquarterof. co.uk sells only sweets: 500 different ones to be precise, including all your old favourites from Aztec bars to Sherbet Fountains. They will mail stuff to Europe by surface mail, airmail or courier. There is no minimum order.

Shopping Hours

Most shops keep long and convenient continental hours, typically from 8am to 7pm (allowing for much regional variation). Small shops take an afternoon break, which lasts longer the further south one travels. In some areas it is usual for shops to be open on Saturday, and part of Sunday, but to close on Monday. In cities, especially Paris, some shops may close for a long summer holiday in July and August.

FOOD AND DRINK

Eating and drinking mean a great deal more than just keeping body and soul together: the French have taken the arts of wining and dining to heights that can only amaze lesser mortals. The whole thing certainly goes too far, perhaps, but there is an undeniable sense of shock when one returns to the UK, a country where many people only eat to live.

Traditionally, one expected a quality of food that was mostly unobtainable in the UK. The French have become complacent about their restaurants, it must be said, and the UK is catching up with France. Contrary to what one might think, it is quite possible to get a bad meal in France; chain restaurants, or those where there are excessive numbers of tourists are generally best avoided. France will always have the edge because the quality of produce in supermarkets and shops is so much better than in the UK. The average French household spends less on going out to eat than does a British family, but a great deal more on buying food to prepare at home. In contrast with the UK, there are still plenty of small supermarkets (*supermarchés*) and greengrocers (*primeurs*). There is also the trend towards hypermarkets (*hypermarchés*) selling every possible kind of product under one roof. Local supermarkets are generally smaller than in the UK; in small towns there is usually only a general grocer's or superette in the town centre. Most people prefer to go to local markets for fresh produce and meat.

One of the positive sides of small country supermarkets is that the produce is often locally sourced. The downside is that fruit is sold ready to eat, and may not keep for very long. French meat is also hung for longer, to be more tasty, and sold lean. French meat appears expensive by weight, but the quality is often far better. Parts of the animal usually discarded in Britain such as pigs' trotters and sweetbreads and other offal, are made into tasty dishes and terrines.

Perhaps through poverty, the French have been inventive about finding things to eat. Everyone knows about frog's legs. Spare a thought for the frogs: their legs are chopped off while they are still alive. It's just as well to know what you are eating. All kinds of small birds are blasted out of the sky on their migratory routes for the sake of their meat, especially larks or alouettes. Larks that have been captured and fattened up are *mauviettes*. Even blackbirds are not safe here. For one of his last meals, the late President Mitterrand is said to have dined on *ortolans,* a protected species of bunting, the last word in extravagance and decadence.

The Etiquette of Eating Out

The etiquette of eating in a high-class restaurant in France is not that different from what you would expect anywhere else. It is considered good manners to eat off the back of the fork, and to keep your hands on the table when you are not eating. You should make sure that your fellow diners' glasses are kept topped up. If you are eating out with French friends, they will know which wines go with different courses, otherwise the wine-waiter – *le sommelier* – can advise you. It is best to be clear about who is going to pick up the tab beforehand. Unless you are in informal company, one person should pay for everyone. Going Swiss – *faire suisse* – as they say, is OK if it is decided in advance. The French like everything to be clear.

Discussing business matters during a meal is acceptable, as long as it is done after the cheese course. Before this time you should stick to other topics. By the time the fruit course comes round everyone should be in a good mood, and you may be able to clinch a good deal. It is rather *mauvais ton* to drink too much alcohol at lunchtime – one glass of wine is sufficient – all the more so if you are trying to negotiate business matters. The evening is the time to indulge if you need to.

There are certain odd rituals in French cafés and *chambres d'hôte* that are worth noting. You may be expected to hold on to the same knife and fork for your hors d'œuvre or entrée as for the main course; in other words: *gardez vos couverts.* If you have bread with your meal, or for breakfast, you are not given a plate to put it on. Leaving crumbs and a few stains on the table is a sign that you had a good meal; the tablecloth is washed daily anyway.

If you order meat in a restaurant it is vital to ask for it to be well cooked: *bien cuit*. Even then it will be undercooked by British standards. The French like their meat bloody – *saignant* – and need to be persuaded that you can cook meat all the way through. There are no such problems with fish.

In cafés and bars, you are not expected to pay for your drinks or food until you are ready to leave. The bar staff will give you a ticket for each item, or you ask for the bill (*l'addition* – colloquially *la note*) at the end. They may ignore you if you ask how much you owe after your first drink. It is all right to ask for free tap water, but be careful about asking for a 'soda': you are likely to get Coca-Cola. If you want fizzy water, ask for *une eau gazeuse*. For flat mineral water, ask for *eau non-gazeuse* or *eau plate*.

Smokers are generally considerate towards non-smokers in bars. There are no particular regulations about providing non-smoking areas. Finally, if you have to, ask for *les toilettes* and not *la toilette*, which means a washstand.

MEDIA

French Television

The main terrestrial channel is the formerly state-owned TF1. FR2 and FR3 are still owned by the state. The fourth channel is Canal Plus, a private subscription channel. Channel 5 shows *La Cinq* – a state-run cultural channel – in the daytime, and the Franco-German Arte after 7 pm. The latter is by far the most highbrow terrestrial channel, broadcasting high-quality films and documentaries in the evening, with no news bulletins. Channel 6 is a light entertainment channel.

High definitition television over the internet (via broadband) which has been on the market barely two years, is growing faster in France than in the UK. The two main providers are *France Télécom* and *Iliad* (www.free.fr) which charges about €30 per month.

The fee for your TV licence or *redevance audiovisuelle* is automatically added to your income tax bill. This is to prevent unlicensed viewing. The charge is €116 (2005) regardless of whether you own a colour or black and white set. If you are liable to pay *taxe d'habitation* (that is you are occupying habitable premises on 1 January of the tax year) then you will be charged. If you do not own a television you will have to opt out by ticking the relevant box in your tax declaration. Those over 65 and invalids (assuming they do not live with someone who is subject to taxe d'habitation) are exempt. It is possible to pay by three-monthly instalments, using direct debit.

Access to British Television

If you want to have access to the BBC and other English-language stations, then the best option is satellite. You can get some CNN and BBC channels with cable. There is no need for a dish with cable TV, but if you live too far out in the countryside you will not be able to connect to cable in any case. *CanalSat* (www.canalsat.fr) are satellite subscription stations also offering English-language channels; the hire of the decoder and dish are included in a monthly charge of around €20-30 depending on the option you choose. There is also the possibility of receiving satellite TV through your telephone connection, via ADSL (only in larger cities). The advantage of cable is that you can have a superfast broadband internet connection included.

The satellite TV situation changed in 2004, insofar as the Astra 2D satellite, which broadcasts British stations, shifted its 'footprint' to the north somewhat. Whilst you will still have reception with a 60 cm dish (*parabole*) in the northwestern quadrant of France, along the Côte d'Azur you will need a 130 cm dish to be sure of receiving UK television. A map of the required dish sizes can be seen at www.satalogue.com. The dish is installed on the exterior of your residence.

To obtain the maximum number of English-language channels you can obtain a Freesat card from Sky in the UK. The first step is to obtain an information pack from Sky; ask for it to be sent a UK address. The Freesat card is valid for 3 years and costs £20. Sky will only send it to a UK address and you will also need to give a UK phone number. The company www.insatinternational.com can obtain a Sky digibox and Freesat card for you. Some people ask a friend in the UK to do it for them. UK company Satalogue can supply a digital satellite system that will receive all of the Sky Astra Satellite and Radio channels plus normal UK television channels anywhere in Europe. Another great advantage of having satellite TV is that it enables you to pick up British radio stations, without the bother of accessing them over the internet.

The Decoder. You will need to obtain a decoder, which costs in the region of £250. The rest of the equipment will cost around £70, and there is still the cost of €200-300 for someone to do the actual installation. If you are technically minded you could buy the decoder for far less on eBay. Where there are large communities of Britons, you may be able to obtain assistance more cheaply. There are numerous British-owned companies who will provide the complete package; they advertise in French property magazines. At all events, it is advisable to download the free guide to satellite TV installation from www.satcure.com.

Satellite Providers & Programme Guide	
Sky	www.sky.com; ☎ 08702-404040
Insatinternational	www.insatinterntional.com; ☎ 020 8886 7155
Satalogue	www.satalogue.com; ☎ 01332-812588
Digiguide	www.digiguide.com. Subscription satellite programme guide

UK Newspapers

For those addicted to the UK press, it is fairly easy to get hold of English newspapers like *The Times* on the day of publication, while the *International Herald Tribune* is published in Paris. Needless to say, British newspapers are expensive in France. An alternative is to subscribe to *The Times* before you move, or *The Guardian Weekly*, which is a compilation in English, of the main articles from *The Guardian* and the *Washington Post* and *Le Monde* (☎ 0870 066 0510 for subscriptions; or arrange online www.guardianweekly.co.uk).

You can also order various newspapers online at www. britishpapers2u.com, which will post any British newspaper or magazine to you anywhere in the world. The easiest way to keep up with the news is to use a computer to read newspapers online. The website www.thebigproject.co.uk/news has a comprehensive list of links to British newspapers (national and regional) where you can do this.

Newspapers in English, Published in France

There are a handful of English-language newspapers published in France, for the British expatriate communities. *French News* (www. French-news.com) based in Périgueux appears monthly. There are separate supplements for Brittany, Limousin, Aquitaine and Périgueux. Also, *The Connexion* newspaper which is of similar quality and type.

A newsletter *Le Réseau Amical* published by Peter and Heather Jeffery, a couple who live in France and the UK, has been going for more than a decade with 300 subscribers. It has useful articles on practical aspects of daily life in France for those living, visiting or house-hunting there and is invaluable for swopping information.

English-Language Newspapers & Newsletter Published in France

The Connexion: ☎04 93 32 16 59; www.connexionfrance.com

French News: ☎05 53 06 84 40; www.French-news.com

Le Réseau Amical: ☎0117-942 1697; www.jefferydesign.com

English Books

There are about a dozen English bookshops in France about half of which are in Paris. A list of them can be found on the Expatica website www.expatica.com. Montpellier has an American Library (www.bibliotheque-americaine.cc). If you are not near a bookshop but like to buy books regularly you could join a bookclub that caters for your tastes and will mail/e-mail regular reviews to you. Check that they will mail books abroad first. The *Good Book Guide* (www.

thegoodbookguide.com) is an online bookseller and will mail world-wide. Amazon.fr has an English books section and delivery is free if you spend more than €20, and don't forget the *London Review of Books* (www.lrb.co.uk; 020-7207 1101) which you can currently read free online and then order books from their online bookshop. The printed version is published fortnightly and costs £76.50 for a year's subscription to Europe.

CARS AND MOTORING

Driving

As already mentioned, the French have their own style of driving, which some call hair-raising, and the French Transport Ministry is always looking for ways to reduce the accident rate which is much higher than the UK's. Stringent measures appear to have had an effect, as the road death toll for 2005 was under 5,000 (3,000 fewer than in 1998). In France it is possible to have your licence taken away at the roadside by the police. There was even a national trial in 2005 to see if keeping car headlights on at all times would reduce accidents. The French equivalent of the MOT is the *contrôle technique,* which is compulsory every two years for cars over four years old. The first test is due within the six-month period leading up to the car's fourth anniversary.

If you live in a rural area it is essential to have a car and, in the case of couples, that both of you are able to drive. Widow Anne Scanlon who lives in the hamlet of Faux in the Dordogne explains why:

There are no public bus services, except for schools, so it is absolutely essential to have a car and to be able to drive. Widows who don't drive are very isolated. I know two; their husbands drove them everywhere. Now they are reliant on friends and taxis for transport and their lives are so restricted.

Those particularly concerned about driving in France, together with those who cannot yet drive, should take lessons with a local driving school (*l'auto-école*). Before you can start with a driving school, you will need to produce some ID such as the (now voluntary) *carte de séjour* and proof of your address (you can use a receipt for rent, or an electricity or telephone bill), and excise stamp and four photographs. It is also advisable to obtain a copy of the French Highway Code before leaving the UK. Some of the fundamental rules are below. The French government's traffic website is www.securite-routiere.gouv.fr.

French Highway Regulations

○ Newly qualified drivers have to sport a sign on the back of the car (a circle enclosing two people) and may not exceed 90km/h (55mph) for a year after passing their test.

○ *Priorité à droite* means you must give way to traffic joining from the right from another road (but not driveway) however minor. Thus, you must stop, as emerging drivers will not; nor will they be pleased if you stop when it is your right of way. This rule generally applies in towns and on minor roads.

○ If you are on a road with the sign *passage protégé* it means you have right of way, which ends when the same sign appears crossed through with a black bar.

OTHER ESSENTIAL ROAD SIGNS	
attention travaux	beware road works
allumez vos feux	switch on your lights
bande d'urgence	breakdown lane
chaussée deformé	uneven road edges or temporary road surface
déviation	diversion
gravillons	loose chippings
ralentez	slow down
rappel	reminding you to heed the previous sign, usually in restricted speed areas
sens interdit	no entry
serrez à droit/gauche	keep to the right/left
Vous n'avez pas la priorité	give way

○ The speed limit on autoroutes is 130kph (80mph); however, this reduces to 110km/h (65 mph) in wet weather, and is 110km/h on non-toll autoroutes. The speed limit on dual carriageways is 110km/h and 90km/h (55mph) on single carriageways – both reduced by 10km/h in wet weather. A new speed limit of 50 km/h has been introduced for foggy conditions where visibility is reduced to 50 metres. *Rappel* means the restriction is continued.

○ Seatbelts must be worn by anyone travelling in the front or back of the car and children under ten are not allowed, by law, to be carried in the front of a car unless they are in an approved, rear-facing seat.

Importing a Car

Under EU regulations, you can bring in one car for your personal use, as long as you can show that you are going to be permanently resident in France. There are few conditions attached to importing a car: you need to have the original registration papers, invoice and proof that you have paid VAT in your home country.

You need to register your car with the local authorities. The local *préfecture* will send you a leaflet explaining how to obtain your French registration document, the *carte grise*. Generally you will need to make modifications to the headlights and the exhaust for your car to pass the required norms. Once you are resident in France you will need to change your number plates. Ask at the nearest *préfecture de police* who will tell you what documents you require as these vary slightly from region to region.

There are very good reasons for buying a left-hand drive vehicle in France; safety when overtaking being the most obvious one.

Buying a New Car in a Third Country

An alternative to buying a new car in France is to buy one in another EU country where prices are low, and then pay the VAT in France. There are dealers in Belgium who specialise in this kind of arrangement and who will do all the paperwork. One could also try Luxembourg, Germany or Portugal. New car dealers are under pressure from manufacturers not to sell to foreign buyers, thus, while Denmark has the cheapest ex-VAT cars in Europe, the dealers will put a lot of obstacles in your way if you try to buy your car there. You may not get the model you want, and you may have to wait a long time. You can buy through a *mandataire* or person appointed to act on your behalf.

Once your car has been delivered in France you have 15 days to pay the VAT to the *recette des impôts du département d'immatriculation* and you will then have a provisional immatriculation. The downside of getting a new car abroad is the potential problems with the warranty in France. A Peugeot in Belgium is considerably cheaper than in France; legally, French garages are required to carry out service checks on French models. A better plan could be to buy a second-hand up-market car in Belgium, where they are very cheap, to import into France.

Buying a Used Car in France

Used cars are also available from franchised dealers. These mostly only sell used cars up to one or two years old, and are usually a reputable source and offer appropriate warranties.

If you choose to buy a used car (*un vehicule d'occasion*) from outside the franchised dealer networks then a great deal of care and caution is required: this applies whether buying privately, perhaps from a newspaper advertisement, or from a dealer.

Few dealers sell models more than five years old. The préfecture in the département in which the car is registered should issue the seller with a *lettre de non-gage*, which means there are no outstanding debts (e.g. hire purchase) on the car. The seller must also provide evidence that the car has been checked and issued with a *contrôle technique* within the last six months, which lists any faults that need to be put right before the sale. The purchase of a used car must be registered at the préfecture. You will need to take with you a certificate of sale which is an official document supplied by préfectures to sellers; the cancelled *carte grise* (log book), and the *autobilan* (test certificate), as well as all your own identity documents are all required for this. Further information at www.carte-grise.info.

If you buy the car outside the area you are living in then you will need to get the car re-registered locally when you are back home.

A useful publication is *L'Argus*, the French car guide. It provides details on how much you should pay for particular models and the purchasing process.

Car Insurance

Car insurance is expensive in France partly because all premiums include taxes at an average rate of 36%. Even higher *cotisations* (premiums) are charged for cities and areas notorious for their high crime rate. Another factor affecting insurance charges is the high collision rate (one every 85 seconds according to one recent estimate). It is particularly important to shop around and to find the best deal possible.

The basic legal requirement for French car insurance is third party *(au tiers)* liability, and many owners of what seem quite new cars risk taking out no greater cover than this, though most will also have cover for accidental damage to the vehicle. Comprehensive insurance *(tous risques)* is available which will cover most risks, including damage to your own car. It is particularly important to examine each policy and to see what is and what is not included, as various policies do not necessarily cover the same risks, and the insurance inclusions and exclusions will certainly vary from a UK or US comprehensive policy.

If you are taking up permanent residence you will require a new policy that complies with French requirements: ask various companies and/or brokers for quotes as they all compete against each other for business. If you are in France, it should be a simple matter to locate local brokers, preferably with subsidiaries all over Europe so that insurance can be continued if you move elsewhere in Europe. Leading French insurers include AXA, AGF, CNP, Generali France and Groupama and a list of their regional agencies is normally given on the company websites. The advantage of insuring through a local office in France is that they are more inclined to treat you as an individual, they know you and this can be useful as you can go and visit them in person to explain any problems you may be having with your documentation.

There are various peculiarities of French motor insurance. Firstly, the *bonus/malus* system: although one gains a useful no-claims bonus and discount for not claiming each year, one also gains a claims supplement and loading if a claim is made, which can make insurance very expensive. Basically, to get the maximum discount (50%), you need to provide the French insurance company with proof of no fault claims for thirteen years. The other party may offer to settle with you directly if they have caused damage to your car and do not want to lose their bonus. If you decide to agree, make sure that you complete the *constat à amiable* (see below) in any case, so that you have this official document to fall back on if the payer defaults.

Another difference is that many comprehensive policies will reduce cover to third party only, if any accident or damage occurs because the driver was breaking road traffic law. If you want a policy that is tailored to the usage of the car, it is possible to arrange insurance based on the car's mileage (*kilométrage*). It is necessary to carry proof of insurance *(une attestation d'assurance)*, which will be issued by the insurer. This should be kept in the car with your car registration papers.

INSURANCE GLOSSARY

English	French
No claim bonus/discount	*bonus*
Third party liability	*au tiers/responsabilité civile*
Comprehensive insurance	*assurances touts risques/tous risques*
Fire and theft	*vol et incendie*
windscreen damage	*bris de glaces*
Accidental damage	*dommages a votre vehicule*
Personal accident/bodily injury to driver	*garantie conducteur*
Policy excess	*franchise*

If you are involved in an accident you have to fill in a report form, which should be supplied by your insurers and kept in the car at all times so that it can be filled in on the spot. This document is known as a *constat à l'amiable* and is a standardized form being used increasingly in various parts of Europe. If there is a disagreement as to who is to blame for the accident, it is usual to call a *huissier*, a legal official who will prepare an official and impartial statement of facts for insurance or legal purposes.

As was highlighted by the car accident that killed Princess Diana in Paris, it is a criminal offence in France not to try to assist persons in danger, or if that is not possible to summon assistance. The maximum penalty is five years imprisonment and a substantial fine.

As with house insurance, it is usually necessary to give a long period of notice (sometimes three months) before cancelling a policy and one is liable for premiums until that notice expires. Overall, the French motorist has good reason to be envious of the comparatively reasonable cost and generous terms of motor insurance elsewhere.

MAIN POINTS OF MOTOR INSURANCE IN FRANCE

- Compulsory cover for third party liability
- No restriction on drivers (vehicle can be driven by any driver with the insured's permission).
- The no claim bonus cannot be protected.
- The maximum no claim discount is 50% (13 years with no liable claim).
- When taking out insurance with a French provider, the proposer must provide sufficient proof of his/her insurance cover 13 years back in order to claim the maximum no claim discount.

Useful Websites – Insurance Companies

AGF: ☎08 10 81 09 63; www.agf.fr.

AXA Assurances: ☎08 11 90 11 01; www.axa.fr.

AZUR Assurances: ☎08 20 01 40 00; www.groupeazur.fr.

GMF : ☎08 20 80 98 09; www.gmf.fr

MAAF Assurances: ☎08 00 16 17 18; www.maaf.fr.

MACIF Assurances: ☎01 55 56 57 58; www.macif.fr.

Main Documents Required by Car Owners

Registration Document *(carte grise)*. This is supplied when you register or buy a new or used car, and should be handed on to the buyer when you sell it. Cars are registered locally in France and if you move to another département then you must re-register your car at a préfecture there within three months: this involves obtaining a different registration number and new number plates.

In order to get a carte grise you will require the necessary documents including proof of property ownership, or a rental agreement or a French utility bill in your name. If you are renting from another owner and do not have any bills in your name then you will probably be refused a carte grise.

Selling a Car

You cannot sell or otherwise dispose of a car imported duty free within 12 months without paying the TVA on the import. As far as documentation is concerned, selling or part exchanging a car in France is probably more complicated than you are used to. You have to obtain the appropriate certificate of sale form from the mairie or préfecture and, complete this in duplicate and then to send one copy back to the registration office. The other copy and the carte grise registration document go to the purchaser.

The main difference between selling a car in France and England is that in France, if the car is five or more years old it must be submitted to a mechanical inspection (*contrôle technique*), after which, if successful, it will be issued with a test certificate (*autobilan*). Thus, no matter how recently another, similar test has been done on the vehicle, you must arrange and pay for this beforehand. Legality apart, no sensible buyer would want to pay very much for a vehicle over five years old, which does not have an inspection certificate.

Breakdowns, Thefts and Accidents

There is no exact French equivalent of the AA or RAC operating on a national basis. However, there are motoring organisations you can join which will arrange for a local garage, rather than their own service vehicle, to attend the breakdown. You can extend your AA or RAC assistance cover to France, or you can join an international help organisation like Europ Assistance (www.europ-assistance.com).

LOCAL GOVERNMENT ADMINISTRATION

Regions

The introduction of a new layer of government between Paris and the departments was initiated in 1972. From 1982 each of the 22 *régions* was given an elected assembly and an executive. This is not really devolution as we would see it in the UK. The regions have powers in the area of culture, education and business. The main purpose was to reduce the power of the *départements*, and to restore some feeling of regional identity, which had been deliberately negated by the organisation into departments after 1789.

Départements

France is logically, and conveniently, divided into 100 départements or departments, four of which are overseas. The rest make up what is called La Métropole, or La France Métropolitaine. Each department has a two-digit number, which is, again very logically, used for postcodes and licence plates. Napoleon placed a prefect or *préfet* in charge of each department, in a deliberate imitation of the Roman Empire, an unelected official directly appointed by the President. Since 1982, the prefect has been replaced by the President of the General Council. The General Council is elected for a period of six years by local councillors. The chairman is elected for three years by the General Council.

Arrondissements and Cantons

The départements are divided up into *arrondissements* and these are again divided up into *cantons*. These units have some significance in organising voting and public services, but no directly elected representatives.

Communes

The level of government that everyone comes into contact with is the commune, of which there were about 36,700 at the last count, many of them with fewer than 1,000 inhabitants. The voters elect a municipal council for six years, while the chief executive officer is the *maire* or mayor, who is not only an official of the municipality, but also a government agent, and a member of the *police judiciaire*. The *maire* is obliged to keep the civil register (*état civil*), and often performs marriages. He or she also draws up the electoral roll and publicises laws. The French government's policy is to encourage, or force, *communes*, to work together in groups or *collectivités*, within the limits of their official competencies, in order to run the country in a more rational and democratic manner. At the commune level the *maire* is an all-powerful figure, someone that newcomers should try to cultivate at all costs, because he has a lot of say in who receives planning permission for buildings and can be very helpful, or obstructive, if you want to start a business.

Pays

Since 1995, following the Loi Pasqua, different regions or communes can band together to form a *pays* (literally 'country'), to promote their economic interests and strengthen cultural ties. By 1996 there were already 200 *pays* in France, a throwback to the pre-Revolutionary *ancien régime*. The more republican French are concerned about the weakening of the departments, and fear a return to the pre-1789 organisation of the country.

RETAINING YOUR RIGHT TO VOTE IN UK NATIONAL AND EUROPEAN ELECTIONS

Electoral Registration from Abroad

If you are a British citizen living abroad you can apply to be an overseas voter in UK Parliamentary and European elections. You must have appeared on the electoral register in the UK within the previous 15 years.

You can register as soon as you move abroad by completing an Overseas Elector's Declaration form from your nearest British consular or diplomatic mission. For more information contact www.aboutmyvote.co.uk or for Northern Ireland www.electoralofficeni.gov.uk.

RELIGION

Catholicism

France is primarily a Roman Catholic country. Despite its influence throughout French history, the Church is now neither as strict nor as strong as in the past and as in other highly-developed western European countries there has been a steady decline in the number of practitioners. 64.3% of the population identify with Catholicism. Although the Church now tends to keep its distance from French politics (the French state was officially secularised in 1905), this did not stop its clerics dabbling in left-wing politics on social issues just after the Second World War. As a result there are many spiritual and charitable organisations that continue to be dynamic today. Some of the best known are *Le Secours Catholique* or *Caritas France*, created after the Second World War has an estimated 68,000 volunteers. Another, *Emmaus*, is an international charity founded by Abbé Pierre that helps the underprivileged and aims at the eradication of poverty.

To satisfy the need for some kind of religion, albeit more relevant than the established one, there are many unofficial religious groups that meet in private homes. These tend to receive less publicity than mainstream rebels such as the Lefebvre faction in Catholicism that continues to celebrate Mass in Latin.

The Catholic Church continues to exercise its influence in education. Most private schools in France are Catholic schools, including primary establishments, *collèges* (first stage of secondary education) and *lycées* (second stage secondary schools). Between them Catholic schools have about two million pupils or 20% of the school age population. And, the church is very forthcoming in upholding the right to state aid for Catholic schools, which are separate from the rest of the French education system. When the French government banned the wearing of the Muslim veil in state (secular) schools, the Catholic schools offered their services and tolerance of the headscarf to Muslims students; in Marseille 70% of female pupils in some Catholic schools are Muslims.

As in many countries, most people frequent church for christenings, weddings and burials only. In France a civil wedding ceremony must be held to validate a marriage legally and this takes place at the mairie and is presided over by the mayor who wears a tricolour sash. A church ceremony is optional and has no legal significance: some couples choose to have both, whereas others settle for a civil ceremony.

The Other Religions

Protestantism. The number of protestants has increased from 1.64% of the French population (about 950,000) ten years ago to about 2.2.% in 2005. This is in large part due to the rise of Pentecostalism. The three regions with the highest concentration of Protestants are Paris, Alsace-Lorraine and the south of the country. The predominant faction is the Calvanist Reformed Church (450,000 members). The only women priests in France are to be found in this church. Other Protestants include: Lutherans, most of whom are in Alsace-Lorraine, and the remainder are a mixture of Evangelicals, Adventists, Pentecostalists etc.

Judaism. There are an estimated 600,000 Jews in France representing a religion, which has been present in France since the first century A.D. The largest populations are to be found in Paris, Marseille and Alsace. About 60,000 Jews have emigrated to Israel from France.

Islam. The second largest religion in France is Islam and France is home to the biggest Muslim community in Western Europe. As statistics calculated on ethnicity or religion are banned in France there is no figure for the exact number of the Muslim community, which is estimated at between five and ten million. More Muslims in France are identifying with their religion and the rise of Islamic militancy is cause for concern because of its potential to throw up extremists. Many of the Muslim community are from former French colonies, who arrived in bulk in the 1950s and 60s. They represent several factions of Islam including Sunnis of Maghrebian, i.e. north African origin; Turkish Islam which incorporates both Sunnis and Shiites, and most recently, African Islam which has marabouts (religious leaders) for the various brotherhoods it tends to form.

Little Canterbury Beyond England

France has several Church of England (or 'C-of-E' as it is commonly known) parishes which are part of its Diocese of Europe. There are at least 50 Anglican (*l'Eglise Anglicaine*) congregations around France, seven of them in the Paris area and others include Poitou-Charentes, Brittany, Lille and the Loire Valley. Services are mostly held in borrowed Catholic churches. Joining a congregation can be a good way of meeting people, especially for families and some are thriving in areas where there are large numbers of expatriates such as the south-west. The Intercontinental Church Society (☎01926-430347; www.ics-uk/org/ churches/France.shtml) can supply maps and contact details directly, or via their website which has a list of Anglican churches in France.

Quality of Life

CHAPTER SUMMARY

O National Museums such as the Louvre in Paris and others in the provinces offer free entrance to all on the first Sunday of the month. Other exhibitions offer free or reduced entry to pensioners.

O The French government is very keen to preserve older citizens' involvement in society and there is a national organisation to promote their interests.

O The local mairie holds details of local clubs and associations.

O French railways, SNCF, offer up to 50% off rail travel for seniors over 60 through the Carte Senior scheme which also gives reductions on excursions, accommodation, car rental and ferries to Corsica.

O France has a network of over 8000 km of inland waterways which are a great way to explore large parts of the country.

O Le Camping is highly evolved in France, but if you don't want to stay on a fancy campsite with all mod cons, it is quite acceptable to ask a farmer's permission to pitch your tent or park your motorhome on his land.

O Many municipalities organise events for the over 60s. These can include trips to see shows and sometimes holidays based at hotels or in a holiday residence; it is worth asking at the mairie to see what is on offer.

O France has 11 national public holidays. At a local level there are thousands of festivals celebrating all kinds of things from truffle fairs to ice sculpture competitions.

O Cheap airfares are provided by over 40 low cost airlines operating in and out of France. There are discount travel specialists that deal in last minute holidays and flights at bargain prices if you are able to travel at short notice.

WHERE TO GET INFORMATION

The Mairie

The first useful port of call is the local *mairie* which you will already be acquainted with, as all the forms and official business required to regularise your settlement in France will have been dealt with there. The mairie also holds details of everything of interest locally to its citizens such as local clubs and associations of all types, so for instance if you are keen on astronomy, you can find the contact details for the local astronomical society. Every year, usually in September, there is an open day in every town when local volunteer organisations present themselves and it is a great time to go around getting information and contacts for anything you might want to get involved with or indeed get help from.

Some Activities and Services of the Mairie

- Welcome and information to incomers (*accueil et information*)
- Social aid (*action et aides sociales*)
- Culture and cultural events (*culture et spectacles*)
- Environment (*environment*)
- Registry services (family etc) and identity papers (*état civil et papiers d'identité*)
- Electoral list and elections (*liste électorale et élections*)
- Housing (*logement*)
- School attendance (*scolarité*)
- Local transport (*transports*)
- Town planning (*urbanisme*)
- Roads department and green spaces etc (*voirie et espaces verts* etc)

MJCs

Another potentially interesting organisation with social and cultural functions is the *Maison des Jeunes et de la Culture* (MJC). A chain of these was established throughout the regions of France in the 1960s with a mission to involve urban and country populations in cultural activities of all types. They provide activities and cultural expositions for all ages. There is no UK equivalent, although they also serve some of the functions of a typical village hall, i.e. as a venue for youth activities and senior activities such as dances, lunches, soirées, club meetings etc. MJC.s as they are usually known, are found in towns, some villages and quartiers of cities. You can find the nearest one to you on their website www.mjc-cmjcf.asso.fr.

Accueils des Villes Francaises

AVF (www.avf.asso.fr) is a national organisation with 350 branches throughout France that help newcomers, regardless of nationality, to settle in to the area. They mainly provide information and advice for matters such as finding housing. They also organise welcome events and language courses. You can find the nearest one on their website. Périgeux, in the Dordogne has its own, unofficial, welcoming facility as Bob Culshaw explains:

> *Périgeux in the Dordogne has a lot of English residents and there is also an English pub, 'The Star Inn,' run by Mike and Bev who have lived here for 20 years and operate as an informal base and exhaustive information centre for residents and newcomers. They helped us a lot when we were starting out.*

MAKING NEW FRIENDS

Of course most people know how to make new friends and do it instinctively or subconsciously, but moving to another place, in another country with another culture and language can be hard on even the most honed social skills and you can suddenly feel like a mute idiot, or as one foreigner implanted into the UK and having mastered some colloquialisms put it 'a complete plonker'. Undoubtedly, language skills are pretty essential and once you have made headway in that area, you can branch out into French Third Age life with zeal. A good starting point can be the numerous clubs and associations for seniors of which there are a considerable variety as Keith Oakley found when he and his wife retired to a village near Périgeux:

It is highly unlikely that one's immediate neighbours will have similar interests and/or become your best friends. Consequently, for retired people, who will not normally meet French people as part of daily life such as schools and work, joining a local activity in which one can meet people with similar interests is essential. Clubs and societies are part of the French culture. Our local town, St. Astier (pop. 5,000) has around sixty, from scrabble to aqua gym.

Bob and Annette Culshaw also found joining a local club and stocking up their garden has expanded their interests:

My wife and I joined a local walking club run by French people and we are just about to go on a snow-walking holiday in the Auverge with them. I am looking forward to putting 'tennis rackets' on my shoes; it will be a new experience for me. We also met an English-speaking Frenchman in the local garden centre who introduced himself and it turned out that he lives a mile from our house. He 'adopted' us and has helped in all sorts of ways including introducing us to his social circle and we now have an enormous one, most of them French locals.

While widow Anne Scanlon, who is in her seventies and lives in Faux, finds her local seniors club very sociable:

You don't have to be a pensioner to join it. The Pensioners' Club, called Temps de Loisirs de Faux, is run by the local commune and they organise evenings of card games, regular lunches, bingo, bridge and so on. We also get a free annual four-course Christmas lunch laid on by the local commune for its pensioners.

If you have an MJC (see above) near you they will have details of local clubs as will the local *Centre Communal d'Action Sociale*. Below are some national organisations that hold details of clubs and associations nationwide for *les retraités* (retired people) and *les aînes* (seniors).

Useful Organisations

L'âge d'or de France: ☎01 53 24 67 40; www.agedorenfrance.com. Organisation formed 30 years ago to bring friendship, culture, leisure (including travel) and creative pursuits to the retired and not so retired. Organises regular activities. Mainly Paris-based but has some useful links.

La Fédération Nationale des Clubs d Aînes Ruraux (FNCAR): ☎01 44 56 84 67. National Federation Of Rural Seniors Clubs. The national union of retired and aged people is the main organisation for the retired in France. It has about three-quarters of a million members belonging to 10,000 clubs in 90 départements. The clubs extend a warm welcome to anyone over the age of 50 including foreigners. It acts as a lobby group, gets retired people involved in the life of the local region and offers a programme of social and cultural events.

L'Union Nationale des Retraités et des Personnes Âgées (UNRPA): ☎01 42 39 21 90.

SENIOR CONCESSIONS

There are the usual range of concessions applicable to seniors over 60 in France which can contribute to your quality of life, not least are the concessions on public and private transport and cultural spectacles. For more budget travelling within France see section *Travelling and Tourism in France*.

○ **Local Buses.** Depending on where you live, from 60 years of age, you can enjoy free or reduced travel on local buses. Small dogs, and cats can accompany you in a basket (maximum 45 cm).

○ **Trains.** SNCF the French railway company offers a Carte Senior for the over 60s which gives a minimum of 25% off and up to 50% reduction on train journeys (depending on times of travel) by TGV and Corail (inter-city trains) and 25% reduction on ferries to Corsica. An example fare: Paris to La Rochelle by first class TGV would cost €46.60 with a 50% reduction. If you combine your train journey with a night in a hotel and or an excursion to an historical monument, museum, theatre or cinema there are reductions of 30-50% for these too. Further details from www.senior-sncf.com or www.sncf.fr.

o **Visits to Museums and Monuments.** There are no reduced entrance fees to national museums in Paris and the provinces for the over 60s; instead they offer free entry to all comers on the first Sunday in each month. Other permanent collections and certain exhibitions offer free entry to pensioners and the disabled so when you visit ask if there is a reduction for seniors. Every year (since 1983) millions of French people take advantage of the *journée portes ouvertes du Patrimoine* which allows entry to everyone, to over 10,000 historical monuments for free, or for a reduced fee, over a weekend in September.

SPORTS

Less than a century ago if you lived beyond 65 you were regarded as aged. These days, 60 is being touted as the new 40 and increasingly retired people are pursuing sports and living fit and active lives into their 80s and sometimes 90s. Sports are the best way of maintaining a healthy cardiovascular system, good reaction time, agility, hand/eye coordination and the unquantifiable benefits from belonging to a club and the social interaction involved. A recent report highlighted the fact that a sixty-year-old can have a cardio-vascular system as efficient as that of a twenty-year-old; sadly this does not apply to joints as well, so it is essential to know your weaknesses and take suitable precautions and medical advice. Certain sports including downhill skiing are more difficult to learn in later life unless you are already used to similarly demanding physical activities. Other sports, such as Tai chi, swimming and even weight training are suitable for beginners of any age. A useful starting point for contacts is your local marie, or you can contact the *Fédération Française de la Retraite Sportive* (FFRS), the national retirement sports association. If the weather forecast is a crucial factor for your preferred sport you can check it on *Allô Météo* (www.meteo.fr).

Most towns have a selection of sports clubs, details of which can be obtained at the mairie, but if you want to find the nearest you can always contact the national organisation of a particular sport; the main ones are given below.

Air Sports – Microlighting – *Fédération Française de Planeur Ultra-Léger Motorisé;* ☎01 49 81 74 43; www.ffplum.com. Gliding – *Fédération Française de Vol à Voile;* ☎01 45 44 04 78; www.fffvv. org; Parachuting – *Fédération Française de Parachuting,* ☎01 53 46 68 68; www.ffp.asso.fr. Flying – *Fédération Nationale Aéronautique,* ☎01 44 29 92 00; www.fna.asso.fr.

Alpine Skiing – *Fédération Française de Ski,* ☎04 50 51 40 34; www. ffs.fr and www.ski.fr. If you have been skiing for years you'll probably want to continue, albeit as less of a daredevil. If you are a beginner desperate to make the most of the French Alps, try cross-country skiing (*ski de fond*).

Archery – *Fédération Française de Tir à l'Arc,* (FFTA); ☎01 48 12 12 20; www.ffa.fr. Suitable for beginners. There are lots of clubs in France and archery is very sociable. Equipment can be provided for beginners at most clubs.

Badminton – *Fédération Française de Badminton,* ☎01 49 45 07 07; www.ffba.org. Light raquets. Played indoors and outdoors. Any age.

Boules – *Fédération Française de Sports de Boules,* ☎04 78 52 22 22; www.ffsb.asso.fr. Almost synonymous with France, boules was being played 3000 years ago. Hugely popular and very sociable. Brilliant for retirees. Lots of rules and regional variations.

Caving – *Fédération Française de Spéléologie,* ☎04 72 56 09 63.

Cycling – *Fédération Française de Cyclisme* (FFC), ☎01 49 35 69 00; www.ffc.fr. Huge in France. Not uncommon to see wiry male octo-genarian devotees sailing up hills in Tour de France manner. Perhaps best not to race them.

Dance – *Fédération Française de Danse,* ☎01 42 74 55 50; also www. france-danse.com and www.cnd.fr. Dancing is big in France, espe-cially amongst the retired all of whom can waltz and foxtrot etc to a high standard and there are normally local opportunities for this kind social dancing organised by the mairie. There are also regional dance groups if you are interested in learning the traditional dances of say the Auvergne.

Equitation – *Fédération Française d'Equitation* (FFE), ☎02 54 94 46 00; www.ffe.com; also look at www.fnc.fnsea.fr and www.lesmetiers-ducheval.com. Brilliant for the spectacular trekking routes in France which can be taken at a gentle pace.

Golf – *Fédération Française de Golf,* ☎01 41 49 77 00; www.ffg.fr. Not as big as some other sports but gaining in popularity. There are around 150 golf courses and you can find out about them from the website.

Gymnastics – *Fédération Française de Gymnastique,* ☎01 48 01 24 48; www.ffgym.asso.fr. You will find that the movements, practised regularly improve your ability at other sports. You can join a group of which there are many all over France.

Pétanque – *Fédération Française de Petanque et de Jeux Provençal,* ☎04 91 14 05 80; www.ffpjp.fr. Similar to boules, but with smaller boules.

Retirement Multisports – *Fédération Française de la Retraite Sportive* (FFRS), ☎04 76 53 09 80; www.ffrs-retraite-sportive.org. Find your nearest departmental committee for sports in retirement.

Swimming – *Fédération Française de Natation,* ☎01 40 31 17 70; www.ffnatation.org. Swimming exercises more muscle groups than any other sport and puts minimum strain on the joints. Can be done at any age. You can find out about your nearest swimming pool from the above website

Tai-Chi-Chuan – *Fédération de Tai-Chi-Chuan,* ☎01 40 26 95 50; www.fed-taichichuan.asso.fr. Movements based on martial arts and done in slow motion. Excellent for older people as practised every day in China. Suitable for beginners.

Tennis – *Fédération Française de Tennis* (FFT), ☎01 47 43 48 00; www.fft.fr. Very popular in France.

Walking – *Fédération Française de la Randonnée Pédestre;* ☎01 40 35 85 47; www.ffrp.asso,fr. Rambling is hugely popular and any local tourist office will give you details of marked trails and local clubs (2,500 of them exist in France). Details of long distance paths (*chemins de grandes randonées*) can be found at www.rando-trekking. com or www.gr-infos.com.

Yoga – *Fédération Française de Yoga;* ☎01 47 00 26 12; www.yoga-paris.com. *Fédération Française de Hatha-yoga,* 50 rue Vanneau, 75007 Paris; 01 45 44 02 29; www.ff-hatha-yoga.com. The ultimate anti-stress remedy that helps you live in harmony with your body and mind as you progress with the breathing and stretching exercises.

LEISURE INTERESTS

Leisure interests are as varied as the people who pursue them and there is not room to cover all of them here. Almost every kind of mainstream interest has websites devoted to it. In any case, being connected to the internet is almost essential, especially if your interest involves a club or a widespread group of enthusiasts so that you can get a group newsletter by e-mail and updates of gala events, special offers, outings, etc as well as making use of an internet forum to exchanges views and request information on subjects ('threads' in computerspeak). For more information about internet and email see the *Keeping in Touch* section. Below are some of the more popular leisure interests and contacts for helping you pursue them in France.

Bridge

Bridge performs the useful dual function of keeping your brain active and providing convivial company as it is both challenging and very sociable. There are about 1,300 clubs in France and you can work upwards from beginner level. The mairie and the MJC will have details of the local club, or you can contact the French Bridge Federation (www.ffbridge.asso.fr).

Collecting/Rummaging in Brocantes (Flea Markets)

Collecting can give hours of pleasure and even excitement if you find something rare and potentially valuable. The variety of objects that are collectible is eclectic and if you choose something small then you will have room to enlarge your collection: buttons, cigarette packets, coins and stamps for instance. Some are pricey such as watches and miniatures and some have enormous human interest such as old documents, postcards, letters etc. which can also help with your French as you learn to translate them. The variety of places that you can pursue additions to a collection ranges from *brocantes* and antique shops to *vide-greniers* (car boot sales).

There may be local groups of collectors which you can join such as those for postcards which have dedicated websites such as www.cpapassion.com

(English version available) where you can swop/sell cards, and exchange information about them; also www.carte-postale.com.

If you are going to go rummaging at brocantes (the French word for this is *chiner*), it is essential to be there either very early, or just before packing up when boxes of stuff are sold off cheaply and sometimes given away. If you think you have made a find there are organisations that can value objects for you. The *Chambre nationale des commissaries-priseurs judiciaries* organises free valuation days in the provinces which you can find out about locally or from their website www.commissaries-priseurs.com. A calendar of brocantes throughout France can be found at www.la-brocante.com.

DIY

Bricolage (pottering, doing odd jobs) is becoming something of a craze in France, probably because of the urge to economise in a country where repairs and maintenance are expensive and from the discovery that it can be therapeutic to work with your hands. Even if you are used to DIY in the UK you may find different techniques and products are required in France. There are plenty of do-it-yourself shops, just as in Britain. The best-known are Castorama (www.le-castor.com) Leroy-Merlin and Mr Bricolage. The main drawback is the terminology, which can make it a laborious task getting what you want. Islay Currie, of Currie French Property Services, has the following story:

I went into a builder's shop and spent an hour and a half explaining all the different stuff I needed, like left- and right-threaded joins and so on. The assistant patiently went back and forth showing me everything they had. As I was leaving he said 'Have and nice day'. So you speak English then', I said. 'Of course', came the reply, 'I lived in New York for 14 years'. But, you know, this is France so you have to learn to ask for things in French'.

For the hardcore enthusiast the magazine *Système D – les bricothèmes* (www.systemd.fr) deals with a different aspect of DIY each month, bathrooms, heating. Another useful website is www.commeunpro.com.

The *Institut d'Art et d'Archéologie* runs a regional programme of archaeology workcamps, but more interestingly for those interested in DIY renovation they run courses in carpentry, mural painting, stained glass window making and stone masonry and more. You can send a stamped self addressed envelope to them at 3, rue Michelet, 75006 Paris or email artarch@paris4.Sorbonne.fr.

Fishing

Inland fishing (*la pêche*) is an ideal retirement pursuit. You can relax and enjoy, and learn the art of patience, in solitude or with others. As in the UK you have to have a fishing permit. Permits are obtainable from local fishing associations or from shops and businesses selling fishing gear (*attirail de pêche*).

However, during annual fishing festivals held in May and June, there are two days of free fishing for all. This provides an opportunity for anyone to discover whether or not they have a vocation for it.

The most esoteric fishing is fly fishing (*pêche à la mouche*) which involves designing or buying your own fake insect (fly) to make the end of your line so visually exciting that it is irresistible to your prey, usually a trout or salmon.

A good source of information is Phil Pembroke's book *Pêche Française: The Friendly Guide to Angling in France*. To order, call or email Phil at: ☎01708-764696; e-mail philippembroke007@hotmail.com.

Useful Contacts

Union Nationale pour la Pêche en France: ☎01 48 24 96 00; www.union. peche@unpf.fr.

Club Française des Cybers Pêcheurs à la Mouche: www.lapecheala mouche.free.fr.

Fédération Française de la Pêche à la Mouche et au Lancer: ☎01 45 21 01 69; www.pechealamouche.com.

Ornithology

Ornithology in France tends to embrace caged as well as wild birds. Bird-based interests include buying and selling, breeding, competitions, festivals and more. Remember also that the French watch wild birds, and also eat a wider range of species than the British.

Useful Contacts

Fédération française d'ornithologie: ☎ 02 51 68 56 23; www.f.f.o.free,fr.
Ligue française pour la protection des oiseaux: ☎ 05 46 82 12 34;
www.lpo.fr.

Photography

The French claim to have invented photography (think of Monsieur Daguerre and his daguerreotype). What would the early photographers make of modern photography based on the digital camera which can store up to 900 images at a time? Of course film-operated cameras are still very much in evidence. Most MJCs run photography courses, which may be free for seniors. The *Fédération Photographique de France* has branches all over France.

Useful Contacts

Société Française de Photographie: ☎ 01 42 60 05 98; www.sfp.
photographie.com.
Fédération Photographique de France: ☎ 01 43 71 30 40; www.fpf.asso.fr.

Reading

Reading is pursued enthusiastically, if not passionately, in France. Books are more expensive than in the UK as they carry VAT. However, the French have their own version of Everyman budget classics, the *livres de poches*. Assuming that you have mastered French sufficiently to venture into a public library, you will find a vast choice of books to read for free. There are 2000 public libraries (*bibliothèques municipales*) throughout France and in localities of fewer than 10,000 inhabitants a mobile library (*bibliobus*) visits on regular dates.

Book groups are on the rise in France as in many countries. This is a great way to share the pleasure of reading, which tends otherwise to be a rather solitary occupation. You can start your own group of about ten to fifteen persons and organise a rotation of book choosers and presenters. It should be possible to negotiate a discount if you are buying books in bulk.

Singing and Other Music

As in the UK there are many local choral groups (*chorales de quartier*) and they are popular with all ages. Singing is particularly good for the memory and you have to master using your breath. You don't necessarily have to be able to read music, but you will probably have to have a brief audition with the choir leader (*chef de choeur*) The genre of music sung by each group may be along a theme such as church, Basque songs, traditional, gospel, classical and so on. France has many choir festivals: one of the largest is the *International Rencontres de Chant Choral* held in Tours. Arles has choir weeks and Lyon and Troyes have regional choral festivals.

Keith and Hannah Oakley found that joining the local choir led on to many friendships:

There are those who choose to integrate with the French and those who prefer to stay amongst other Brits. We wanted to integrate. This is quite difficult unless you get involved in local activities, because at our age, you do not make friends at the school gates. We love music so we joined the local French choir where we have made a lot of friends. The French are very polite at first and they wait until they know you better, probably longer than in England, before inviting you to their homes. Our friends are mainly people who have moved around a bit and who don't have family in the region.

There are a number of organisations you can contact for more details but try first the MJC, parish church and the Centre d'art polyphonique regional for choral groups in your region and the Association des musicians amateurs for those that want to play, or who already play an instrument.

Useful Contacts

Association des Musicians Amateurs: ☎ 04 72 41 90 82.

Les Centres d'Art Polyphonique Régionaux: ☎ 01 42 85 30; www.ariam-idf. com. There are 22 of these centres. You can obtain a list of them all on the website of the CAP in Alsace at www.cap.musicanet.org/missions_addresses.htm.

> **Fédération des Centers Musicaux Ruraux:** ☎01 48 73 06 72; www.cmr.
> musicites.org. A useful organisation if you are looking for singing lessons or
> courses.
> **Le Mouvement a Coeur Joie:** ☎04 72 19 83 46; www.acj.musicanet.org.
> An organisation of 600 choirs, 20 of them reserved for seniors. Organises
> courses, meetings and festivals including des voix d'or du troisième age for
> choirs of seniors.

Theatre, Concerts and Ballet

Known collectively as *spectacles,* you might consider these rather
expensive leisure pursuits, but there are discount tickets available
on websites or at the actual venues. Music and theatre and festivals are a part of everyday life throughout France. Details of local
events will be posted in the municipality and the local MJC will
have their own programme of events. Free concerts are often given
in churches.

If you are not watching it, you can be doing it: English amateur
theatricals are thriving in the Dordogne as Anne Scanlon who lives
near Issigeac explains:

*I know that the drama club at Issigeac has 260 members, because I am
the membership secretary. We put on two plays a year in the Château
at Issigeac, which is the munipality's Salle des Fêtes, the venue for
organised events. The drama club even organises an annual shopping
trip by coach, to Bordeaux. There are lots of other clubs including an
excellent music club.*

Reduced Ticket Websites – Cultural/Spectacles

All kinds of reduced tickets	www.billetreduc.com
All kinds of reduced tickets	www.carrefourspectacles.com
Theatre	www.theatreonline.com
All kinds of reduced tickets	www.ticketclic.fr
Various reduced tickets	www.ticketnet.fr
Tickets for cultural events	www.viafrance.com

TAKING COURSES

The French Government is as keen as any other First World country's government to keep its seniors mentally astute and fully active members of society, as this contributes greatly to their quality of life in retirement. There is a wide range of courses on offer for the older student, so there is every chance you can find one that interests you or develops an earlier interest that you have not had time to pursue in more depth: from IT to theatre, and from art history to socio economic theory and everything in between, there are both academic and practical courses on offer. Courses can be based locally, for instance in MJCs, or at academic institutions in towns and cities. Educational institution courses are part of France's programme of continuing education (*la formation continue*), which has been operating for over 30 years. Costs vary depending on the number of modules (*cycles*) you take and how many hours the sessions cover, typically twelve to seventeen hours. Classes can be taken in the evening or during the day depending on the course and the institution. The international organisation *Association Internationale des Universités du Troisième Age* is a good starting point; also *Universités de Tous Ages* and *Universités de Temps Libre*, which are all part of the *formation continue* programme. Some useful contacts and sources of information are listed below:

Course Providers

Association Internationale des Universités du Troisième Age, c/o AG2R,1 rue Augustine Variot, 92245 Malakoff, Cedex, France; ☎01 46 73 12 13; www.aiuta.asso.fr.

Centre d'Enseignement à distance, 7460 Blvd du lycée, 92170 Vanves; ☎01 46 48 23 00; www.cned.fr. Correspondence courses which allow for home study leading to nationally recognised diplomas.

Formation Continue de l'Université de Nantes, 2 bis, Blvd Léon-Bureau BP 96228, 44 262 Nantes Cedex 2; ☎02 51 25 07 25; www.fc.univ-nantes.fr.

Institut Universitaire Tous Age de Picardie Jules Verne, 47 Blvd de Cange, 8000 Amiens; ☎03 22 23 11; www.u-picardie.fr. One of the first universities for continuing education along with Toulouse. Has over

50 conferences, 60 courses and workshops and physical activities annually. Oldest student 82 years.

Université Inter-Ages Safire University of Poitiers, 5 rue Raoul Follereau, BP 635, 86022 Poitiers; ☎05 49 45 44 6; www.safire.univ-poitiers.fr.

Université Tous Ages de Lyon, Université Lumière Lyon 2, 86 rue Pasteur, 69365 Lyon, Cedex ☎04 72 76 84 30; www.uta.univ-lyon2.fr.

Université Vie Active, UNIVA, Université Catholique de Lyon, 74 rue Pasteur, 69365 Lyon, Cedex ☎04 72 32 50 29; www.univ-catholyon.fr.

Universités du Temps Libre, Université de Rennes 1, Ave. du Général Leclerc, 35042 Rennes Cedex; ☎02 99 63 66 76; http://perso.wanadoo.fr/ufuta/.

There are about 45 universities and colleges around France which offer courses to mature students who are retired or not. A list of them can be downloaded at the above http address also the courses they offer.

GARDENING AND HORTICULTURE

The French love gardens but don't have the reputation for gardening enthusiasm that the British do. Many of the most admired French gardens tend to be of the formal and grandiose variety. One famous exception is Claude Monet's garden at Giverny, which is planted along the lines of an impressionist painting, i.e. a floral palette of fairly unconstrained colours. However, there is an increasing perception of gardening as a creative pastime; a recent online poll suggested that 37% of French retired people counted gardening amongst their regular relaxation activities, roughly the same number as are keen DIY enthusiasts.

When French people garden, the result is often something edible, or convertible into alcohol, as if what they are actually doing is rediscovering their pre-industrial roots. When Anglos buy properties in France they often come with what in Britain would be considered a lot of land: one, several or dozens of hectares. This may already have orchards, olive trees and sometimes vines on it, for which the new foreign owners usually lack the required horticultural knowledge. This is a great opportunity for a new hobby such as fruit growing, viticulture etc., as well as offshoots like beekeeping. There is much satisfaction to be derived from creating something that is both bountiful and beautiful. There is of course the probability that some crops will fail. Pests, which come in all species and sizes from olive worms to wild boar, may decide to munch their way through your prize crops, or even your rose garden. When successful however, growing your own fruit and vegetables can help to keep down the cost of living in France, while giving away the surplus does much to endear you to the neighbourhood.

Useful websites for gardening include www.jardinez.com which includes a calendar of garden events in France, a list of nurseries for plants and trees, and schools of horticulture and landscape gardening, all arranged by region, while *Jardiniers de France* (www.jardiniersdefrance.com) has a list of 4,000 gardening clubs throughout France and online garden shopping.

TRAVELLING AND TOURISM IN FRANCE

Most foreigners retiring to France expect to travel widely within their adopted country as indeed the native French do. France will never disappoint travellers as it has everything in terms of landscapes, coasts and history that you could possibly want to explore and see.

Keith and Hannah Oakley are two retired French residents who agree:

> *We don't feel the need to travel much outside France, as there is so much variety here. We like Perpignan on the Mediterranean. We sometimes go by train. With a* Carte Senior *we get a 50% discount on train travel which means a single journey to Paris from the Dordogne costs €20. Even without a Carte Senior anyone over 60 can get 25% discount.*

A recent tourism survey in France found that 40% of French people aged 50+ took their holidays in France, which means that seniors are an important part of the home tourism industry, and travel companies are being encouraged to target their custom. Travel agents are being guided by the government, which is also keen for seniors to stay involved in French society, to create more products for the over 50s including offering them lower rates for holidaying in the off season. *Vacances Bleues*, famous for 35 years for traditional seniors' holidays, now offer a *Faites-Vous Plaisir* brochure aimed at active seniors.

Villages de Vacances

France has a small industry of holiday villages (*villages de vacances*), about 700 of them, and the majority welcome seniors. Villages de vacances are mostly non-profit associations and their charter includes the proviso that they should promote enjoyment and appreciation of France's most beautiful places. They are currently evolving specific attractions for older holidaymakers. They are traditionally enjoyed by families, including children with grandparents but the children tend to get most of the *animateurs'* (activity organisers) attention. Holiday villages are usually good places to make friends. Vacances Bleues run some villages and have a new programme of holidays aimed at seniors. They and several other providers are listed below. There are too many to list here but details of other villages de vacances associations can be found at www.franceguide.com or from your local MJC, marie or tourist office.

Camping Caravanning

For those who own a tent, caravan or a motor-home, the landscape of France offers wonderful opportunities for exploring, so it is well worth investing in any of these if you haven't already done so. Suitably equipped, you are free to enjoy the open road, and the least expensive, and possibly most enjoyable way of travelling in France. In the last few years camping-caravanning has exploded in France which has campsite facilities of all types to suit all purses and requirements. It is up to you to choose the camping style that you prefer from no cost to low cost and from one to four stars, the latter having all mod cons and activities laid on. There are campsites that take tents and caravans, or sometimes just caravans and they may be called *camps de tourisme, camps de tourisme saisonnier* (seasonal only), *camps de loisirs* (with activities) or *parc residentiels de loi-*

sirs (mobile home parks with activities). You can find out the latest information on all of these by consulting the guides and magazines devoted to them (you will find some on the camping federation's website www.ffcc.fr) and from brochures supplied by the local tourist office. Prices are usually based on two people, with supplements for additional guests. Most sites accept animals but there is usually a charge for this and they are not allowed to run free around the site. If you want a quieter ambience, there are also gîte campings offered by local farmers or municipalities, but the facilities are usually very basic. For almost total liberty (*camping sauvage*), it is perfectly acceptable to ask a farmer if you can camp on his or her land and you will help your case if you ask if you can buy eggs and other fresh produce from him.

You can find out everything you need to know about camping in France from the *Fédération Nationale du Camping et de Caravanning.*

Rivers and Canals

France has over 8000 km of navigable waterways (rivers and canals) nearly all managed by *Voies Navigables en France*. Taking a pleasure boat (*bateau de plaisance*) or barge (*péniche*) on the rivers and canals of France and indulging in *la navigation fluviale* is undoubtedly the most tranquil way to go with the flow through the interior of France. The navigable network of waterways unites the main French rivers (Seine, Loire, Garonne, Rhine and Rhône) with a series of canals (the oldest built in 1642), by means of junctions involving artificially raising or lowering water levels. This marvel of a navigable network has recently been awarded UNESCO World Heritage status. The smallest boat (*coche de plaisance*) which is approximately 10 metres by 3, does not require a permit and is similar to a caravan in style and amenities. A half-hour lesson is normally sufficient to learn the principles of steering and navigation before you are given the freedom of the water.

You can also arrange to go on a river cruise on a crewed barge, which may sleep up to twelve people. Further details on hiring boats can be found on the websites www.crown-blueline.com, www.locaboat.

com and www.rivedefrance.com and www.nautic.fr which deals with the southern waterways. The monthly magazine *Fluvial* carries much useful information about travel on the internal waterways of France and has a classified section with boats for sale.

Where to Get Travel and Holiday Info

There has been a noticeable change in the last ten to fifteen years in the range of holidays that are now of interest to the over 50s. Cruises, holidays *en famille* with the grandchildren, and conventional seaside breaks retain their popularity, but there is an increasing demand for more challenging holidays. As the marketing agencies would have it, '50 is the beginning of second adulthood'. According to tourism agencies in France, seniors are now looking for mountaineering, deep-sea fishing, trekking, and scuba diving holidays (among other things) as couples, singles or in groups.

Details of travel and tourism in the regions can be obtained from local *Offices du Tourisme* and *Syndicats d'Initiative* or from the *Fédération Nationale des Offices du Tourisme et des Syndicats d'Initiative* (FNOTSI).

Useful Contacts

Batipaume: ☎04 67 94 11 47; www.batipaume.com. Village de Vacances in the Languedoc.

Fédération Française de camping et de caravanning: ☎01 42 72 84 08; www.ffcc.fr. Produces a guide to all the campsites in France.

Fédération nationale des office du tourisme et des syndicates d'initiative (FNOTSI): ☎01 44 11 10 30; www.tourisme.fr. Head office for all the tourist offices in France.

Renouveau Vacances: ☎04 79 75 75 75; www.renouveau-vacances.fr. Has 21 villages vacances, residential accommodation and a hotel. Many themed holiday weeks including painting and thalassotherapy.

Vacanciel: ☎04 75 82 45 40; www.vacanciel.fr. Villages de vacances, camp sites, tourism residences and small hotels. Offers holidays based around regional tourism, arts, festivals etc.

Val-VVF Villages: ☎04 73 43 00 43; www.valvvf.fr. Has 30 villages des vacances offering all-year-round stays.

Vacances Bleues: ☎04 91 00 96 30; www.vacancesbleues.fr.
Voies navigables en France: ☎03 21 63 24 24; www.vnf.fr. Spearheads
tourism on the waterways and manages the waterways, dams, locks and
riverbanks etc. Employs 6000 people. Publishes the useful guides *Le Petit
Futé du Tourisme Fluvial* (the cunning little fox of waterway tourism) and *La
France au Fil de l'Eau* (downstream France).

Green Tourism

Green tourism (*tourisme vert*), is a way to lose yourself deep in rural
France. In the last few years this form of tourism, also referred to as
l'agrotourisme, has been developing throughout France partly as a way
to support rural and agricultural communities and give them an extra
source of income. As a green tourist you will need your own transport
to reach the accommodation and eating places such as *fermes auberges*
(farm restaurants), *table d'hôtes* (literally, table of the host), *gîtes ruraux*
etc, which come under the banner of green tourism.

Gîtes (lodgings) come under the direction of the *Fédération Nationale
des Gîtes de France* (www.gites-de-france.fr) and they are categorised *gîtes
ruraux, d'etape* (overnight), *de séjour* (longer stay), *gîtes de charme* etc.

Farm-based hospitality comes under the direction of ACPA
(*Assemblée Permanente des Chambres d'Agriculture – Service
Agriculture and Tourisme*) which has 3000 farms throughout
France registered on its farm hospitality scheme. Member farms
subscribe to a charter of standards and display a roadside sign
bearing the words *Bienvenue a la ferme* and a yellow flower logo.
Farm accommodation, and where applicable, farm-based activities
are offered. Where meals are provided they will be prepared from
home-grown produce. You can also buy the farmer's produce for
self-catering if you are camping on a farm belonging to this scheme.
Look out for different classifications such as *fermes auberges, fermes
de séjour* (farms where you can stay), *fermes de chasse* (with hunting),
camping de ferme accueil (camping with a welcome service), *fermes de
découverte* (learn about farming) etc. More information is available
at www.bienvenue-a-la-ferme.com.

Another rural support scheme is *Accueil Paysan* (www.accueil-paysan.
com), which has 1000 members countrywide under the direction of

the *Fédération Nationale Accueil Paysan*, and is similar in structure and offerings to Bienvenue a la Ferme. Members of either scheme are required to be earning their principle living from farming and using green tourism to supplement this. Useful addresses are given below.

Assemblée Permanente des Chambres d'agriculture (APCA), 5 Avenue George V, 75008 Paris; ☎01 53 57 11 44. Produces two guides: *Bienvenue à la ferme* and also *Fermes Auberges*.

Maison des Gîtes de France et du Tourism Vert; 59 rue Saint-Lazare, 75009 Paris; ☎01 49 70 75 75. Produces a guide *Le Guide des gîtes de France.*

CAP France (Fédération Nationale des Maisons Villages Et Gites Familiaux de Vacances); 28, place St. Georges, 75009 Paris; ☎01 48 78 84 25; www.capfrance.com. Another federation of gîtes.

Clevances (Fédération Nationale des Locations de France) P54 rue de l'Embouchure, BP 52166, 31000 Toulouse Cedex 02; ☎05 61 13 55 66; www.clevacances.com. Vacation rentals (*locations*) and chambres d'hôtes (bed and breakfasts).

Fédération Nationale Accueil Paysan, 9 rue de la Poste, 38000 Grenoble; www.accueil-paysan.com. Publishes annual guide *Accueil Paysan* (€10 including postage) giving details of hosts throughout France. You can also look these up on the website.

Fédération Nationale des Logis de France, 83 av. d'Italie, 75013 Paris; ☎01 45 84 83 84; www.logisdefrance.fr. Produces *Guides des Logis de France* containing details of 3,500 places to stay with a centralised booking service.

Rail

As already mentioned there are concessions for seniors on travel by train and other forms of transport. As well as the Carte Senior, SNCF offers fares as low as €19 on the TGV line from Paris to Marseille, if your booking is made four months in advance under its iDTGV (*interactif-Détente Train à Grande Vitesse*) schemes; more details at www. idtgv.com. iDTGV is open to all ages but is useful for seniors as they are usually freer to plan in advance.

Tickets. Train tickets can be bought at stations from machines (*les billetteries automatiques*) as well as the ticket offices. Some travel agents will also book train tickets. The SNCF has a computerised booking system at www.sncf.fr or www.voyages-sncf.com. It is also possible also to book tickets via the telephone Minitel system. TGV seats must always be booked in advance and there is a supplement.

All rail tickets must be validated (*composté*) in the orange machines labelled *compostez votre billet*. The machines automatically date-stamp and clip tickets and are located at platform entrances. Ticket collectors do not appear on platforms, only on the trains. They will fine you 20% of the fare if your ticket is not *composté* and being a foreigner is not considered an excuse.

Air

There are also reductions for various categories of passenger on the airlines. Seniors are offered cheaper fares than normal on domestic flights operated by Air France and its subsidiaries. Independent budget airlines are on the increase in France and have no need to offer concessions as all their fares are cheap anyway. Air France, the national airline with a regional network of flights, reorganised its fares in November 2005 to compete with no frills French carriers, and offers cheap return fares (from €129/£88) between various French cities. Some airlines offering internal (*métropolitaine*) flights have regular special offers and also may offer an *abonnement* (season ticket) ranging in price from €299 to about €500 a year, but you still have to pay for fares, albeit at a reduced (up to 35%) rate. Most companies also offer a loyalty air miles scheme called Flying Blue. A useful website giving details of all the airline companies in France, as well as air travel news and updates on special offers is www.belvedair.com.

Bear in mind that budget airlines companies operate on a very fine margin of profitability and competition is cut-throat so companies and routes come and go. Some internal flight providers are listed below with their contact deals.

Air France: www.airfrance.fr; ☎0820 820 820. National carrier with internal network of flights between main French cities organised with affiliates Brit Air, City Jet and Régionale. Internal return fares from €120.

Airlinair: www.airlinair.com. Based at Paris (Orly) airport, Airlinair runs a fleet of 23 turbo-prop aircraft flying between Paris and about eleven French cities; in addition it offers the cross-country route Lyon-Poitiers-La Rochelle. One-way fares from €50.

Air Turquoise: www.airturquoise.com. From its base at Rheims, Air Turquoise flies shuttle routes to Bordeaux, Marseille and Nice. Fares start at €50 one way.

Régional: www.regional.fr/English/html; .www.airfrance.fr; ☎0820 820 820. A low fare subsidiary of Air France, Régional links 20 French cities via its hubs of Paris, Lyon, Clermont-Ferrand and Bordeaux. New routes added every year. More details of the network on the regional.fr website but bookings are made directly through Air France via internet, or through a travel agent.

Twin Jets: www.twinjet.net; ☎0892 707 737. Scheduled flights aimed primarily at the business community and based around a dozen airports including Paris Orly, Cherbourg, Jersey, Metz-Nancy, Epinal, Marseille, Toulouse, Lyon, Angoulême and Toulouse. Best to plan ahead as fares booked a week in advance are double or more fares booked 30 days in advance e.g. Paris Orly to Epinal €83 (one-way) goes up to €174.

Ferries to Corsica

If you tire of mainland France then the French island of Corsica in the Mediterranean is accessible by SNCM (*Société Nationale Corse Méditerranée*; ☎0891 701 801; www.sncm.fr) ferries which depart from Nice, Marseille and Toulon. Journey times from three hours. Partly privatised in 2003, SNCM has revamped its fleet and services with better on board facilities and off season special offers. Seniors get 25% discount at any time. In the off season such as February this can be excellent value. For instance two seniors plus two young grandchildren can get a first class cabin for €230 (€356 with own car). SNCM also offer short Mediterranean cruises (see *International Travel* below)

The other ferry provider is Corsica Ferries (www.corsicaferries.com) which has eleven ships. Seniors can check for special offers on their website.

INTERNATIONAL TRAVEL FROM FRANCE

Vast and varied as France is, you are bound to want to travel back and forth to the UK, around Europe and even further. France has good connections to its former territories in Africa and Indo-China and its exotic overseas departments in the Caribbean and Indian Ocean, as well as francophone destinations such as Québec. If these are not to your taste then connections all over Europe and beyond can be made by train or no frills, charter and scheduled flights. Or you can cruise the Mediterranean, or use the ferries from France to Italy, North Africa and so on. If you prefer minimum scheduling, then going abroad by car leaves you free to choose your own route and explore and stop off as you wish.

You can book holidays and travel through travel agents (*agences de voyage*) but increasingly the internet is the booking method of choice, as it is so versatile, informative and instant. You can search for travel ideas and special offers, make ticket reservations for trains, boats and planes, buy tickets for shows and festivals, book rooms and rental cars, take out travel insurance, compare prices online, and plan your itinerary, all almost effortlessly. If you want to be certain that the travel or holiday you are booking is suitable for your age group you can look at the detail of what is on offer. Some useful companies and websites are given below.

Bargain Travel

Senior concessions and no frills air and train fares are not the only *voyages en solde* (bargain travel) opportunities that France has to offer. About two weeks before departure dates, agents and air travel companies put unsold flights and holidays directly on the market at discounted prices. Sales can be either through agents themselves or through bargain travel specialists. Discounts from 20% to 40% are usual, but offers can be half price or less. Any'way was offering seven nights in Djerba (Tunisia) for €99 (down from €399) in December 2005 and up to 60% discount on Air France flights. The only problem with such bargains is that you have to decide pretty much on the spot, i.e. without sufficient time to research if it is really what you want, and you do not always know which hotel you will be staying in until you arrive. It is also worth trying discount websites including www.promovac.fr, www. opodo.fr, www.lastminute.com and www.voyages-sncf.com.

Specialist Discount Travel Agents

Any'way: ☎ 0892 894 008; www.anyway.fr. Last minute cheap hols & flights

Dégriftour: ☎ 0899 785 000; www.degriftour.fr. Part of Lastminute.com

Directours: ☎ 0811 90 62 62; www.directours.com.

Look Voyages: ☎0892 788 778; www.lookvoyages.fr. Specialises in all inclusives.

Nouvelles Frontières: ☎0825 000 747; www.nouvelles-frontieres.fr. Frequent special offers.

Travel Agencies

Nouvelles Frontières; ☎0825 000 747; www.nouvelles-frontieres.fr. One of France's best known travel companies. Their agencies throughout France can be found on website. Cheap flights, packages etc from France worldwide.

Fram; www.fram.fr. Founded in France over 55 years ago, Fram has only recently added travel beyond Europe to its repertoire of holidays. Huge range of holidays throughout Europe. Also specialises in holidays in France.

Frantour; www.frantour.ch/fr. Swiss-based but has been operating in France for 30 years. Specialists in city-to-city (*intervilles*) travel to 18 countries in Europe. Offers seaside, spa and theme park holidays throughout Europe by plane and train. Children go half price or free on some offers. Has special offers section.

Syndicat National des Agences de Voyages; ☎01 44 01 99 90; www.snav. org. The national association for travel agencies. You can get a list of all the travel agents in France at their site.

Travel and Cultural Ticket Websites

www.ebookers.fr	Cheap flights and all kinds of holiday bookings
www.abm.fr	Aventure du Bout du Monde, Globe Trotters Association
www.vdm.com	Also phone ☎0892 688 363. All kinds of travel tickets
www.cityvox.com	Event tickets & accommodation France and Europe

Air

If you have become accustomed to low cost no frills flying from the UK to all over Europe you will not be disappointed if you try to speed away on cheap wings from France. Over 40 low cost no frills airlines, nearly all of them foreign, operate in and out of France between points almost as various as you could wish e.g. Dinard to Jersey (Rockhopper), Nice to Gothenburg (Snalskjutsen) and Lyons to Bucharest (Blue Air). The UK no frills airlines easyJet and Ryanair between them cover the most routes between the UK and France while Danish airline Sterling has the most routes between France and the Nordic countries.

www.attitudetravel.com/france/lowcostairlines/ is a useful website that answers all your questions about which low cost airlines fly to and from France and their routes and has links to all the airline websites.

PUBLIC HOLIDAYS AND LOCAL FESTIVALS

France has 11 national public holidays (*jours fériés*); they all com-memorate something, rather than being just bank holidays.

PUBLIC HOLIDAYS	
1 January	New Year's Day (*Jour de l'an*)
Easter Monday (*Pâques*)	As UK
1 May	Labour Day (*Fête du Travail*)
8 May	Victory in Europe Day (*Fête de la Victoire 1945*)
May	Ascension Day
May/June	Whitsun (*Pentecôte*)
14 July	Bastille Day (*Fête Nationale*)
15 August	Assumption
1 November	All Saints Day (*Toussaint*)
11 November	Remembrance Day (*Jour d'armistice*)
25 December	Christmas Day

Festivals

France has an extraordinary number of festivals each year. Many of them are put on to promote tourism in remote areas. The French love any excuse for a party and they know how to put on a good show. Festivals are important for anyone who is thinking of running *gîtes* or *chambres d'hôte* as a way of pulling in the customers. There are thousands of concerts, plays, happenings and festivals advertised on the internet on sites such as: www.culture.fr, www.francefestivals.com (music), www.festival-saoste.com, www.viafrance.com (all kinds of festivals and spectacles) – and on tourist office websites. The following is only a small selection of what is available. The phone numbers are sometimes only in use during the month before the festival.

FESTIVALS IN FRANCE

Month	Festival	Telephone/Website
January	Ice Sculpture Competition. Valloire, Savoie.	☎04 79 59 03 96 www.valloire.net
	Foire Grasse, Limoges, Haute Vienne. Foie gras, truffles, goose, duck products. Also February.	☎03 55 34 46 87 www.tourismelimoges.com
	Journée de la Truffe - Truffles Day, Uzès, Gard.	☎04 66 22 68 88 www.ville-uzes.fr
February	International Festival of Short Films in Clermont-Ferrand.	☎04 93 12 34 50 www.clermont-filmfest.com
	Carnaval, Nice.	☎04 93 92 82 82 www.nicecarnaval.com
	Fête du Citron - Lemon Festival, Menton, Alpes-Maritimes.	☎04 92 41 76 76 www.feteducitron.com
March	International Carnival, Mulhouse, Alsace.	☎03 89 35 48 48 www.ot.ville-mulhouse.fr
	Grenoble Jazz Festival.	☎04 76 51 00 04 www.jazzgrenoble.com
April	Laughing Spring Festival of Humour, Toulouse.	☎05 62 21 23 24 www.mairie-toulouse.fr
	Musicora Classical Music Festival, Paris.	☎01 49 53 27 00 www.lesalondelamusique.com

May	Cannes Film Festival.	☎01 53 59 61 00 www.festival-cannes.fr
	St Émilion Open Door Days, Gironde.	☎05 57 55 50 55 www.saint-emilion-tourisme. com
	Chocolate Days, Bayonne, Pyrénées Atlantiques.	☎05 59 46 01 46 www.bayonne-tourisme.com
	Wine And Food Festival, Plombières, Vosges.	☎03 29 66 01 30 www.plombieres-les-bains. com
June	Summer in Bourges Music Festival, Bourges, Cher.	☎02 48 24 93 32 www.ville-bourges.fr
	International Garden Festival, Chaumont-sur-Loire, Loir-et-Cher.	☎02 54 20 99 22 www.chaumont-jardins.com
	Jazz en Franche-Comté.	☎03 81 83 39 09 www.besancon.com
	Bordeaux Fête Le Vin - Wine Festival.	www.bordeaux-fete-le-vin. com
	Fête de la Tarasque, Tarascon, Provence. Folklore, concerts, bullfighting.	☎04 90 91 03 52 www.visitprovence.com
	Vinexpo, Bordeaux. Wine and spirits exhibition.	☎05 56 56 00 22 www.vinexpo.fr
July	*Festival de Cornouaille* - Celtic Festival, Quimper, Brittany.	☎02 98 55 53 53 www.festival-cornouaille.com
	La Félibrée-Occitan Festival, Dordogne.	☎05 53 07 12 12 www.felibree.fr.st
	Fête de l'Agneau - Lamb Festival, Sisteron, Alpes-de-Haute-Provence.	☎04 92 61 36 50 www.provenceweb.fr
	Festival International de Folklore, Gap, Alpes-de-Haute-Provence.	☎04 92 52 33 73 http://paysgavot.free.fr
	Fête des Géants-Festival of Giants, Douai, Nord.	☎03 20 14 57 57 www.crt-nordpasdecalais.fr
	Les Tombées de la Nuit, Rennes, Brittany. Theatre, music, dance.	☎02 99 67 11 11 www.ville-rennes.fr/tdn

	Festival Européen du Pain - European Bread Festival, Brantôme, Périgord.	☎ 05 53 05 80 52 www.ville-brantome.com
	Bataille de Castillon, Périgord. Spectacular re-enactment of 1453 battle. Also August.	☎ 05 57 40 14 53 www.batailledecastillon.com
	Festival d'Avignon, Provence. Also August.	☎ 04 90 14 14 14 www.festival-avignon.com
August	Inter-Celtic Festival, Lorient, Brittany.	☎ 02 97 21 24 29 www.festival-interceltique.com
	Mimos International Mime Festival, Périgueux, Dordogne.	☎ 05 53 53 18 71 www.ville-perigueux.fr
	Tournois de Joutes - Water Jousting, Sète, Hérault.	☎ 04 67 74 71 71 www.ville-sete.fr
	Fête de la Lavande - Lavender Festival, Digne, Hautes Alpes.	☎ 04 92 36 62 62 www.ot-dignelesbains.fr
	Feria-Catalan Fiesta, Collioure, Pyrénées Orientales.	☎ 04 68 82 15 47 www.collioure.com
	Jazz à Montauban, Tarn-et-Garonne.	☎ 05 63 20 46 72 www.jazzmontauban.com
September	Fêtes Médiévales, Arles-sur-Tech, Pyrénées-Orientales.	☎ 04 68 39 12 22 www.ville-arles-sur-tech.fr
	International Music Festival, Besançon, France-Comté.	☎ 03 81 25 05 80 www.besancon.com
	European Sand-Yachting Championships, La Barre-de-Monts, Vendée.	☎ 02 51 68 51 83 www.ville-labarredemonts.fr
	World Puppet Festival, Charleville-Mézières, Ardennes.	☎ 03 24 59 94 94 www.marionnettes.com
October	*Octobre en Normandie*; throughout major cities of Normandy. Starts September.	☎ 02 32 10 87 07 www.octobre-en-normandie.com
	Fête des Vendanges - Grape Picking Festival, St Émilion, Gironde.	☎ 05 57 55 28 28 www.saint-emilion-tourisme.com

November	*Jazz dans les Feuilles*, Côtes d'Armor, Brittany.	☎ 02 96 78 89 24 www.jazzdanslesfeuilles.com
	Journées Mycologiques - Mushroom Festival, Entrevaux, Alpes-Maritimes.	☎ 04 93 05 46 73 www.entrevaux.info
	Fête de l'Olivier, Manosque, Haute Provence.	☎ 04 92 78 68 80 www.provenceweb.fr
	Salon International du Livre Gourmand, Périgueux, Dordogne. Cookery book fair.	☎ 05 53 53 10 63 www.ville-perigueux.fr
December	*Fête aux Santons*, Marseille, and Provence. Nativity crib figures.	☎ 04 91 13 89 00 www.marseille-tourisme.com

KEEPING IN TOUCH

Communications

It has never been easier to keep in touch with friends and family. Wherever you live, modern technology is making it possible to maintain regular contact without the vast telephone bills that this once generated. For the cheapest new way to communicate, which doesn't tie you to a landline and costs the same whether you call next door or next country, you will need a broadband internet connection and the latest innovation VoIP (Voice over the internet protocol), though this may not be available depending on where you are in France. There are other options for communicating, which are detailed below.

If you are bemused by the technology, ask your niece, nephew, children or grand-children to help you get connected to the internet and show you the basics of using the internet and e-mail. Master this before leaving the UK (if you need to). Both Sir Tim Berners-Lee who invented the internet, and Bill Gates are now in their fifties, so this is no longer new technology and ignoring it will be a big missed opportunity to keep up-to-date with your family, friends and relations. In addition to preventing huge telephone bills, use of the internet will greatly increase the efficiency and enjoyment of your life in France giving you access to all the information you want on every possible subject and preventing you from feeling isolated.

Telephoning Using Landlines

For the moment the telephony scene in France is straightforward: France Télécom is the only company that can install your phone and all calls go through them. You can benefit from cheaper rates by signing up to a rerouter (companies that buy communication time in bulk and sell minutes on to customers at much cheaper rates). Such companies are well-established in France and include AXS, Accord, Westel, First Télécom, Onetel, Phone Systems, World Xchange, Tele2, Cegetel and 9 Télécom. Price comparisons can be found on the website www. comparatel.fr. There are plans to privatise France Télécom, and this may not be entirely positive, especially if you live in a country area. Sooner or later, it will become more expensive to install a connection if you live in the countryside.

British handsets need an adapter to work in France; the British variety have three wires, while the French ones have only two. The keys on French telephones are much the same as on British ones. The only point to note is that the hash symbol is called *dièse* – the same as a 'sharp' in music – needed for cheap-rate telephone cards.

Both business and private phone numbers are on the Yellow Pages site: on www.pagesjaunes.fr. Private subscribers are listed on the same site under *pages blanches*. A telephone directory is an *annuaire*. There is also Minitel, which is expensive but can be used free in post offices. There is always Directory Enquiries: dial 12. Telephone boxes mostly work with cards; those that work with coins are inside cafés or other private buildings, so it is useful to have a card with you. The best one seems to be Kertel, sold by post offices and particularly good for phoning abroad.

Mobile Phones

If you spend any amount of time in France you will want to rent or buy a mobile phone there, but before you sign a contract it is worth considering the small print. Unless you are prepared to stay with one company for a certain time, you will not be able to keep the same phone number or list of numbers if you buy another phone. You can try to have the

SIM card in your phone replaced with a French one, so you can carry
on using the same phone. If your phone is 'SIM-locked', i.e. the card
cannot be changed, then you would have to obtain a French mobile.
Unless you are officially resident in France, then a French mobile
phone company will only let you use a phone with a pre-paid card, on
production of your passport. To buy a mobile phone you need proof
of identity and proof of address. You also have to produce an RIB – a
bank account number – which is in any case unavoidable if you pay by
direct debit. You may also be asked to produce a cheque written out to
you that has gone through your account, or a French credit card. Out
of the three main phone companies, Orange and SFR are supposed to
have better coverage than Bouygues Télécom in country areas. They
generally claim to cover 98% of the population and 87% of the land
area. There is even a plan to have small aeroplanes flying 24 hours a
day over the countryside to ensure better coverage.

The mobile phone market is competitive and rapidly changing.
Some mobiles can receive and send text messages, operate as a diary,
connect to the internet and receive e-mails and take photographs
and send them by e-mail. For a reasonably clear overview of the
different deals on offer, look at the website www.comparatel.fr.
The three main companies are: www.orange.fr, www.sfr.fr and
www.bouyguestelecom.fr.

Internet and E-mail

It would be fair to say that France is some years behind the UK in
terms of internet use and availability. This is to some extent because
of the pioneering system known as *Minitel* started in 1985, which
provides a service similar to the internet. Minitel is a keyboard and
screen that sits alongside your telephone; it is expensive to use but
still popular. You can access Minitel from the UK, by logging on to
www.minitel.fr. If you are travelling around in France it is difficult
to find cybercafés outside tourist towns. Internet terminals in post
offices can only be used for very basic internet searches, and will not
allow you to send e-mails or use interactive sites like railway time-
tables. The French post office offers a useful e-mail address: www.
laposte.net, but you cannot set this up in a post office, only from a

fully functioning internet terminal.

Once you have settled in to your new home in France, you can look at the different internet service providers' offerings, which are fewer than you would find in the UK. If you are connected to cable, you can get good deals with Noos. You can have ADSL (broadband) in some densely populated areas; remote country areas may never have broadband, although the French government are looking for ways to cover the whole country. You could try installing a dish on your house. For more information about different ISP charges look at the website www.comparatel.fr.

Telephoning Using the Internet

To make an internet phone call you will need to rent broadband (£15-£20 per month), download the relevant software from Google, Skype etc., draw up a list of contacts on your computer, plug a telephone headset (cost about £5) into your computer and click on a contact's name. If they are online, they click to accept your call. You should either agree a time in advance when you will both be online, or see from your computer whether they are online. You can talk for as long as you like to anyone anywhere who has software compatible with yours. Hopefully you will have coordinated with friends and relations before leaving the UK about using the internet for telephony.

Internet telephony (VoIP or Voice over the Internet Protocol) is evolving and some providers enable callers to talk from a cordless phone anywhere in their house and garden without the need to switch on their PC. Some providers charge a monthly subscription fee (£5-£10 per month) or nothing at all. If there is no monthly subscription there will be tiny charges for calls to landlines (typically 1.2 to 3p per minute) and if there is a monthly subscription (e.g.Vonage charges £9.99) the calls will be free. Providers in France include Skype, Vonage, Google Talk, Yahoo Messenger, Glophone and Buddytalk. All providers at present charge for calls to mobiles.

Having Friends and Family to Stay

The chances are, when you retire to France you will have friends and family coming to stay on a fairly regular basis. It is important for you to buy the house that suits you, rather than being obsessed with any potential visitors. Estate agents may try to sell you a larger house than you can afford citing regular family usage and visitor space as a selling point. There are alternatives to having a four-bedroomed house. Your guests and family can stay in a local guest house or you may have outbuildings that you can convert to guest accommodation, and possibly even a gîte so that you can let it when family and friends are not staying. Also, if friends and family visit for longer periods then it may be preferable for all to have them living in separate accommodation on your land or nearby. Details of the types of rural accommodation in France are given above under *Travel and Tourism in France*. For information about renovating a building see *Renovating a Building* in the chapter *Your New Home in France*.

Another factor that may influence your visitor flow is accessibility. If you are not far from an airport which is on a no frills fare route, or within easy driving of the Channel ports, or near a train station the chances are that you will get more visitors, or more frequent visits than if you are in a remote country location.

STARTING A SMALL BUSINESS

Converting Outbuildings

Many people imagine themselves making a little money from their property when they retire to France. The details of property conversion are beyond the scope of this book, but there is no shortage of places to get advice not least from books such as David Everett's *Buying and Restoring Old Property in France,* which is mainly about restoring, not buying. It is worth enquiring about grants (*subventions*) for restoration from the *Association Nationale pour l'Amelioration de l'Habitat* (www. anah.fr) which offers grants of about 20% towards the cost. Conditions include that the property restored must be a principle residence for at least nine years after restoration. There are more possibilities if you are planning to run *gîtes*. Grants for *gîtes* are distributed by the local *Conseil Général* (the departmental government) through *Gîtes de France* which is organised on a regional basis and there are conditions attached: such as if you sell the property within ten years the grant has to be returned. Whatever kind of work you plan to do, all the plans and estimates must be approved first before any work is started. Many people take fright at the thought of dealing with French builders if there is a language barrier. A service called Renovate in France (www.renovateinfrance.com) lists hundreds of local artisans who can speak English. Alternatively you can buy gîtes as a going concern as Ann and Alan Barrett did, when they bought a farmhouse (www.lesgrezes.com) with four gîtes :

We didn't have to do anything to the gîtes when we bought the property, they were already up and running. We have occupancy year round, although summer is busier as you might expect. As a lot of English people come to buy property here, so we regularly get longer lets of three or four months as it can take this long for property purchase to be completed and people need somewhere to stay in the meantime.

Running Gîtes or Chambres d'Hôtes

These are the two most popular options for running a small business. Gîtes are self-catering lodgings, often converted from farm outbuildings, while *chambres d'hôtes* involve opening your home to bed and breakfast guests, and possibly providing them with an evening meal as well. Gîtes are normally let for a week or longer, but weekends may also be possible. You can get further information and advice from the local tourist office or *syndicat d'initiative*, and also the local *chambre de commerce*.

It is important to be realistic about the income that can be made from *gîtes* as Ann Barrett (see above) explains:

Many people have unrealistic expectations of the income from gîtes. We do not make a lot of money from them but they help support our comfortable lifestyle. I should say I am semi-retired really, although the work involved is only for short bursts and is really busy on changeover days.

It is important to note that chambres d'hôtes and gîtes come under national schemes that have set minimum standards, regulations and restrictions, also that running them is a seasonal business and there is usually a lot of competition in popular tourist areas.

You will have to declare any income earned from offering accommodation to the French tax authorities. You may get away with not declaring income from a week or two's letting, but more than that and you run considerable risks and penalties. You should also consider all the possibilities for tax deductions. If you have taken out a loan, the interest may be tax-deductible. The local tax office or an accountant will advise you. For further information on running a gîte and many other small businesses, see *Starting a Business in France* published by Vacation Work (www.vacationwork.co.uk).

Finding a Part-time Job or Voluntary Work

For whatever reason you may find yourself more isolated than you wish to be in France, or you may have organised your life there well enough to have time to spare. Bear in mind that paid work may be hard to come by. France has high unemployment, particularly amongst the young, and job opportunities in rural areas may be almost non-existent. If you have a skill or trade and can speak French your chances may be slightly better. If you are an author, artist or musician you can probably create your own job. By law, all employers have to register vacancies with the national employment service ANPE (*Agence nationale pour l'emploi*) so you can start your search at the nearest branch of ANPE. You should also ask around locally to see what might be on offer. You should have some idea of how much of your time you wish to allocate to a part-time job as it will be a regular commitment.

Voluntary Work (*le bénévolat*) is much more easily available. This can take almost any form though your good intentions will be restricted if you do not have a grasp of French, although you could offer English lessons or help as a classroom assistant during English lessons. If you do speak French, you will almost certainly find something that ties in with your interests such as environmental protection, animals, children, cookery, schools, hospitals,etc.

Although you should not expect payment, travel expenses are usually reimbursed.

Your local mairie maintains a list of organisations, needing helpers and every year each mairie organises a day of presentations by local voluntary organisations (*forum des associations/journée des associations*), usually held in September. Members of the public can go along and ask questions, collect details etc.

> ### Useful Contacts
>
> **Espace Bénévolat:** www.espacebenevolat.org; Helpful website that lets you key in your post code, type of volunteer work you are interested in and when you are available and gives you a list organisations in your area.
>
> **France Bénévolat National:** ☎ 01 40 61 01 61; www.benevolat.com. Does much the same as *Espace Bénévolat.*

Personal Finance

CHAPTER SUMMARY

O It is advisable to maintain a bank account in the UK as well as opening one in France if you still have property or income in the UK.

O The French Post Office offers all banking services except wired bank transfers.

O If you are living permanently in France, you can open an offshore savings account and get interest tax-free. Some offshore banks offer a dual currency (e.g. euros and sterling) cheque account .

O Most offshore banks require you to maintain a large minimum balance and charge an annual fee.

O You must not go into the red with your bank account in France without a prior arrangement as it is a criminal offence to write a dud cheque and you may be banned (an *interdit bancaire*) from having a French bank account for 5 years.

O If you have a pension lump sum due to you on retirement, it will be taxed in France if you are resident there. You can avoid this by taking the lump sum while you are still a UK resident.

O France has succession laws which stipulate that blood relatives automatically inherit your French assets which means that if you want your spouse to inherit you need expert legal advice.

O Grandparents can gift grandchildren €30,000 tax-free every ten years. Such gifts may be treated as part of inheritance (if their existence is known to the tax office) after the donor's death. Having the gift witnessed by a notaire and formalised in a legal document precludes the risk of being penalised by tax later.

FINANCIAL ADVICE

For those who intend to take up residence in France, the importance of good financial planning cannot be stressed enough. Although both the United Kingdom and France are members of the EU, there are significant differences in their approaches to residence, domicile, taxation and succession matters.

You are deemed to be a French resident on the day that you arrive in France if your intention is to live there permanently. As a French resident you are liable to income tax and social tax on income, wherever it is earned, so ignoring tax is not an option.

Independent Financial Advisers for the British Expatriate in France

• **How can I produce tax efficient income in France?**

John Siddall Financial Services Ltd
Lothian House, 22 High Street, Fareham, Hampshire,
PO16 7AE **t:** 01329 288641 **f:** 01329 281157
e: france@johnsiddalls.co.uk **www.siddalls.net**

• **How can I protect my capital from French inheritance rules and taxes?**

John Siddall International Ltd
Parc Innolin, 3 Rue du Golf, 33700 Bordeaux-Mérignac
t: 05 56 34 75 51 **f:** 05 56 34 75 52
e: bordeaux.office@siddalls.com.fr **www.siddalls.fr**

Siddalls also advises that assets are potentially liable to capital gains, wealth and inheritance taxes wherever they are situated. ISAs and TESSAs are not classed as tax free in France and withdrawals will be taxed. It is also worth noting that current UK investments often give no protection from any of the French taxes and, in particular, French Inheritance Tax.

However, it is possible to minimise or remove exchange rate risk, inheritance tax and succession law issues by getting the right advice on how to restructure your investments, savings, and property.

Expatriate Financial Planning

Axis Strategy Consultants: *76/78 Avenue Champs Elysées, 75008 Paris;*
☎ 01 39 21 74 61; e-mail dcooney@axis-stratefy.com; www.axis-strategy.com; www.axis-strategy.com/personal – finance.htm. Specialises in financial advice for expatriates living in France.

Blackstone Franks LLP: Barbican House, 26-34 Old Street, London EC1V 9HL; ☎020-7250 3300; www.blackstonefranks.com. Also offices in France. Specialists in the expatriate financial sector.

Blevins Franks: Specialists in the expatriate financial sector. For a list of partners in France contact: Philip Marshall (Senior Partner) ☎05 53 522 09 75; phil.marshall@blevinsfranks.com; www.blevins.franks.com. Publishers of the book *Living in France* available from Blevins Franks partners.

Brewin Dolphin Securities: Cross Keys House, The Parade, Marlborough, Wilts. SN8 1NE; ☎01672-519600; fax 01672-515550; e-mail info@brewindolphin.co.uk; www.brewindolphin.co.uk. Services include international portfolio management with off-shore facility for those domiciled or resident outside the UK.

Dixon Wilson: 19 avenue de l'Opéra, 75001 Paris; ☎01 47 03 12 90; fax 01 47 03 12 85; e-mail dw@dixonwilson.fr. Rotherwick House, 3 Thomas More Street, London E1W 1YX; ☎020-7680 8100; fax 020-7680 8101; e-mail: markwaterman@dixonwilson.co.uk. Chartered Accountants, provide strategic financial and tax planning services to businesses, companies and high net worth individuals resident either in France or the UK

Hansard Europe Ltd: Enterprise House, Frascati Road, Blackrock, Co. Dublin, Republic of Ireland; ☎01 278 1488; fax +353 1 278 1499; www.hansard.com. Hansard has products aimed at the French market and designed to be tax efficient with regard to French tax and life assurance regulations.

John Siddall Financial Services Ltd (Siddalls): Lothian House, 22 High Street, Fareham, Hampshire PO16 7AE; ☎01329-288641; fax 01329-281157; e-mail france@johnsiddalls.co.uk; www.siddalls.net. Independent financial adviser providing investment, retirement and tax planning for those people moving to, or already living in France.

John Siddall International Ltd (Siddalls): Parc Innolin, 3 rue de Golf, 33700 Mérignac; ☎05 56 34 75 51; fax 05 56 34 75 52.; e-mail: Bordeaux.office@siddalls.com.fr; www.siddalls.fr. French office of John Siddall Financial Services (above) with regionally based advisers throughout France.

PKF (Guernsey) Ltd: P.O. Box 296, St. Peter Port, Guernsey, GY1 4NA; ☎01481-727927; fax 01481-710511; e-mail french.tax@pkfguernsey.com; www.pkfguernsey.com. Chartered accountants and French tax specialists.

Smith and Williamson: 2 Athenaeum Road, Whetstone, London N20 9YU; ☎020-8446 4371; fax 020-8446 7606; www.smith.williamson.co.uk. A UK chartered accountant, experienced in dealing with most tax matters relating to expatriates and non-UK residents.

BANKING

There are several types of bank in France: clearing banks such as *Crédit Lyonnais*; co-operative banks such as *Crédit Agricole*; corporate banks, e.g. *BNP Paribas;* and savings banks (*caisses d'epargne*). *Crédit Agricole* has an immense advantage in that it has the largest number of branches, 7,500 in France alone. The departmental branches of CA function as separate banks and issue their own shares. Other co-operative banks include *Crédit Mutuel* and *Banque Populaire*; if you want to take out a mortgage with a co-operative bank you are usually required to buy shares in the bank, but not if you just want a cheque account. The post office, *La Poste*, has 17,000 branches in France and longer opening hours than banks, so it could be convenient to have a post office account, or *Compte Courant Postal (CCP)*, which you can access from any post office.

The French bank you choose will depend a lot on whether there is a branch near you, and whether you need specialised services. It is worth finding out if there is anyone who speaks English in your branch; where there are large concentrations of English-speakers some banks are trying to recruit English-speaking staff.

The Calvados region of Crédit Agricole operates a service called Britline with offices in Caen, Normandy, which allows you to open a non-resident bank account in France by post. Britline sometimes has a stand at French property fairs in the UK. Britline cannot open a business account for you. The only exception is an account for a Société Civile Immobilière, a type of company specifically set up to own property.

Generally banking is not free in France, even if you keep your account in credit. However, the situation is improving. In 2005 after a change in the banking laws, the Caisse d'Epargne (4,700 branches) became the first major commercial bank in France to pay interest on current accounts under the product name Satellis. You pay a small monthly subscription on the account but you get interest of one or two percent which is still revolutionary in French banking.

Online banking is not widespread but is growing in France. Providers of internet only accounts include Axa Banque (www.axabanque.fr), ING Direct (www.ingdirect.fr) and Egg (www.egg.fr).

Important Points About Banking

o If you are moving abroad there are several possibilities, some of which are possible to do conjointly, such as having a bank account in the UK, and also in France.

o You can keep your current account in the UK (you will need to do this anyway if you still have property and income in the UK)

o If you are selling up and moving permanently to France you can open an offshore account through UK high street banks and building societies. Most require a large minimum balance to be maintained and charge an annual fee but there may be advantages (see below).

o You can open an account in France with a local branch of a French bank (no UK High Street Bank has arrangements with French banks to open a local account in France but Barclays has a UK helpline for those planning to buy property abroad).

o You need a local bank account in France to gain access to important services such as utilities. You will probably also find it useful to have a French cheque book to use in rural areas where acceptance of credit/debit cards is not universal.

o It is best to open an account in France with a bank that has a lot of branches, as this will be useful if you travel around.

o Most UK High Street banks will charge you to access your money outside the UK. Many people do not realise this until they start withdrawing cash from ATMs abroad.

o Nationwide is popular as it does not charge its current account holders for accessing their money at ATMs abroad.

o Some UK banks conceal commission charges for accessing your account abroad in a loaded exchange rate.

o The French post office (*La Poste*) has a banking department that offers almost all the same services as a bank (except wire transfers from an overseas bank) but is cheaper. The website www.lapostefinance.fr has a banking section in English.

Major French banks

Barclays Bank SA: ☎ 0845 675 0555; www.barclays.fr.

Banque Populaire: www.banquepopulaire.fr.

BNP Paribas: www.bnpparibas.fr.

Britline: ☎02 31 55 67 89; www.britline.com.
Caisse d'Epargne: www.caisse-epargne.fr.
Caixa Bank: www.caixabank.fr.
Crédit Agricole: www.credit-agricole.fr; http://www.ca-(name of department).fr.
Crédit Commercial de France: www.ccf.com.
Crédit du Nord: www.credit-du-nord.fr.
Crédit Lyonnais: www.creditlyonnais.com.
Lloyds Bank SA: www.lloydstsbiwm.com.
Société Générale: www.socgen.com.

Credit Cards

While you are still looking for property, you can use a cashpoint or credit card. Credit cards (*cartes bancaires*) in France operate with a microchip. You need to know your PIN code otherwise you may not be able to use your card in shops.

Because of the French laws against usury France technically has charge cards with a deferred debit rather than credit cards of the type, which allow you to run up enormous debts as in the UK. In France, every 30 days the amount you owe is automatically debited from your bank account, meaning that you may pay for something the day after you bought it. In the UK, credit is for 30-60 days, in France for 0-30 days. If you want to defer payment you will need to open a sub-account, which allows you to borrow money at a lower interest rate than you would pay in the UK on a credit card. There is an annual charge for credit cards in France. A Gold Card costs about €90 a year.

The national French debit card, the *Carte Bleue* (CB) can only be used in France. Debit/credit cards are useful for automatic ticket machines at stations and for car parking, motorway tolls etc. Also in an emergency (because it is an expensive method) you can make calls abroad from public telephones with a credit card. If you need a credit card that functions abroad, you can ask for Carte Bleue/Visa or Mastercard.

Bank Accounts

Opening a bank account is not difficult. If you are resident in France then you simply take along your passport, and proof of your fiscal address in France. For non-residents the bank will ask to see proof of income. The basic form of bank account is the *compte de chèque* which comes with a cheque book. If the bank thinks that you are not a good bet because of some previous misdemeanour, or because you cannot prove your income, they may only give you a *compte de dépôt,* an inconvenient form of account that only allows you to take out cash and has no cheque book or cashpoint card. If at the end of the day you cannot find a bank to open an account for you, then you can go to the Banque de France (there are branches in big towns) who will assign a bank to you.

When you open a bank account you will be offered a Carte Bleue, originally conceived as a substitute for writing cheques. The CB is a cashpoint card, which can also function as either a debit card or credit card; you choose one of the two. CB also stands for *carte bancaire,* i.e. any kind of bank card. You key in your PIN number when making transactions.

As well as the bank's own number, there is one central number for reporting lost bank cards: 01 45 67 84 84.

Resident and Non-Resident Accounts. Whether you are considered resident or non-resident from the bank's point of view, depends on where you are fiscally resident, i.e. where your centre of interests lies. If you spend more than 183 days a year in France you will normally pay your taxes there, so you are fiscally resident. As a non-resident you can only open a *compte non-résident.* Correspondence will be sent to you in your home country. After choosing your branch in France, you need to supply a reference from your UK bank, a legalised copy of your signature, photocopies of the main pages of your passport, and a draft in euros to start you off. You should open an account in person in France after talking to the local bank staff.

Banking Practices

Banking services are not as sophisticated or as liberal in France as in the UK or US; banks are not at all keen to lend money in a hurry. The main rule to remember is that you must never go into the red without prior arrangement, otherwise you risk becoming an *interdit bancaire.*

It is also worth bearing in mind that if you do go into the red any standing orders that you have will automatically be stopped, so your telephone and electricity could suddenly be cut off.

When you open your account you opt for monthly or fortnightly bank statements, or whatever arrangement suits you. There are charges for most transactions, apart from statements. You can authorise utility companies to debit your account automatically (*prélèvement automatique*) for bill payment, but this is not obligatory. This is not the same as a standing order (*ordre permanent/virement automatique*). With the internet you can see what is going on with your account. The antiquated French version of internet, Minitel, is still used for some on-line banking services.

Bank opening hours are a favourite gripe with foreigners in France; there is a law that prevents banks opening more than five days a week, so your bank may close on Mondays. Very small branches (*permanences*) in country areas may only open one morning a week. Internet banking is making things easier.

Cheques

Cheques are used for half of all financial transactions in France; there are no cheque guarantee cards, but you can be asked for other identification. Cheques are written out in a similar way to those in the UK or USA, with the information positioned differently. Your bank will send you your first cheque book once there are funds in your account. French cheques are not negotiable to a third person. The basic form of cheque is the *chèque barré* (crossed), which is only payable to the payee (*destinataire*); the bank has to inform the tax inspectors if you want to use open cheques. When you pay a cheque into your account or cash it then you sign it on the back (*endosser le chèque*).

Bouncing Cheques. Known in France as a 'wooden cheque' (*chèque de bois*) you will be given 30 days to rectify the situation. The Banque de France is informed immediately, and you are not allowed to write any further cheques until matters are resolved. You not only have to pay money into the account to cover it, but also a fine of 15% of the amount that goes to the French treasury. There is also a form to fill in, declaring that you have dealt with the problem or '*incident*'. If the money is not paid you are put on a Banque de France blacklist, and are barred from writing any cheques in France for five years. Bank cards and cheques have to be surrendered.

A cheque is considered the equivalent of cash and cannot be cancelled, unless it has been lost or stolen or is deemed to be fraudulent by the bank. A police report has to be submitted to the bank in such cases.

Business Accounts

Everyone agrees that you should have a separate business account – *compte d'entreprise* – from your personal account if you are earning money in France. If you are self-employed you require a *compte professionnelle*. Actually persuading the bank to let you open one may be less simple than you might expect. You need to show your creditworthiness, and try to get the backing of a chamber of commerce. A further consideration is that charges are higher on business accounts than on current accounts, and the more money that goes through your account the more you pay. There are risks in mixing private and business finances, so there is no alternative to opening a separate account.

Offshore Accounts

Offshore banks are based in places where the tax rules are different and can be exploited when there is a legal opportunity to minimize tax liability. They have advantages and disadvantages. Amongst the former is the fact that you can operate them in two currencies. For instance if you are living in France, you could open an account which provides a euro chequebook and debit card, but you could also maintain the facility of paying UK bills in sterling. This would be useful if you are no longer able to maintain accounts in the UK (i.e. you are no longer resident there).

The disadvantages include the fact that you may (depending on the bank) have to maintain a large minimum balance and there are annual charges. Offshore product providers include include, Alliance and Leicester International, Lloyds TSB Overseas Club, Abbey Gold and NatWest/Royal Bank of Scotland Advantage International. Among the items to compare when considering offshore banks are the annual charges, the permanent minimum balance required and the facilities offered with the account.

The European Savings Directive came into force on 1 July 2005 and means that tax is now deducted at source from the next interest payments. This does not affect the rate of tax for those already declaring their worldwide income but it has caught a few offshore account holders who were happy to ignore the tax rules or were ignorant of what they were. If offshore savers do not accept deduction of interest at source, they will have to opt for having their interest paid gross and participating in 'an exchange of information' and have details of their interest passed to the tax authorities of the country in which they are resident. The latter option is the route currently recommended by some leading tax advisors as it will avoid the possibility of paying too much tax.

All the major British high street banks and some building societies offer offshore banking. Customers of such accounts are not normally liable for UK taxes, but they may be required to pay tax in the country where they are resident. Unless you are a financial expert you should get independent advice from someone qualified to analyse the advantages of offshore banking in your particular circumstances .

Offshore No Notice Savings Accounts

Abbey International: ☎01534-885100; www.abbeyinternational.com

Alliance & Leicester Int.: www.alil.co.im/ofshore

Anglo Irish Bank IOM: ☎01624-698000; www.angloirishbank.co.im

Derbyshire IOM: ☎01624-663432; www.Derbyshire.co.im

Nationwide International: ☎01624-696000; www.nationwideinternational.com

Northern Rock Guernsey: www.northernrock-guernsey.co.gg

Portman Channel Islands: ☎01481-712004; www.portmanci.com

Tax Advisors

Blevins Franks (advisors): ☎+356 21 347 347; www.blevinsfranks.com

Fry Group (advisors): ☎01903-231545; www.thefrygroup.co.uk

John Siddall Financial Services Ltd: ☎01329-288641; www.siddalls.net

John Siddall International Ltd: ☎05 56 34 75 51; www.siddalls.fr.

Towry Law (advisors): ☎01344-828000; www.towrylaw.com

UK Companies/Trusts

This is an immensely complex area that also requires expert advice and it is usually linked with tax planning and asset management. You can buy French property in the name of a UK company or trust but this means it would be locked into a vehicle that has some advantages but is not suitable for the majority of second home buyers.

Advantages/Disadvantages of UK Companies

○ It is a fairly simple matter to transfer the shares of a UK company to say, another family member
○ There is no requirement to involve a French notary in transferring shares to another party
○ If you are not a French resident, the shares are not liable to French inheritance tax; rather they come under the UK tax regime because they are a UK company. This means that if they are willed to a surviving spouse, that person will not normally have to pay inheritance tax.
○ The UK company will be taxable in the UK for capital gains. There may be additional tax liabilities should you liquidate the company or distribute the net sale proceeds.
○ Potential buyers are normally put off at the idea of buying shares in a company and will probably want the property transferred to their name, which means liquidating the company, which is expensive and carries tax liabilities.

Disadvantages of Buying French Property with an English or Offshore Trust

French law does not recognise trusts and because of the uncertainty about how the French tax authorities will view the trustees for tax purposes (probably as owning the property outright or as a partnership), and because it will be liable to French inheritance and gift tax which could be very hefty, it is not currently recommended that French property should be put into a trust.

An offshore structure may however, be useful to anyone whose assets total more than a million pounds as in this case, financial advantages should outweigh the high cost of setting up and maintaining an offshore structure.

Things to Know Before Selling Your UK Property

○ If you are resident in France, you can let your UK home for a few years and then sell it. You will not be liable for UK capital gains tax if you are no longer a UK resident.
○ At the time of selling your UK home you should arrange to be resident nowhere (i.e. take a long holiday anywhere but the UK or France) to take advantage of the fact that the UK tax year runs from April 6 to April 5 and the French tax year is the calendar year. While not being resident anywhere, you may be able to dispose of your assets into a discretionary offshore trust to avoid paying capital gains. This has to be done after you have left the UK and before you are resident in France. If you have made large gains, this could be an astute move. Professional advice is essential as timing is crucial.

UK PENSIONS AND BENEFITS

Pensions and Benefits

As already described in the *Basics* chapter in *Preparations for Departure* if you are already receiving a UK pension, you should make arrangements to have it paid directly into your French bank account before you leave the UK. The UK State Pension is payable in full anywhere in the European Economic Area. Note that Pension Credit is not payable outside the UK. UK War Pensions can also be paid in full to people living permanently outside Britain.

If you are retiring to France before the official retirement age, you can get a UK State Pension forecast by completing form BR19 available from a Jobcentre Plus (or download the form at www. thepensionservice.gov.uk/resourcecentre/br19/home.asp). If you are already living abroad contact HM Revenue and Customs in Newcastle for form BR19 (or download it) and send the completed form back to HM Revenue and Customs.

Note that nearly all other UK derived social security benefits cannot be paid to those who are living permanently outside the United Kingdom. Instead you will be able to claim local benefits and social assistance on the same terms as French citizens from their social services. Most of these benefits are related to health and wealth (or lack of it). Further details of French medical benefits and E forms 106 and 121 which give you access to French state healthcare if you have paid National Insurance in the UK, are given in the *Healthcare* chapter.

Things to Know About UK Pensions and French Tax

○ If your pension is derived from British Armed Forces or the Government it will be taxed in the UK and will not be taxed in France.

○ All other types of UK pension paid in France, are taxed in France, not the UK.

○ If you have a pension lump sum that is paid to you on retirement this will be taxed in France. You can get round this by taking your lump sum while you are still a UK resident.

PERSONAL TAXATION

As a result of the different tax regimes, which exist in different countries there are complications involved in a move overseas. This does not just apply to tax affairs in the host country; a move also has tax implications in one's home country. The situation is rather simpler, however, if you are leaving the UK, and thus the UK tax system, for good. Tax regulations are more complicated if you are buying a second home (*une résidence secondaire*) with a view to retiring in France later, because then you are obliged to become involved in two very different tax systems.

It is advisable to take individual and independent financial advice before committing yourself to a move to France. This will ensure that no unnecessary tax is paid, and should also minimise eventual tax bills. If you do not already have an accountant who is experienced in expatriate taxation then the addresses of Franco-British tax consultants can be obtained from the French Chamber of

Commerce in Great Britain (197 Knightsbridge, London SW7 1RB; ☎020-7304 7021; fax 020-7304 7034).

Procedure for Residents in France

Any person who spends more than six months (183 days) per year in France has to pay French tax on his or her worldwide income. The situation is reasonably straightforward if you are moving permanently to France.

○ You should inform the UK Inspector of Taxes at the office you usually deal with, and you will receive a P85 form to complete.
○ The UK tax office will usually require certain proof that you are leaving the UK for good.
○ You may be eligible for a tax refund in respect of the period up to your departure in which case it will be necessary to complete an income tax return for income and gains from the previous 5 April to your departure date.
○ It may be advisable to seek professional advice when completing the P85.

For further information see HM Revenue and Customs publications IR20 *Residents and non-residents. Liability to tax in the United Kingdom* which can be found on the website www.hmrc.gov.uk/. Booklets IR138, IR139 and IR140 are also worth reading; these can be obtained from your local tax office or from the *Centre for Non-Residents (CNR):* St John's House, Merton Rd, Bootle, Merseyside L69 9BB; ☎0151-472 6196; fax 0151-472 6392; www.hmrc.gov. uk/cnr/contact_a.htm.

Non-Residents of France

If you are buying a second home in France, whether for long holidays or retirement, etc. then the situation as regards taxation is more complicated in that you remain liable to UK tax but may also acquire liability for French tax. This may also be the case if you are maintaining any sort of financial connection with the UK, e.g. if one still owns and rents out a home in the UK, thus generating an income. If this is the case then an accountant in the UK must be consulted for individual advice.

Personal Income Tax

Known in France as *IRPP (Impôt sur le Revenu des Personnes Physiques)* this tax goes as high as 40%, but this gives a somewhat misleading picture, as most tax is collected in the form of social security payments and VAT. While everyone pays social security contributions, only half of French families pay *impôt sur le revenu*.

Tax Returns, There are several different types of tax return – *déclarations fiscales* – for different types of income. The forms can be viewed on the government website www.service-public.fr, and can also be obtained at any time from your Centre des Impôts or *mairie*. The basic form is No.2042, the *déclaration des revenus*. If you are self-employed, have capital gains to declare, or rent out property, you also have to fill in No.2042C, the *déclaration complément*. For business, see below.

TYPES OF INCOME SUBJECT TO IMPÔT SUR LE REVENU INCLUDE:

Wages, salaries, remunerations, pensions, life annuities	*Traitements, salaires, remunérations assimilées, pensions, rentes viagères*
Investment income	*Revenus de capitaux mobiliers*
Capital gains (short-term)	*Plus values à court terme*
Industrial and commercial profits	*Bénéfices industriels et commerciaux (BIC)*
Property income	*Revenus fonciers*
Agricultural profits	*Bénéfices agricoles (BA)*

Profits from running *chambres d'hôtes* and *gîtes* come under BIC (see below).
   Property income concerns the letting of houses, offices, factories, etc, agricultural land, lakes, forests, as well as hunting rights.

Exemptions. Certain kinds of income are exempt from income tax, notably:

○ Rental income, if you rent out rooms in your own home on a long-term basis, as long as the rent is considered 'reasonable'.

○ Up to €760 rental income generated from short-term letting of rooms in your house.

○ Income from certain savings plans, and investments in industry, under certain conditions.

○ Social security benefits, such as disability benefits, incapacity benefits.

Methods of Calculation. The basis of the calculation is the total income of the household added together. In order to compensate tax-payers with dependants or low earners in their household, the French use a 'family quotient' system – *quotient familial* – calculating tax according to *parts* assigned to members of the family. The total income is divided by the number of parts, which has the effect of calculating the tax as if each member of the family earned the same amount. Once the tax has been worked out on a sliding scale, it is multiplied by the number of parts to arrive at the final figure.

As a single person, you have 1 *part*. If you are married then you have 2; if one partner is disabled the couple receives 2.5 parts; if both are disabled 3 parts. There are other parts including ones for disabled dependants living in your house.

As a rule, each additional child or dependant gives a further 0.5 parts. Three children or dependants give 1 part apiece, plus 0.5 *parts* if one is an invalid. There is a limit to the amount that you can save with this system. If your saving is more than €2,086 (indexed) *per half part above your base parts, then you do not qualify for the quotient familial,* and your tax has to be calculated differently. Single parents and those with disabled dependants are treated more generously.

Tax Calculation by Tranches. The French tax system resembles other systems in that tax is calculated progressively on the amount per part. The amount per slice or *tranche* has to be multiplied by the parts to arrive at a final figure before tax credits and rebates are applied. They are revised annually depending on inflation. There are five rates and from 2006 the top tax rate will be 40% (reduced from 48.09%).

Tax Credits

There are various tax credits and reductions, too numerous to go into in great detail. Note that these are all subject to conditions and limits. All are subject to having the correct paperwork. The more usual ones include:

- ○ 50% of the cost of domestic help, child-minding, gardeners, cleaners, etc. up to a maximum credit for all employees of 50% of €15,000.
- ○ Child-minding expenses outside the home.
- ○ Charitable donations; but no more than 10% of your taxable income.
- ○ Renovations, extensions, repairs to the principal residence, and to tourist accommodation in certain rural areas, up to 15% of the purchase price of the property.
- ○ A 25% tax credit for the costs of installing heavy equipment for the home.
- ○ Environmentally friendly vehicles.
- ○ Investments in small and medium-sized businesses.

Complete Exemption from Income Tax. Certain persons are completely exempt from paying income tax. If your income after deduction of professional costs is below €7,250 you pay no tax.

MAIN TAX DEADLINES

	Declaration	Form	Payment
IR *Micro*	31 March	No.2042	3 instalments/ final payment 15 September
Réel simplifié BIC	30 April	No.2031	as above
Réel normal BIC	30 April	No.2031	as above
BNC	30 April	No.2035	as above

Other tax annex forms.

There are a number of other tax forms that one **may** be required to fill in:

- ○ No.2044 for *revenus fonciers* – property income
- ○ No.2047 for foreign income
- ○ No.2049 for capital gains (IPV)
- ○ No.2065 for corporation tax (IS)
- ○ No.1810 for fixed minimum corporation tax (IFA)
- ○ No.2074 for capital gains on investments

Where Do You Pay Your Taxes?

Tax declarations and demands are issued by the *Centre des Impôts*. There are two different organisations that collect your taxes, the *Trésor Public* and the *Centre des Impôts*, and each has its own inspectors and controllers. Since 2004, the term *Recette des Impôts* is no longer officially used, having been replaced by the term *Centre des Impôts*; people will continue to refer to the Recette des Impôts. You can now fill in your tax return on-line, but this is not permitted for the first year.

Type of Tax	Where to Pay
IR	Trésor Public
IS	Centre des Impôts
ISF (wealth tax)	Trésor Public
Taxe d'habitation	Trésor Public
Taxe foncière	Trésor Public
Taxe professionnelle	Trésor Public
Taxes sur les salaires (payroll tax)	Centre des Impôts
TVA	Centre des Impôts

Social Security Taxes

The basic tax is the CSG (*Contribution Sociale Généralisée*) which is applied at a rate of 7.5% after a deduction of 5% for professional costs (i.e. 7.5% of 95% of gross income). All earned and unearned income is subject to this tax, which is in many cases a withholding tax. A contribution to repaying the social security system's debt, the CRDS or *Contribution pour le Remboursement de la Dette Sociale,* is levied at 0.5% on similar terms to the CSG. Most types of income are also subject to an additional 'social contribution', the *Prélèvement Sociale* at 2%.

Social security contributions are entirely separate from social security taxes.

Paying in Instalments

The French tax system works on the basis that you pay income tax (IR) in instalments on your income for the previous year, calculated on the basis of your income in the year before that. If you come from abroad you will pay for the first time by September 15 **in the year after you start up.** You are then hit with the entire tax bill in one go for the previous year.

Businesses pay IR in three instalments in February, May and September – the *tiers provisionnels,* as do many salaried workers. Since 2003 you are required to pay within 45 days of an assessment. If you fail to pay in time then there is a 10% penalty.

All French residents must be registered with the local *inspecteur des impôts.* You are liable for tax on your worldwide income from the day you arrive in France. It is up to you to request a tax return (*déclaration fiscale*) if you do not receive one automatically. Small businesses are given more time to submit their tax returns. For the micro regime the final date is 31 March. For BIC and *déclaration controlée* (BNC) it is 30 April. If you file your tax return even one day late, you automatically receive a 10% penalty.

Wealth Tax (ISF)

ISF or *Impôt de Solidarité sur la Fortune* only affects those with net assets over €732,240 (indexed) if they are resident or have assets in France on 1st January of any tax year. The tax is levied on the fiscal household, defined as:

○ Single persons, divorced, widowed, unmarried or separated from their partners.
○ Married persons, including dependent children under 18.
○ Persons who are known to be living together (*concubinage notoire*), and children.
○ Those who have entered a PACS (partnership contract) and children.

Variations in the value of your assets during the year cannot be taken account when calculating your liability. All your assets, including cars, yachts, furniture, etc. must be taken into account. There are a number of items exempt from wealth tax, of which a few are given here in a simplified form:

○ Antiques over 100 years old.
○ Copyrights on works of art, literature, music.
○ Personal injury compensation.
○ Movable and sometimes immovable property that you require to carry on your profession.
○ Shares in companies of which you are a director, with more than 25% voting rights.

Since the basis on which ISF is calculated is your net worth, any debts can be deducted from the total. This includes any property loans. Any money you owe to builders or other tradesmen can be deducted, as can the taxes you owe for the previous year (including the ISF itself). Money that is owed to you is added to the total. There is a limitation on wealth tax, inasmuch as your total tax liability (including income tax) cannot exceed 85% of your net taxable income for the previous year. This unpopular tax that has caused the richest French people to emigrate to countries with less rapacious tax regimes including Switzerland, Belgium and even the UK.

Useful Addresses

Franco-British Chamber of Commerce: 21 Dartmouth Street, Westminster, London SW1H 9BP; ☎020-7304 4040. Will provide a list of Franco-British tax consultants.

French Fiscal Attaché: French Embassy, Tax Department, Kingsgate House, 115 High Holborn, London WC1V 6JJ; Tues & Thurs 2pm-4pm ☎020-7831 9048; fax 020-7242 9439; www.finances.ambafrance.org.uk

Direction des Résidents a L'Etranger et des Services Généraux: 92 bvd Ney, 75878 Paris, Cedex 18; ☎01 49 25 12 45; fax 01 49 25 12 49. Further tax information.

Conseil Supérieur de l'Ordre des Experts Comptables et Comptables Agréés (CSOEC): 153 rue de Courcelles, 75017 Paris; ☎01 44 15 60 00; fax 01 44 15 90 05. Chartered accountants professional organisation.

WILLS AND INHERITANCE TAX

The subject of succession tax (*droits de succession*) and gift tax (*droits de donation*) needs to be carefully considered before you buy a property in France. Failure to take the right steps before signing an *acte de vente* can have serious consequences for your heirs; it is difficult to make changes to the *acte de vente* once it has been registered. If your family situation is at all complicated – many foreign property-buyers have been married more than once – then legal advice is a necessity, and highly desirable even in straightforward situations. This means dealing with an English-speaking lawyer who understands French and UK law, which generally implies a UK-based lawyer. See *Firms Dealing with French Property* in *Your New Home in France*.

The French system of inheritance tax – strictly speaking 'succession rights' or 'succession taxes' (*droits de succession*) – is very different from the British one: you are not free to leave your assets to anyone you please. Blood relatives always come first, while your spouse or partner is treated almost as though they were strangers. The logic behind this is simple. Napoleon saw that too many men were leaving their properties to their mistresses or their wives, so he instituted a system that would ensure that property remained with the blood family.

The first issue to consider is that of domicile, a concept that is not defined in the UK Tax Laws, but which rests on legal precedent. Domicile is something like nationality, but harder to lose. Generally speaking, your country of domicile is the one where you have had the longest-lasting ties during your lifetime, or the country you intend to return to after living abroad. If you were resident in France on your decease, the French tax authorities will claim that your heirs should pay French succession taxes on your worldwide assets, or at the very least on your assets in France. The British tax authorities are very reluctant to concede that a British citizen is no longer domiciled in the UK. Foreign domicile can only be established after 'exhaustive enquiries'.

There are potential advantages to being taxed in France if the inheritance exceeds the UK inheritance tax threshold. The top rate in France of 40% only kicks in on inheritances over €1.7 million

(£1.2 million), while in the UK it starts at £285,000 (indexed). In 2005, succession tax was abolished on estates below €100,000. If you are relatively wealthy, you will want to disperse your assets in good time, leaving as little as possible for the taxman. The good news is that there is a double taxation agreement between France and the UK concerning inheritances, so as long as you are open and honest about matters you will not have to pay inheritance taxes twice. There is also a general principle, however, that you pay IHT in the country which has the higher rate.

French Succession Taxes

Under French law, one part of your assets has to be left to specified members of your family (*la réserve légale*), while the rest is yours to do with as you please (*la quotité disponible*). Blood relatives are entitled to inherit in descending order:

> ### Reserved Heirs
>
> **Children:** 50% for the first child; 66.6% between two children; 75% between three and above. No distinction is made between children from a first and subsequent marriage.
> **Parents:** Where there are no children, parents receive 25% each. A single surviving parent can only receive 25%.
> **Spouses:** Only become reserved heirs if there are no direct ascendants or descendants.

Grandchildren become reserved heirs if the children are no longer living. Brothers and sisters can be disinherited. They only inherit automatically if there are no descendants, ascendants or spouse. If the former are deceased, nephews and nieces can inherit in their place. Children of the current marriage are treated equally with children of previous marriages, and children born outside marriage, including half-siblings of the deceased's children. The principle that children born out of 'adultery' have equal rights with their half-siblings has only recently been accepted in France. In the absence of the above then relatives take precedence over strangers, depending on their relationship to the deceased, up to the fourth degree. Relatives beyond the fourth degree are considered to be unrelated for the purpose of inheritance tax.

The 2005 French Finance Act changed succession tax rates to favour the children of the deceased. In the first place, estates up to €100,000 are free from any inheritance tax. Children now benefit from an abatement of €50,000 (increased from €46,000). The surviving spouse benefits from a tax-free amount of €76,000 as previously. Note that 'spouse' only refers to your marriage partner; other rules apply to common-law partners. Inheritance and Gift Taxes are levied at the following rates:

Tax Percentage	Spouse	Children/Parents
5	the first 7,600	the first 7,600
10	7,600-15,000	7,600-11,400
15	15,000-30,000	11,400-15,000
20	30,000-520,000	15,000-520,000
30	520,000-850,000	520,000-850,000
35	850,000-1,700,000	850,000-1,700,000
40	1,700,000 and over	1,700,000 and over

Brothers, sisters and grandchildren pay at rates of 35% (0-€30,000) and 45% on the excess. More distant relatives up to the fourth degree pay at 55%. Anyone else pays at 60%.

CHANGING THE INHERITANCE STATUS QUO

Most people are surprised to learn that in France you are not free to leave your French assets to whomsoever you wish and that you cannot leave your assets to your partner. In fact, surviving spouses are treated as little better than strangers under French law. Instead, France has 'succession rights' which ensure that blood relatives always come first and that you cannot disinherit your children. There are legal ways around this, which involve changing your matrimonial regime; these are outlined below. Expert legal advice is essential as there are disadvantages as well as advantages with the legal remedies listed below. These may affect your partner's children from their first marriage. The website *Notaires de France* (www.notaires.fr) has some useful information in English on transferring an estate.

Matrimonial Regimes and Inheritance

If you do nothing about your marriage regime, your partner has the option of remaining in the marital home for the rest of their life (see below). The partner can also choose to move out of the property, and receive their part of the assets of the deceased. This is often the best solution where several children jointly inherit a property and want to dispose of it. It can be too much of a headache staying on in a property, which is owned by children of your partner's previous marriage whom you do not get on with.

French law recognises three different types of married and non-married partner: a marriage partner; a *concubin*, also known as *union libre* which is roughly equivalent to a common law partner; and a PACS (*Pacte Civil de Solidarité*) under which contractants make themselves liable for each other's debts and agree to support each other (originally conceived for gay couples but applicable to any two people who are not closely related but who just live together.) PACS contractants file a joint tax return. A PACS can be dissolved at any time by mutual consent.

Changing Your Marriage Regime

If you become resident in France, you can change to a more suitable marriage regime specifying how assets are divided on the death of one partner. In all there are five different marriage regimes, making the system very complex.

Things to Know About Changing Your Marriage Regime

- ○ Changing marriage regime is costly, at least €1500
- ○ Evidently, you need to take professional advice if you want to change your marriage regime
- ○ You can only change your marriage regime if you are actually resident in France, and it needs to be done before you buy a property

Types of Marriage Regime

O If you go for the *communauté universelle avec clause d'attribution intégrale* your partner acquires all your assets on your death without any succession tax being paid; only 1% registration duty is payable. No declaration has to be made for succession purposes. Your children and other heirs then have to wait for the second partner's decease before they can inherit their rightful share. This solution cannot be used to disinherit children from the deceased's previous marriages. This is the option that was chosen by most French married couples in the past.

O There are several disadvantages with the communauté universelle avec clause d'attribution intégrale. Firstly, the children of the marriage will pay a higher rate of succession tax than they would have if they had received their inheritance directly. Secondly, each partner is liable for the debts of the other. Thirdly, the surviving partner can do what they want with the assets, and may use them to benefit his or her new partner.

O Another possibility is the *communauté légale réduite aux acquêts* – where only the assets acquired during the course of the marriage are common property. In this case the surviving partner pays succession tax on half of the deceased's part of the common property.

O A simpler solution is the *régime de séparation des biens* – separation of estates – where the marriage partners' assets before and during the marriage remain completely separate. The French authorities assume that you are married under the régime de séparation des biens if your marriage was contracted in the UK, and for most marriages in the USA (a few states influenced by French law have a different system).

O A common way to improve the marriage partner's lot is to make a *donation entre époux* (gift between spouses), an act which can be registered with a notary for a minimal cost.

Buying En Tontine

This is where two or more people whether married or not, acquire assets, on the understanding that the one who lives the longest acquires the whole, thus entirely cutting out the inheritors of the other members of the *tontine*. For legal purposes deceased members of a tontine – and, by extension, their inheritors – are treated as though they never had any share in the assets. The survivor is treated as though they owned the property from the day that it was bought. Where the partners are unrelated, or concubins, the 'winner' of the tontine is subject to succession tax at 60% on half the value of the property, unless the property is worth less than €76,000 and it is their principal residence, in which case the survivor only pays 4.89% transfer taxes. If there is a PACS between them, the succession tax is only 50%. Married partners pay the usual succession tax applicable to them.

Things to Know About En Tontine

○ Partners can enter into a tontine if they have roughly the same life expectancy and can therefore profit equally from the tontine.

○ They should also contribute equal amounts to the purchase.

○ It is not allowed to buy *en tontine* with your children as partners, or with someone who is likely to die soon.

○ A disadvantage of a tontine is that it is impossible to sell your part of the tontine since the buyer will lose everything if the person they bought their share from dies before the other members.

○ If your partner in the tontine is also your spouse, then any dispute becomes very unpleasant. All the members have to agree to dissolve a tontine and it is still a costly and slow process.

○ Spouses married under the separate estates regime – which means everyone married in the UK can enter a tontine and could benefit from this arrangement. The main advantage is that it allows you to decide who will inherit your property. It is very effective in cutting the family of the partner who dies first out of the will. It is not actually tax-efficient (except for very cheap properties), since there is only one heir in this situation, and no flexibility as to who inherits. The tontine clause has to be put into the *acte de vente* before it is signed; afterwards is too late.

Setting up a Société Civile Immobilière (SCI)

A potentially useful way of minimising succession taxes is to buy your property through an SCI (property owning company) which you have set up yourself. You are then the owner of the shares which you can give to your children during your lifetime. This is best done at the start, otherwise you will have to pay transfer taxes if you sell the property to the SCI later. There are considerable costs involved; setting up the SCI costs on average €2500. There will also be Capital Gains Tax (*l'impôt sur les plus values immobilières*) to pay when the property is sold .

Seek expert legal advice if you are thinking of setting up an SCI. While it is not that difficult to set one up, the terms under which it is set up must be carefully considered. The SCI is useful for expensive properties. It is also very useful where unrelated people wish to buy a property together, for instance in the case of co-ownership.

Buying En Indivision

The concept of *indivision* is fundamental in French law. Where two or more persons buy a property jointly they automatically enter into an indivision, unless they opt for another regime, such as the tontine or the SCI. While the members of the indivision have separate shares, the assets themselves are not divided up. Members of the indivision can leave if they wish, or ask to have the indivision dissolved through a court of law. Couples married under the regime of common property – *communauté des biens* – automatically have equal shares in a property, given that their names are on the acte de vente. There is also the possibility that only property that is acquired during the marriage is commonly owned. Under the regime of separate estates – *séparation des biens* – the property can be divided up unequally, or only one partner may own it.

Once the members fall out with each other the only solution is to break up the indivision. Serious problems can arise if one member dies. The positive side of the indivision is that it is easy to enter into; no written agreement is required. Each member retains their share of the property and benefits proportionally from the income generated.

Gifts to Grandchildren

Grandparents can give grandchildren €30,000 tax-free every 10 years. Gifts that are not revealed to the tax office will not be subject to gift tax, but if their existence becomes known after the donor's decease then they will be treated as part of the inheritance and will be subject to full succession tax. The gift can be witnessed by the notaire, who will make up an *acte authentique,* a document which has legal force and which is recognised by third parties. The notaire can put certain advantageous clauses into the gift act, and there is then no risk of being penalised later when succession tax has to be paid.

WILLS

Making a will in both the UK and France is essential. While it is possible to pay your Inheritance Tax on a second home in France to the UK taxman, this may not be in your interests and could get you into trouble with the French authorities. One procedure is to make a UK will, after taking advice from someone familiar with French inheritance law, and have it translated into French and notarised, but having a will translated by an official translator can be very expensive, and the results may not even be that accurate. The other possibility is to make up a UK will with no mention of your French property. The French will only relates to your French assets. Before you make a will in France, you should take professional advice to make sure that it does not conflict with, or invalidate your UK will. Provisions in your UK will can be taken into account by the French authorities, as long as they are not in conflict with French law. Care needs to be taken if you make another will at a later date: clauses such as 'this will invalidates all previous wills' can be disastrous if you have two wills. Remember to leave copies of your will with the notary in France and to inform your heirs of this. Hunt the will is an all too common occurrence, which adds to the distress of the bereaved.

TWO MAIN TYPES OF WILL

○ Holographic (*testament olographe*): entirely in the person's handwriting, it is best done in French, and is generally not witnessed. If you choose, you can register it with the central register of testaments, the Fichier de Dernières Volontés. Most wills in France are in this form.

○ Authentic (*testament authentique*): can be printed or written and has to be witnessed by two notaries or one notary and two other persons. Automatically registered with the Fichier de Dernières Volontés.

The holographic testament is generally the best, with the proviso that someone needs to know where it is kept. There us also the secret testament which has virtually fallen out of use.

Inheritance Procedures

Once someone has passed away, the family and/or partner need to visit the notary who dealt with the deceased's will as soon as is practically possible after registering the death at the town hall. The surviving partner, potential inheritors, the executor or creditors can request a *greffier en chef* (chief clerk) from the local civil court to put seals on the deceased's property (*pose de scellés*) if they believe there is a risk of theft or fraud. The greffier can make up a list of the goods and conduct a search for a will.

Legally, the reserved heirs, and anyone with a power of attorney, have the right and duty – known as *saisine* – to use the deceased's assets from the moment of death, to pay debts or bills as they arise. The deceased's bank account is automatically blocked, but money can still be taken out for bills, the funeral, and standing orders.

Documents required to start the inheritance process:

○ The death certificate.
○ A copy of the French will.
○ A copy of the British will, translated into French.
○ The names of all the potential inheritors.
○ Marriage/divorce certificates.

○ Death certificates of deceased former inheritors still mentioned in the will, if any.

For a detailed overview of French succession law, see Henry Dyson's *French Property and Inheritance Law,* published by Oxford University Press. This is a technical work written for lawyers, but still comprehensible to laypeople. If you read French, then you can find the latest information on the website www.lesechos.fr or the government website, www.service-public.gouv.fr.

Funerary Formalities and Afterwards

Deaths in France must be certified by a doctor and registered within 24-hours at the mairie with the death certificate and proof of the deceased's identity. A funeral cannot take place until the mairie gives its approval. If you do not know of a reliable funeral director who will take care of all the formalities, you can contact the *Association Française d'Information Funeréraire* (☎01 45 44 90 03; www.afif.asso.fr), which represents the funeral trade in France. Their website lists funeral directors throughout France, costs and everything concerning funerary rites and rituals. You will probably be invited to view the body and to witness the sealing of the coffin with a red seal in the presence of a police official as is customary in France.

France is predominantly a Catholic country, burial facilities for other faiths are comparatively rare; the nearest British Consulate will provide the address of a Protestant church or synagogue. Cremation is much less common than burial in France, but is becoming more prevalent; there are now about 116 crematoria which are listed at www.afif.asso.fr. A request previously signed by the deceased or by the person dealing with the ceremonies is required for cremation.

Despite the expense of such an undertaking, a spouse and family may prefer their deceased relative to be buried or cremated back in their country of origin. If this is the case, then the nearest Consulate should be contacted as soon as possible for information and guidance on the appropriate way to carry out this procedure.

It is much less expensive to bring ashes back to the UK and to have a memorial service for friends and family there, but of course it depends on personal preferences. A list of UK and US Consulates may be found in the *Residence and Regulations* section of the *Basics* chapter.

Presumably you will have considered what the situation would be if your spouse should die after moving to France. It may well be that the survivor would want to return to the UK to be closer to family and friends: provision should be made for this at the outset, perhaps by arranging life assurance which will cover the costs of returning home. In a forced situation these costs could be much greater than those involved in the original move out.

Healthcare

CHAPTER SUMMARY

- The French health system is rated first in the world by the World Health Organisation, is funded by very high social security charges, yet is permanently in deficit and still not free.
- Anyone who leaves the UK to live abroad is no longer automatically entitled to free treatment with the British NHS and may be removed from their GP's list after three months.
- If you are of official retirement age and are living permanently in France, you are entitled to the same health benefits as a French pensioner.
- However, even as a pensioner, you still need a top-up insurance for the portion of medical expenses not covered by French social security as even for pensioners, medical treatment is not entirely free (except in the case of chronic diseases where costs are refunded in full).
- France has good provision for the elderly and the government encourages responsibility for them at commune level. This means that there are usually social-medical facilities locally so the elderly can maintain their links with their own community.
- During the 2004/2005 season there were over 160,000 skiing injuries in the French Alps. For over 50 years France has had an Association of Doctors specializing in alpine-induced injuries. Their members are stationed throughout the Alps during the skiing season.
- Liver disease, often brought on by, or aggravated by alcohol is the third biggest killer in France after cancer and heart disease.

THE FRENCH HEALTHCARE SYSTEM

How the System Works

In general the French hospital and health care system is very good; so good in fact that the World Health Organisation and the French themselves consider it the best in the world. The system is so liberally funded you can see the doctor you want when you want. Waiting to see a GP, or a hospital consultant, or wondering if you are going to get the best treatment depending on what it costs, is therefore unimaginable. Such high standards come at a price, which includes 9.8% of French GDP (7.7% in the UK) and even then, healthcare is not free.

The French healthcare system is a combination of private and public services: the national healthcare service is available to all, but it functions in a particular way. In most cases you cannot obtain free treatment at the point of delivery. Patients pay for treatment and then reclaim most (usually about 70%) of the cost, and have insurance (*une mutuelle*) for the rest. The recent changes to health service provision mean that more of the tab will be picked up by the mutuelles, which in turn means higher premiums. Many of the mutuelles in France are linked to particular professions.

Julian Roberts, who is 67 and retired to the Dordogne reckons it may not be worth older pensioners paying for a mutelle top-up insurance:

> *My wife and I registered with CPAM. However, we have not taken out top up insurance for the 30% of costs that you have to pay yourself. Because of our ages such insurance is very expensive and so we pay as we go for minor ailments, as it works out cheaper. The cost of expensive treatments such as those for chronic or life-threatening illnesses is in any case refunded 100% by the state.*

Bob Culshaw, who also retired to the Dordogne, has nothing but praise for the health system but realises, that it comes at a price:

> *You cannot avoid health expenses, even if you use the French National health service, but there are no complaints because the service in my*

experience is second to none. The only problem with the health service is that it is losing billions.

Accessing French Healthcare

If you are going to be in France for a visit exceeding three months, you should, before you leave the UK, ask the Department of Work and Pensions (0191-218-7777/7367; www.dwp.gov.uk), for the reciprocal health agreement forms which allow you to access French healthcare: these are the E121 if you are a pensioner and E106 if you have retired before the state retirement age. You then register at the CPAM (see below). You will need to take with you your E106 or E121, your passport and proof of your UK address. These forms exempt you from paying French social security contributions as you are still attached to the UK system.

A foreign individual who is resident in France permanently and has no UK address, should register at the local sécurité sociale or CPAM (*Caisse Primaire d'Assurance Maladie*) health insurance office, The address can be obtained from the local mairie. If you have not reached retirement age you will also have to make contributions (if you are not eligible for an E106). These contributions provide for a range of health and social security benefits for the contributor and his or her dependants. UK pensioners living in another EU country will be entitled to the same healthcare benefits as a citizen of that country. The alternative to plugging into the state stystem is to go completely private and take out commercial healthcare insurance but this is not usually necessary in France as public and private healthcare overlap and public healthcare is of a very high standard. See sections below for more details.

Medical Treatment for Non-resident Foreigners

Foreigners who are non-residents, even though they are from elsewhere in the EU will only receive doctor/hospital treatment if they pay first and then apply for reimbursement. British expatriates working in France while continuing to pay UK national insurance contributions will be covered if they have applied for form E101 or E106 (depending on their length of stay). Maximum cover is for two years.

Anyone just visiting France should apply for an EHIC (for details of how to get a European Health Insurance Card see below) which covers emergency treatment only, or they, or the person looking after them, will have to choose between returning to the UK for free treatment or paying up front to go to a French hospital. Charges would be in the region of £750 per day for an in-patient (non-serious) including treatment and drugs, accommodation and food and up to £20,000 for more intensive treatment (e.g. a heart operation requiring intensive care). Note that anyone requiring unexpected emergency treatment will still be treated without paying first.

Continuing to Use the UK NHS While Living in France

During visits to the UK, Britons can also continue to use the British National Health Service for the first three months while they are living in France, provided that they are still registered with the Department for Work and Pensions in Britain. However, this dispensation is only while they remain technically UK resident. Once they have become a French resident, if they have not reached retirement age: they will have either applied for an E106, or be paying French social security contributions, in order to be able to use the French health service.

If you retire early (i.e. before the UK pensionable age)you must continue to pay social security contributions, but you will not be covered by French social security until you start contributing to their social security system. During this time you may continue to pay into the UK NHS System for a period of up to two and a half years, during which you can still receive UK National Health treatment, provided that your British National Insurance contributions are up to date, and you have obtained form E106 from the DWP in Newcastle upon Tyne, before you leave the UK. Special rules apply if you have an industrial injury or occupational disease.

While you are still paying UK contributions, the French social security system classes you as *détaché*. The advantage of continuing to pay social security contributions in the UK for as long as possible is that they are much lower than in France. Eligibility for the E106 and how long it lasts is something of a fudged area and your best bet is to try to get as much clarification of your particular case with the DWP before you leave the UK for good.

What Social Security Entitles You To

Entry into *sécurité sociale* entitles both you and your dependants to medical treatment, and other expenses, free of charge up to a statutory limit for each type of treatment. Usually, sécurité sociale pays for only a percentage (usually 70%-90%) of the treatment and (35%-70% for medicines) and the patient is liable for the remainder. Sécurité sociale will only pay the full cost of treatment for more serious illnesses and in specific hospital practices. Hospitals and general practices are basically allowed to charge what they like for their services. However, in each locality a group of doctors from certain hospitals and general practices agree to charge fees within the limits set by sécurité sociale. Therefore, if you use the facilities that these hospitals and practices (known as *conventionné*) offer, treatment undertaken should not cost any more than is stipulated by the authorities. However under new reforms, specialists and some general doctors are allowed to charge an excess, if they judge this to be 'reasonable and tactful'. These excesses are known as '*dépassements.*' Unfortunately CPAM still only reimburses the conventionné charge.

Anyone who has already reached UK pensionable age, will benefit from the EU reciprocal health agreement which means they can use the French health service on the same basis as French pensioners. This still does not mean all health treatment is free. For instance French pensioners still pay for prescriptions, minus the component paid for by social security.

Private Versus Conventionné Treatment

If you want to check the rates for conventionné treatments, you can do so on Minitel (3614 Infoprat). The alternatives to this are either to opt for totally private treatment, or to make up the difference between conventionné rates and whatever the hospital or practice which you have chosen charges. Private health treatment is extremely expensive and the vast majority of people choosing this option take private health insurance (see below) to pay for it. The facilities in conventionné hospitals tend to be basic but are generally considered good so there is no need to feel that you have to pay for a full private healthcare plan.

French Private Health Insurance (Mutuelles)

As we see, there is an element of personal contribution involved between the cost of treatment, even in conventionné facilities, and the percentage (usually 70%) that sécurité sociale pays. In certain cases this difference could amount to quite a lot of money and consequently most people take out an insurance policy specifically to cover this shortfall. The premiums involved are quite low and most industries, occupations and professions in France have special plans (called *complémentaires* or sometimes *mutuelles*).

Choosing a *Complémentaire*. Gordon Eaton of Agence Eaton advises that, in choosing a provider it is important that they are able to provide a direct liaison with the securité sociale and be certain that the policy recognises the Loi Levin, a French law designed to protect the subscriber. He says you should also be sure that your complémentaire provider can and will intervene on your behalf to ensure you are correctly registered by the sécurité sociale and promptly reimbursed.

Apart from Agence Eaton (www.french-insurance.com), which is based in France, you can arrange a top-up policy with a company in the UK through: Friendly Society www.exeterfriendly.co.uk), Amariz (www.amariz.co.uk) and Goodhealth Worldwide Limited (www.goodhealthworldwide.com).

The EHIC

In the initial moving period, or on reconnaissance visits, or while on a speculative visit to France to look at property, you will not be covered by sécurité sociale, and in such cases, you should take out private travel insurance. It is also possible to obtain mainly free, treatment under a reciprocal agreement, which exists between some EU countries. To qualify for such treatment you need an EHIC (European Health

Insurance Card) formerly known as the E111 or E-one-eleven. The form T6 *Health Advice for Travellers* available in post offices, contains the application form for the EHIC or you can download it at www. dh.gov.uk/travellers, or contact HM Revenue and Customs, National Insurance Contributions Office (International Services, Longbenton, Newcastle upon Tyne, NE98 1ZZ; ☎0191-225 4811; international services helpline ☎0845-606 2030; fax 0845-9157800; www.hmrc. gov.uk/nic/intserv/ose.htm

CHANGE FROM E111 TO EHIC

During the course of 2005, the E111 was replaced by the European Health Insurance Card (EHIC) which will be sent automatically to anyone who had the new E111 form and who ticked the box for this on their application.

Once in France, anyone who requires emergency treatment should go to a conventionné doctor, dentist or hospital. Although they will have to pay up front for treatment, up to 70% of this can then be refunded, as long as the procedure for the EHIC is followed. However, you should note that as a percentage of treatment costs are not covered by the EHIC, is still essential to have travel health insurance cover for the balance. For expensive treatments this could amount to a considerable sum.

An EHIC is not valid once you have left the UK permanently (or if you are employed in France). It is very useful if you make frequent trips abroad. However, once residency has been applied for (i.e. after three months in France) permanent arrangements should have been made (see information on the E106, E121 and CPAM above).

Bob Culshaw explains how he transferred from the EHIC to the French national health system:

We used our E111 (now EHIC) for two years after we arrived in France. After that, if you are not at state retirement age, you have to pay into the French system. The contributions are related to your income. I have to pay €3000 per year, for three years, until I am retired. I am paying this by quarterly direct debit. I also pay top-up insurance of €90 per month. Until I shopped around a bit I was paying €150 per month.

Explanatory leaflet SA29 gives details of social security, health care and pension rights within the EU and is obtainable from main post offices and also from the Department of Work and Pensions, Overseas Directorate, Tyneview Park, Whitely Road, Benton, Newcastle-upon-Tyne NE98 1BA.

Private Medical Insurance

If you already hold full private health insurance you will find that most companies will switch this for European cover once you are in France. With the increase of British and foreign insurance companies offering this kind of cover, it is worth shopping around as cover and costs vary. If you do not have complete private medical insurance you must, by law, be registered with the French CPAM.

Private Health Insurance Providers

Agence Eaton: ☎02 97 40 80 20; www.french-insurance.com. Bilingual insurance bureau. All types of insurance.

Amariz Ltd.: ☎0117-974 5770; www.amariz.co.uk.

AXA PPP Healthcare: ☎01892-612 080; www.axappphealthcare.co.uk.

British United Provident Association (BUPA): ☎01273-208181; www.bupa-int.com. BUPA International offers a range of worldwide schemes for individuals and companies of three or more employees based outside the UK for six or more months.

Exeter Friendly Society: ☎01392-353535; www.exeterfriendly.co.uk.

Goodhealth Worldwide (Europe): ☎0870-442 7376. Offices in Antibes, Bordeaux, Nice, Paris area, Sellians, St. Raphael and Toulouse.

IHI – International Health Insurance Danmark: ☎04 92 17 42 42; www.ihi.com.

Tredinnick Insurance: ☎05 45 82 42 93; www.charente-properties.com. Bi-lingual insurance brokers. Private health and 'top-up' policies to the French social security system and other types of insurance.

Using Doctors and Dentists

It is as well to line up a doctor/GP (*médecin généraliste*), dentist or optician who can be consulted if necessary, soon after arrival. Most people will obviously choose a doctor near where they live for convenience.

Before making an appointment you should check the charges in advance of any medical or dental practitioner since if they are not conventionné .(i.e part of the French national health system), a very large contribution will have to be made. Most of these services will provide immediate treatment in the case of an emergency. Night and Sunday duty doctors can usually be contacted through the local police station (*commissariat de police*).

There are not a great many English-speaking doctors in France and although your local British Consulate will be able to direct you to a suitable doctor or hospital, obviously, the majority of medical staff will speak French only. A useful publication in this respect is Alan S. Lindsay's *Glossary of French Medical and Health Terms* £12.50 (£11.88 from www.Global-Investor.com; ☎01730-233870).

La Carte Vitale

Residents of France are issued with a *Carte Vitale* (*carte d'assurances maladie*), a smart card (*une carte à puce*) i.e. with a microchip which makes the whole process of reimbursement from the state and mutuelle faster and simple as information can be transferred directly to the data centre at the *caisses d'assurances maladie* via a terminal operated by the health professional. The Carte Vitale has replaced the previous system of filling in forms and sending them to the local *Caisse Primaire d'Assurance Maladie* which would be followed by a refund of the appropriate percentage of the charges – a minimum of 75% of the cost of treatment and 40%-70% of the cost of medicines. With a Carte Vitale reimbursements can arrive in your nominated bank account within five days. Note that a refund cannot be obtained for medicines, which are bought without a doctor's prescription.

In 2006 a new version of the La Carte Vitale was introduced (Vitale 2) which carries more information such as medical conditions, blood group etc. and includes a passport type photograph of the holder. In a continuing automation process it is intended that by 2007 each patient will have an electronically stored medical dossier (*dossier médicale personnel/DMP*). The personal medical dossier will not be stored on the carte vitale, but Vitale 2 will be used to access the dossier by a registered health professional. The aim of this new system is to prevent the duplication of medical tests, which patients have habitually demanded from several different doctors under the previous unregulated system and thereby help to put a dent in the health service's enormous deficit. Individuals may inspect the information on their Carte Vitale and correct any mistakes that may have been made. There are a number of informative French websites which deal (in French) with the issues surrounding the carte vitale and the personal medical dossier including www.assurancemaladie.sante.gouv.fr/ and www.ameli.fr (L'Assurance Maladie enligne).

Alternative Medicine

Homeopathy and acupuncture are well-respected alternative medical treatments (*les médecines douces*) in France. They are recognised by French social security although only 35% of reimbursement is paid for homeopathic medicines. As the charges for médecines douces are generally higher, full costs are not usually reimbursed by independent health insurance (i.e. *les complémentaires*). Normally you will find such doctors by word of mouth or ask in the *pharmacie*. A law passed in 2002 officially recognised osteopathy and chiropractic as regulated medical disciplines. Ayurvedic medicine (an Indian system of holistic treatments) is not medically recognised in France, but there are a number of practitioners. There are an estimated 50 types of alternative medicine (*médecines parallèles*) available in France.

The contacts below can give you details of their practitioners in your region.

Contacts for Alternative Practitioners

Association Française d'Acupuncture: ☎01 43 20 26 26; www.acupuncture-france.com.

Association Française de Chiropractique: ☎08 20 88 83 77; www.chiropractique.org.

Association des Ostéopathes de France: ☎01 47 66 86 76.

Syndicat Nat. des Médecines Ostéopathes: ☎01 46 22 35 54; www.medicines-osteo.org.

Médecine Âyurvédique: www.ayurveda.free.fr.

Pharmacies

French doctors have a wonderful selection of remedies at their disposal and there is a tendency to prescribe elaborate pharmaceutical cocktails, when an over-the-counter remedy would be just as beneficial. All medicines in France are expensive so you should ensure you are covered for the cost by the combination of EHIC plus travel insurance, or French national and private top-up health schemes.

French pharmacists (*pharmaciens*) fulfil an important function in France and they are qualified to give advice (but not diagnoses). Since 1999 France has been reducing the number of brand name drugs (*médicaments classiques*) with so-called génériques (generic drugs which are the same pharmaceutically, but cost far less than branded drugs) This means that the pharmacist may supply you with a drug which does not seem to correspond with what the doctor prescribed. In fact, the pharmacist has a chart where he or she can check which generic drug corresponds to a branded one. However, if you have any queries about a prescription do not hesitate to ask the pharmacist.

If you need prescriptions and your local chemist is closed at a weekend, holiday etc. there will be a sign on the door, as in the UK, of the nearest duty chemist (*pharmacie de garde*). These are also usually given in the regional newspaper.

Emergencies, Accidents and Hospitalisation

In an emergency, aid can be obtained from any hospital with casualty facilities. The emergency ambulance will select the closest. If less urgent treatment is needed then your doctor or specialist will refer you to an appropriate hospital: this might be a conventionné hospital, or a private one if such a preference has been indicated. Out-patient treatment is charged for and the cost must be recovered as for doctors and dentists.

In the case of in-patient treatment the system varies. Some hospitals are publicly run and some are private clinics. They may charge the full cost and provide a certificate, which can be used to reclaim a part of the charges as described above. Other hospitals may claim the sécurité sociale contribution direct from the Caisse Primaire, and just expect you to pay the balance (e.g. about 25% for medical treatment). Note that emergency treatment for serious illnesses is refunded at 100%. Some hospitals make a fixed daily charge (*forfait journalier*) for accommodation, which sécurité sociale does not cover and this could be up to the equivalent of £90 to £120 per day. If you are in a public hospital you may have to supply your own towels and soap. Modern hospitals, even public ones, have en suite bathrooms and two or four beds per ward.

Sometimes it is possible to agree in advance with social security that they will pay your expenses for an operation or treatment in a private clinic under a *prise en charge* if the amount is in excess of a certain price. This amount is subject to annual revision more or less in line with inflation.

In France, there is no national ambulance service but each area has its own *Service d'Aide Médicale Urgence* (SAMU); national telephone number 15. Once you, or the person assisting you dials this number the operator takes down the name, address and symptoms of the patient and connects the caller with the doctor on call (*docteur de permanence*). According to the demands of the situation, a doctor or ambulance team will be sent to administer first aid or transport to hospital. Charges are levied correspondingly.

Reclaiming Medical Fees

At the end of a course of treatment any expenses which have been paid out and which are recoverable under sécurité sociale need to be reclaimed (see La Carte Vitale above). Ensure you claim for everything that is covered.

It is advisable to be privately insured for the portion of medical expenses that are not covered by sécurité sociale. These can then be reclaimed separately from the insurance company. Under this arrangement, if extra insurance has been taken out, the medical treatment will cost nothing except perhaps a small policy excess. The general rule to remember in France is that everyone is entitled to fairly good, cheap medical treatment under an effective national health service. However, most people take additional steps to improve the level of care to which they are entitled and to gain further protection against costs involved.

Returning to the UK for Treatment

One point to bear in mind is that once Britons have retired to (i.e. are permanently resident) in another country and are attached to that country's social security system, they are no longer entitled to use the British NHS free of charge. If they decide to move back to Britain permanently and re-enter the British social security system they can start to use the British NHS again on a no charge basis.

Of course, free treatment is available in the case of any accident or other medical emergency suffered while on a visit to the UK (under the EU reciprocal health agreement), but routine treatment cannot be claimed free of charge.

COMMUNITY CARE FOR THE ELDERLY

Retirement Homes

The care of the frail elderly is of some interest to anyone intending to retire to France where they may be spending the rest of their lives. Fortunately, social concerns are generally given high priority. The number of centenarians is growing by hundreds per year in the post-industrial developed countries and France is no exception. In 2005 France had 6,000 centenarians (compared with 200 in 1960). France also boasts the longest-lived person in the world, Mme. Jeanne Calmont of Arles whose birth was officially recorded in 1875 and who died, aged 122, in 1997. One of her often-quoted remarks is 'I've only got one wrinkle and I'm sitting on it'.

With increasing longevity, retirement homes (*maisons de retraite*) are understandably prolific in France (there are over 9,000 of them). They may be private or publicly operated. Occupants for public homes are means tested and social aid (*l'aide sociale*) or *l'aide au logement* provided at departmental level, will subsidise the least well off. Many private homes are funded by pension schemes.

There are many different forms of retirement home: *logement-foyers, maisons de retraite, residences avec services, hospices* etc. all with slightly different facilities. You should ask your family doctor for advice as he or she will know the difference between the types of establishments and recommend the best for your needs. Also for further information on retirement homes for dependant-aged people contact your local *Centre Communal d'Action Sociale* or the mairie.

Day Hospital

France is keen to maintain its elderly citizens as part of the community and once they have been hospitalised at an advanced age, the natural tendency is to keep them institutionalised because many of them are too frail to live entirely independently. In order not to resort to this measure too soon, the day hospital (*hôpital de jour*) provides a midway step that may be recommended by a hospital, which has been treating the patient, or by his or her doctor. The patient spends 8am to 5pm, Monday to Friday, at the hospital receiving medical treatments and assessment during the mornings. Lunch is provided at the hospital and the afternoons are for organised recreation (*l'ergothérapie*) and stimulating activities which are part of the programme designed to stave off isolation and the deterioration that often accompanies it. Day hospitals are closed at weekends.

Day Care

There are structures called *Établissements d'Accueil de Jour* which welcome elderly people who are living in their own homes or with their relatives. Often they are part of a retirement home (*maison de retraite*), which caters for both residential and day only clients. They act as social centres with organised social events and communal activities. There is no specific government funding for day welcome centres but they are often subsidised by local funds. Some will also incorporate a restaurant or club, specifically for elderly people.

Personal Carers

Elderly or disabled people who need help to live in their own home can ask about having a personal carer (*garde-malade* or *garde a domicile*) who helps them dress, bath, does their shopping and prepares their meals and so on. For more information contact the Centre Communal d'Action Sociale who will advise you further. Carers can be residential or non-residential and have to be paid for except by the least well off who can apply for social assistance.

Remaining in Your Own Home

The majority of the elderly express a preference to remain in their own home rather than to be moved to a communal home where they may have to share a room with one or two others and succumb to an institutional regime. In order for this to be achieved, diminishing physical capacity has to be addressed and the accompanying safety issues have to be dealt with. You can get help and advice on adapting your home from *Les Centres d'Information et Conseil sur Les Aides Techniques* (CICAT) a state-funded organisation which specialises in gadgets to make life easier for the elderly, or *la réadaption fonctionnelle* in their parlance. CICAT can also put you in touch with your nearest centre, (often hospital based) where you can learn how to use and practice with the gadgets available. This is not a cheaper option for local services; in fact it usually works out more expensive. It may be that you will be asked to pay a 'rent' towards the cost of your specially adapted house. Charges for this service also depend on local resources and various other factors.

You can ask for further advice on adapting your home, from your local social services at the mairie or, if there is one, the local *Association d'Aide à Domicile*.

LOCAL HEALTH ISSUES

Creepy Crawlies and Things That Go Bump

Make sure that your French doctor knows if you have an allergy to any animals or bugs. The fatal disease rabies, once the scourge of many European countries is virtually non-existent as all domestic animals are vaccinated against it. If an isolated case occurs it is usually connected with illegally imported animals or alpine wildlife.

The biggest threats to life and limb in France come not from the animal but the human world and they include the very high rate of traffic and skiing accidents. Enough has been said of French driving habits and the best advice is keep out of range if possible, and on no account emulate their stunts.

Skiing is a French passion and the millions of French who ski are more liable to accidents than ever. From over 140,000 skiing accidents (mostly sprains and fractures) in 1997 the rate rose to over 163,000 in 2004/5. In 2005/6 there were 49 deaths by avalanche in the French Alps; the highest figure for 35 years. The hazards of the piste have warranted their own branch of medicine, and since 1953 there has been an association of doctors (*Médecins du Montagne;* www.mdem. org) who specialise in treating skiing injuries. Throughout the season they are posted throughout the ski stations in the Alps. So as you feel your knee ligaments rip, you can take comfort that the doctor treating you has a lot of experience in your required type of treatment.

MENTAL HEALTH

Mental illness and problems with mental well-being can affect anyone during the course of their lives. However, expatriates with high expectations of retirement can suddenly find themselves overwhelmed by feelings of isolation once they have moved abroad, and find it difficult being so far away from loved ones that they previously saw often and whose support they relied on. Additionally, life-changing events such as bereavement or a marriage break-up are usually hard to cope with on your own, and may be even harder if you feel isolated in a foreign country with no support network around you.

There is no need to despair. There are sources of help for all kinds of problems within the expatriate community on chat forums, English-speaking help organisations that you can contact for face-to-face support and counselling and also English churches in France. If your French is good you can also deal more easily with French medical and social services and independent French organisations such as *France Dépression* (www.france-depression.org).

Ways to Keep Your Chin Up

○ **Contact your local expat group.** Either look on the internet and find a specialist support group, or join an expat forum, or contact a local expat group on the internet and arrange to go to a gathering.

○ **Contact the local *Accueil des Villes Francaises* (AVF) group.** In areas where there are a lot of English-speaking residents, these may be run by English-speakers. A list of them nationwide is at www.avf.asso.fr

○ **Get out more.** Join a local village club, take up a sport or volunteer work. If you don't feel you can cope with humans try offering to help with an animal charity. (see *Quality of Life* chapter for ideas)

○ **Join a French class.** If you can't speak French now is the time to begin. If you speak a little, now is the time to improve.

○ **Take a hobby or interest to the next level, or develop a new interest.** There are some ideas in the *Quality of Life* chapter, or just see what goes on locally.

○ **Gardening.** If you don't already garden, now is the time to start. Gardening can be a great mental soother.

○ **Don't be afraid to contact a counsellor.** Counsellors can be contacted via the internet or you can visit in person. Professional counsellors countrywide are listed at www.counsellinginfrance.com.

○ **Take up one of the mind and spirit disciplines.** Yoga is one of the best known and it is not all about being as bendy as India rubber. There are many yoga groups in France and places you can go to for yoga weekends. Tai Chi is also very popular. Also dancing classes. A useful website for body, mind, spirit providers is www.karinya. com/france.htm.

○ **Talk to a stranger.** There is always someone you can talk to; strike up a conversation with a perfect stranger, and see what happens. In extremis remember that you can always call the Samaritans from France ☎ + 44 8457 909090.

Alcoholism

France is a country where regular drinking of alcohol is part of the culture. Although the benefits of drinking red wine in moderation have been extolled by the medical profession, it is also a fact that France has one of the highest incidences of liver disease: 13% of illnesses in France are attributed directly to alcohol either as the cause or aggravation of illness. Unfortunately, there is a well-known tendency for those living an expat lifestyle to socialise, which while an essential ingredient of a happy retirement, may involve a lot of liquor consumption. This may build up a tolerance to alcohol or in some cases slide into alcoholism. The other causes of alcoholism may be loneliness, or a devastating bereavement The French take alcoholism very seriously not least because, despite the draconian traffic laws, drink-driving, is frequently a cause of appalling accidents. The French version of AA is *Alcoolique Anonymes* (http://perso.club-internet.fr/aafr/; ☎01 46 21 46 46 helpline in English) which has 310 branches in France with 7,000 members who have sobered permanently and who counsel others.

Contacts for Dealing with Alcohol & Narcotics Dependency

Alcoholics Anonymous: ☎01 48 06 43 68; aafr@club.internet.fr.

Alcoholics Anonymous online: www.aa-intergroup.org.

Alcoholics Anonymous: ☎01 46 34 59 65; www.aaparis.org.

Narcotics Anonymous: ☎01 48 58 38 46 ; www.na.org.

Drug, alcohol, tobacco info: ☎113

Crime, Security and the Police

CHAPTER SUMMARY

○ Crime rates vary considerably around France. Typically, villages have minimal crime, whereas some resorts and cities have rocketing levels of burglary and violent crime.

○ An ongoing problem is unrest among young Muslims and Africans living in city peripheries. The biggest flare-up so far was in November 2005 when riots spread from Paris to other cities and continued over several days.

○ French police are generally well-equipped, armed, ruthless and have far-reaching legal powers.

○ Isolated properties are particularly at risk of being burgled so extra security precautions are needed.

○ Insurance companies usually have a list of security requirements such as window shutters and certain types of bars and locks that have to be installed before they will insure your home.

○ If you are unfortunate enough to be burgled, it is a condition of insurance policies that you must report thefts to the police within 24 hours and to the insurers within two days by registered post.

○ Insurance policies are renewed automatically, so if you do not want to take on the previous owner's insurance then you have to actively cancel it.

○ The latest scam: beware anyone who pays by cheque for a larger amount than you agreed, then claims it was a mistake and asks you for an immediate refund of the excess. They are just trying to get you to part with your money before their bogus cheque bounces.

CRIME

France has a similar number of crimes to the UK overall, but there are crime hotspots in areas such as Paris and the Riviera and other places where there are masses of tourists and ostentatious displays of wealth which attract criminals in search of rich pickings. In the seventh UN survey of crime trends worldwide, France comes fifth for the level of burglaries and fourth for total crimes overall (Spain is sixteenth). On the other hand, the majority of rural areas experience minimum crime as Keith and Hannah Oakley, who retired to France, explain:

We feel safer here than in the UK. There is hearsay of burglaries but not much of it seems to happen in the countryside, which is more than you can say for the New Forest, our former home in the UK. Another thing I would say is that yob behaviour by people having fun is almost unheard of. We went to a music festival and there were several thousand visitors, and lots of young people having a good time at night and not a rowdy person or a policeman in sight.

By contrast, outbreaks of violence amongst rival city gangs and riots against the establishment are becoming more common in the community-less suburbs of Paris and many other cities. Discontented Muslim and African youths carried out the worst riots so far in November 2005, when the suburbs of Paris 'burned' for 11 consecutive nights and thousands of vehicles were set alight and sparked similar outbreaks in other French cities. This type of unrest is becoming more common on the fringes of cities such as Paris, Lille, Marseille and Dijon and will continue as long as there are formless masses of unemployed disparate groups living together in high-rise ghettos. There is a widespread feeling that *'l'insécurité'* is a big problem along with immigration and asylum seekers. The result was to make the neo-fascist Front National France's second party ahead of the socialists at the presidential elections in 2002. Recent rightwing governments have tried to be tough on crime, mainly by passing illiberal legislation. The interior minister, Nicolas Sarkozy has taken advantage of this shift to the right to gain support for his campaign to become the next President of France in 2007.

Statistics show that Paris has the worst rate, with 147 crimes per 1000 inhabitants in 2001, but these are heavily concentrated in the depressed areas such as St-Denis. Nice and the Côte d'Azur are not that far behind; muggings and car-jacking are serious problems. A disturbing new trend in the Côte d'Azur is the use of gas to render victims unconscious so that their mobile home or villa can be stripped bare. Avignon is one of the most crime-ridden cities in France. Strasbourg, Mulhouse, Lyon, Bordeaux, Marseille and La Rochelle also have very high crime rates. The presence of large numbers of tourists generates a lot of crime in the summer. The Riviera has a heavy concentration of private security staff to protect the rich, but this does not help the average person on the street. Crime rates are publicised by the magazine *Le Point* in its annual survey of French towns: see www.lepoint.fr. For a small payment you can access data on major French towns.

POLICE

French police are generally well equipped (and well-armed) to tackle the crime problem: they are strict, efficient and have far-reaching legal powers. French police have a reputation for ruthlessness. Although this reputation has improved of late, they are generally not regarded as a user-friendly force and few people care to ask them for help except in cases of absolute necessity. The exception is the special mountaineering section of the police, *Peloton de Gendarmerie de Haute Montagne* (PGHM) who are responsible for providing rescue services and guidance to the public. They have an excellent reputation for being courteous, helpful, and heroic when circumstances require.

A popular misconception seems to be that all French police (*agents de police*) are *gendarmes*. As their name (rough translation 'armed men') would suggest, The *Gendarmarie Nationale* is a paramilitary police force and comes under the control of the Ministry of Defence. It may be the only police force evident in many quiet country areas. The Gendarmarie Nationale also patrols roads and undertakes other specialist duties including motorcycle escorts and sea patrols. The National Police (*Police Nationale*) are responsible for order in larger towns. These forces have equal powers but different jurisdictions.

Dialling '17' in France will connect you with the appropriate police service. The pan-European emergency number which you can dial anywhere in the EU is 112.

City Police. Towns and cities have their own police (*police municipale/ corps urbain*) who deal mainly with petty crime, traffic control and offences and road accidents.

MEASURES AGAINST BURGLARY

Burglary is a problem in some areas particularly in resorts, but is relatively rare in villages, where any stranger tends to be under surveillance by suspicious villagers until their purpose is revealed as harmless. If you are in a known high risk area, or if your home is isolated and full of expensive furniture and possessions you should take sensible precautions. In any case, insurance companies will give you a list of security modifications they require before they will insure the property. You can find addresses and contact details of brokers and insurance agents in English-language newspapers including *French News* (e-mail subs@french-news.com) which comes with regional supplements and French property magazines.

Insurance (Assurances)

The French insurance market is very competitive and high profile. AXA and the state-owned GAN are household names in Britain. Received wisdom suggests that is that it is better to insure with a local company in France, (who are able to handle claims in English if necessary), so that you get a quick response in case of problems; rather than trying to transfer a policy from the UK to France (even supposing that it fulfils French legal requirements). There are English-speaking agents in many parts of France who can arrange insurance for you. There are agents who only sell policies for one company (*agents généraux*), and those who deal with several (*courtier d'assurances*). For further information on insurance see *Insurance* in the chapter *Housing Finance*.

SCAMS

Just because you have moved to France doesn't mean that you are out of reach of fraudsters and scam artists trying to divest the gullible of their money and enrich themselves with minimal effort. The advent of foreigners owning property abroad and the open market of the EU has resulted in similar types of scams operating in many different countries; the international scam has never been more active. An area of current vulnerability is with internet-based transactions. Doorstepping is not entirely out of fashion though: as in the UK beware of unannounced callers who claim to be from utilities companies, and who demand access to your home; you should always ask for proof of identity and if you are at all suspicious then do not let them in. Likewise, if you are introduced socially, or cold-called by someone offering financial advice and investments you should check into their background. The Dordogne is currently reeling from the effects of a previously convicted (in the UK) fraudster who operated in and then fled the Dordogne taking investors' cash with him. He offered retirees in the Dordogne the chance to invest in a genuine *Société Générale* fund. Exploiting a loophole in French banking practices, which allows the recipient of a cheque made out to a bank to pay it into a personal account by signing it on the reverse, he thus paid investors' money into his own account.

According to the authorities battling fraud, bogus investment schemes are on the rise. Punters may be offered worthless or non-existent shares by a crooked share dealer usually based overseas and who contacts potential victims by phone. Usually he (it normally is he) is charming, English and well spoken. One of the main sources of these financial parasites is Spain, and they are extremely adept at mimicking how genuine businesses operate. Others entice their target prey to invest in fine art, wines and rare gems.

There is also a scam that is plaguing property owners who advertise their homes or gîtes for letting. The fraudster makes an arrangement to rent your property, sometimes by booking it on the internet. They will probably arrange to rent for several months, which amounts to a lot of money. They then send you a cheque for double the amount you have requested. It is at this point that alarm bells should go off, as who on earth overpays their rent? The fraudster then explains that they have made a mistake and asks you to refund the overpayment (which could be thousands of pounds). Of course the cheque they have sent you is fraudulent; their aim is to obtain the money before the cheque bounces. They are aided by the rather slow French banking system. French banks do not validate cheques before crediting them to an account. To be on the safe side you should give any cheques 21 days to clear, or preferably not accept cheques at all, but insist on a bank transfer via the SWIFT system. Note that the same practice of overpaying and requesting a refund, can be applied to other transactions such as buying and selling of goods. Do not be caught out.

With the growth of internet selling including from small ads on expat websites there is plenty of opportunity for fraud. How do you know that if you pay the money you will get the goods? For some the answer is to use an escrow account where a third party holds the money in order to protect both buyer and seller. Do not use an online escrow account unless you know that it is genuine, as most of them are scams. One that is genuine : www.esrow.com.

If you want to find out if something is a scam you could do worse than check out the website www.scamvictimsunited.com which is full of cautionary tales. If you want to know what various scams are called in French try www.voilelec.com.

Returning Home

CHAPTER SUMMARY

O According to the Office of National Statistics, of the 190,000 people who move abroad each year, many will return home.

O Many of those moving abroad do not plan their retirement finances before departure and overspend on property purchase and renovation. They are then forced to sell up and return to the UK.

O Trailing spouse syndrome is another cause of returning, where one partner is much keener on moving to France than the other.

O When you return to the UK you should contact HM Revenue and Customs (the Inland Revenue as was) and request form P86. This is the form for re-entering the UK tax system if you have been resident abroad.

O Pensioners who have returned to the UK through financial hardship may be able to claim UK benefits such as Pension Credit aimed at pensioners on low incomes.

O If you rent out your French property after moving back to the UK and you are tax resident in the UK you will still have to declare your rental income to the tax authorities in France and the UK.

O Longer lets of French property give the landlord/owner a lot less leeway than short lets. For instance if you were to get involved in an eviction the process can take years. Short holiday lets (up to 3 months) through an agent would probably be preferable if you are going down this route.

O If you sell your French property within 15 years of having acquired it, then you will be liable for French capital gains tax at 15% unless it is your principal residence.

REASONS FOR RETURNING

According to the Office of National Statistics 190,000 British people left the UK to live abroad (most popular destinations Spain and France) in 2003, but since then many have returned. Failing health and intimations of mortality make people homesick and want to return to the old familiar UK. Some like 74-year-old widow, Anne Scanlon, feel that if middle-aged children start having to spend a lot of time visiting them in France for care duties arising from frailty or serious illness, she would have to go back to the UK. She explains:

> *I am enjoying myself so much living here that I hope never to have to return to live in the UK. However, I see British women I know rushing backwards and forwards to the UK because their elderly parents are very ill, or dying. I wouldn't want to put my son through that, in reverse as it were. If I couldn't cope here on my own, I'd go back.*

Financial strain is often a cause as is the difficulty of abandoning the habits of a lifetime and living like the locals in France for ever.

Common Causes of Returning

- Not enough research and preparation
- Unreal expectations
- One partner is not in harmony with the other about moving
- Financial problems
- Illness of one partner
- Homesickness
- Death of a spouse or partner

No Escaping From Problems

Some people decide to leave the UK as a way of escaping problems they may be having in their lives. Expectations may be too high of how moving abroad can change a life around. They may be disappointed to find that they and their problems are inseparable and that they cannot change their lives until they themselves change. Changing yourself usually requires shedding emotional baggage and altering the way you think and perceive the world the around you. In some ways, it would be better to start this process before leaving the UK. You could then move abroad as the next step. You might then be less likely to give up and come back to the UK.

Rose Tinted Glasses/No Preparation

A surprising number of people have decided to move to France on the basis of spending a holiday there. Having had a memorable week or two admiring the beauty of France and meeting picturesque locals, they suddenly think how wonderful it would be to live there permanently, forgetting that all the mundane details of daily life would be just the same in France (probably worse because of the bureaucracy). The hot weather, which seemed so perfect for dining outdoors at night, is not so brilliant when you are rushing about your daytime chores, or sitting baked in your car. In fact, the lack of rain is a severe problem in parts of southern France. It is as well also to remember that every country has its issues, which drive its populace mad. In the case of the French this can result in multiple *manifestations* (demonstrations), which may not affect country dwellers unduly, but they are very inconvenient for city folk. Oh, and there is the minor problem of hardly anyone in France being able to understand your English. When the rose tinted glasses are removed the vision does not match up to the reality and returning to the UK seems to be the only solution.

Before moving abroad ask yourself why? Why would living abroad be better than holidaying there. What would change in your life if you moved abroad? Once you have made up your mind, then you should research what living in France on a day-to-day basis entails in practical terms and work up to retiring there gradually.

Trailing Spouses and Relationships

This is a common expatriate problem, where moving abroad suits one half of a couple much better than it does the other half. Once out in France the strain in the relationship begins to show as one partner begins to resent that they were forced into the move, feels isolated and cannot cope without their network of friends around them. Of course it is possible to make new friends but if you don't speak French you will be cutting out half your potential acquaintances and in your day-to-day life in France this can cause untold frustration. Couples will either decide to part, or they will return to the UK to try to save the relationship.

It is very important that both partners are in harmony about the wish to retire abroad and that they discuss their aims and expectations in advance of making the move to France.

Financial Pressures

Retiring abroad is not cheap: property purchase, renovations, transporting personal effects, buying a car, trips back and forth to the UK, mean that the first part of your retirement is hugely costly. What happens after that depends on how well you have done your calculations. A large number of expatriates get carried away with the property aspects of living in France and buy a house that they have to beggar themselves to renovate. Unable to live comfortably in France they are forced to sell up and move back to Britain.

It is essential when you move abroad to have done your retirement financial planning before you leave and have a substantial emergency fund that is not part of your budget for moving but is for unexpected expenses only. That way you will have a much better chance of surviving the initial hit of the move financially. After that, expenses will even out on a year-to-year basis and you should be able to budget more accurately from experience.

TAX, SOCIAL SECURITY & HEALTHCARE

Whether you move back to the UK as a result of things not working out, or because a partner has died or you have parted from them, or for any of the other reasons that expatriates decide to return home, there are practical and financial implications. Before you return to the UK you should go through all of your financial affairs including bank accounts, pension schemes and other income and consider the effect the return to the UK will have on your financial situation. If you have offshore accounts, you can continue to use these but when you move back to the UK, i.e. become UK resident, you will have to declare them and pay tax to HM Revenue and Customs on any interest.

HM Revenue & Customs

When you arrive back in the UK you should request HM Revenue and Customs/Inland Revenue form P86 or download it from their website (www.hmrc.gov.uk). According to HM Revenue & Customs (the new name of the Inland Revenue, which merged with HM Customs in 2005) 'This form should be completed if you have come to the UK for the first time or after a period of absence.' After you have completed the tax form you should return it to the local tax office (consult HMRC if you do not know which this is). You will need to know your UK National Insurance number as this is requested on the form.

You will need to keep proper financial records from the time you return to the UK and remember that tax returns in the UK have to be in by 30th September if you want the tax office to work out the figures for you, or January 31st if you are doing the sums yourself.

Pensions and Social Security

You need to contact the Department of Work and Pensions (www.dwp.gov.uk) as soon as you arrive back in the UK in order to switch payment of your pension to a UK bank account. Follow up any telephone calls to the DWP with written confirmation.

Pensioners on low incomes and with limited savings may qualify for income-related state financial assistance on their return to the UK. Benefits include Pension Credit (towards weekly income) and Housing Benefit (help towards rent). You can enquire about these from the DWP on your return. They are not usually payable outside the UK.

Useful Contacts for Pensioners	
Benefit Enquiries	☎ 0800 88 22 00
Help the Aged	www.helptheaged.org.uk
Pension Assessment	☎ 0845 3000 168
Pension Credits	☎ 0800 99 1234

NHS Direct	☎ 0845 4647 (www.nhsdirect.nhs.uk)
Winter Fuel Payments	☎ 08459 15 15 15
	(www.thepensionservice.gov.uk/winterfuel)

Healthcare

Worsening health combined with financial pressures is a frequent cause behind expats returning. As said already, pensioners are entitled to free prescriptions, eye tests, chiropody (but not dental care) in the UK; whereas in France, pensioners pay for these things and have to take out a top-up medical insurance to cover the cost, or pay the 30% not covered by social security as they go. There is also the fact that as the health of one partner worsens, the other one often finds the strain easier to handle by returning to where there is a family support network. As health worsens, there may also be a wish to see the UK again.

Once resident again in the UK you can use the British National Health service without charge by registering with your nearest GP or healthcentre.

Healthcare Useful Contacts

| Care Homes | www.nursing-home-directory.co.uk (by areas) |
| Retirement Homes | www.bettercaring.co.uk |

LETTING YOUR FRENCH PROPERTY

Holiday Lettings

Many people only rent out their second home occasionally to people they know, or privately through placing small ads in the UK. Short-term lets of holiday homes come under the *Location Libre* regime, which protects the owner as long as they observe certain conditions. If the right conditions are not observed, and the tenants refuse to leave the property, there will be major legal costs involved in evicting them. To be able to let your property under the Location Libre regime, the following conditions need to be met (amongst others):

- The property should be fully furnished.
- The rental is for no more than three months.
- The tenants have a principal residence elsewhere.
- The property is only to be used for holidays.

Taxation of Rental Income

If you are not tax-resident in France, letting income from French property still has to be declared to the French tax authorities by April 30 of each year, on the usual income tax forms: No.2042, and No.2042C (specifically for rental income). These are sent to the *Recette des Impôts des Non-Résidents*, 9 rue d'Uzès, 75094 Paris Cedex 02. You can choose to be taxed under the *Micro-BIC* regime, which is the smallest and simplest form of business registration. Tax on your letting income, also includes an amount calculated on the basis of how much you have used the property yourself. The net letting income is taxed at a flat rate of 25%, unless the income is very small. You should declare your rental income to the UK taxman, and you will have to pay the difference between the 25% tax in France, and higher rate tax in the UK if it applies to you. You may be able to obtain tax relief on the mortgage interest from the UK tax authorities.

You can also opt to be taxed under the '*régime réel*' in which case you deduct your expenses, mortgage interest, and 4% annual depreciation from your gross income – *pro rata temporis* – to arrive at your taxable income. The régime réel requires you to present a lot more paperwork, but may be advantageous in the end.

There are considerable risks involved in not declaring letting income to the French authorities. If they discover that the property has been let, they can choose to tax you on 52 weeks' letting income, and you will lose the right to tax deductions. While you may get away with not declaring the odd week or two, it is not worth risking a much higher tax bill by not declaring.

Whether resident or non-resident, if you let your French property unfurnished, you become liable to the *taxe sur les revenus fonciers*. For this you fill in blue form No.2044. If your income is under €15,000 you can be taxed under the *micro foncier* regime; otherwise it is the *foncier normal*. There are numerous deductions. The tax is charged on unbuilt land, lakes, factories, and everything that stands on land.

Long-Term Lets

Longer lets give the owner/landlord a lot less leeway, for instance if they wanted to sell the property, they would have to give a reasonable amount of notice. Tenancy agreements (*bail* or *baux* in the plural) can come under one of four possible legal regimes, of which only one is relevant to holiday properties. This is the so-called *Location Libre* (free tenancy), which is subject only to the articles 1708 to 1762 of the *Code Civil*. The rental agreement can be for a defined or indeterminate period of time, and can be verbal or written. Because the provisions of the Code Civil are in the lessor's favour, the state has imposed certain conditions to prevent abuses. In the first place, it is only applicable to fully furnished premises (fully furnished meaning that the tenant has everything they need to be able to live on the premises), or to second homes or holiday homes.

Most longer-term rental agreements now come under the law of 6 July 1989, which gives tenants considerable protection against eviction, but proprietors can still eject tenants who behave unreasonably, after obtaining an injunction from a civil magistrate (*juge d'instance*). Eviction is a long-winded process. If tenants cannot pay their rent then social services will be called in. It can take years to get to the point of forcible eviction; the police are generally very reluctant to get involved.

Proprietors may be held liable for losses caused by theft if it can be shown that the construction of the house makes it easy for burglars to enter.

Uses of Property Not in the Rental Agreement. It is normal to carry on a profession in a rented property, such as working as an architect or doctor, while also living there. Since 2003, you have an absolute right to register a business at your home address for five years; you are only required to inform the landlord. Tenants are permitted to run their business from home, on condition that:

○ They do not receive customers at home
○ There are no deliveries
○ They are working from their principal residence.

Rental Payment. Payment intervals can be set by agreement with the owner of the property, but the prospective tenant can legally insist that payment should occur monthly. The tenant can ask the owner to come to the property once a month to collect the rent in cash; owners cannot compel tenants to agree to pay by bank transfer, or other non-cash form of payment. In practice, payment will most likely be by standing order but this does not follow automatically.

The repayment of the rental deposit (*dépôt de garantie*) will only take place after the tenant has vacated the premises and left them in good condition.

SELLING YOUR FRENCH PROPERTY

When you buy your property, it is well worth thinking about how easy it will be to sell on. There are parts of France where prices of old property are not likely to increase in the future, namely Alsace-Lorraine and much of central France, especially Auvergne. On the other hand, Provence and the west coast are generally a very safe bet. More and more people are moving to western France, so Brittany and Normandy should see some price rises. Paris is more uncertain, as the population is going to get younger according to the projections of the French Institute of Statistics. If you are selling on to other Brits, then prices may be affected by what is happening in the UK housing market.

Selling Your Property

It is usual to place the property with an estate agent or a *notaire,* who will add their commission to the selling price (8% in the case of the estate agent and 1% in the case of the notaire). There are British estate agents in many areas, who will do a better job of marketing your property than a French one would. The main thing is to have a good photograph of your property; this is not as easy as it sounds, and you may be best advised to use a professional photographer. Unless the photo is taken in the right way, the lines of the house tend to look distorted.

You can try to advertise it privately, or put your house on an English website featuring private sellers, such as www.1st-for-french-property. co.uk. Most British sellers try to sell to other foreigners, on the basis that they can expect to obtain a better price. In the current economic situation, the British are more likely to pay a little over the odds, while the poverty-stricken Germans will pay less. It is normal to emphasise the amount of attic space that could be converted, and to mention the proximity of railway stations and airports.

SHARP PRACTICES

At one time the Masheder family owned a house in a village near Uzès in the Gard. In 1992, when the property market was very sluggish, they let a local agent know that they wanted to sell the property. What happened next took them by surprise:

We received a phone call from a local Frenchman who was very excited about buying the property from us and asked us to come down to meet him as soon as we could. We got on the first plane and rushed down there, but were amazed to find that the supposed buyer had put up his own For Sale sign at a higher price than he was offering us. He was obviously hoping to find another buyer and pocket the difference. He used the excuse that he hadn't found a mortgage, which allowed him to get out of the contract. We never met the so-called buyer, and he removed the For Sale sign while our backs were turned. In the meantime, of course, we had lost a lot of time, and we couldn't sell the property until the following year. In the end we sold it to some Swiss.

From the seller's point of view, you can choose to give the estate agent a *mandat simple* or a *mandat exclusif.* In the first case, you can place the property with as many estate agents as you like, or find a buyer yourself. The agent is paid a commission if they introduce a successful buyer to you. With a mandat exclusif only one estate agent will look for buyers. You have to specify whether you wish to retain the right to look for buyers yourself – a *mandat exclusif simple* – or whether you give up that right – the *mandat exclusif absolu.* In the first case, the agent's commission is reduced if you find a buyer yourself; in the second, you would have to pay the agent an indemnity if you found a buyer yourself.

A mandat is for a limited time period. The seller can withdraw from the mandat, subject to certain conditions. After three months, a mandat exclusif can, in all cases, be cancelled through a registered letter. It is normal these days for the seller to pay the agent's commission.

Defects in the Property

Owners are required to have reports drawn up on the possible presence of asbestos, termites and lead paint. As a general rule, the seller cannot be held liable for *vices apparents,* or visible defects in the property. The issue of *vices cachés,* or latent defects, is more complicated. It is normal to insert a clause into the final contract freeing the seller of responsibility if the buyer subsequently discovers latent defects, but this does not protect the seller from claims for compensation if it can be shown that the seller could reasonably have been expected to know about the defect.

Taxation on Property Sales

If you sell your French property within 15 years of having acquired it, then you will be liable for French Capital Gains Tax, unless it is your principal residence. There are potential ways around paying French CGT for instance if the property is owned by a company. You are not subject to French taxes on proceeds if you sell a property outside France.

ARRIVAL BACK IN THE UK

Must Do List

- Open a UK bank account as soon as possible so that you have access to funds for daily expenses without paying unnecessary charges.
- Contact the Inland Revenue/HMRC for a P86 form or download it from their website in order to reinstate yourself in the UK tax system.
- Keep proper financial records from the time you arrive back in the UK as these will be essential for your self-assessment tax form.
- Contact the Department of Work and Pensions as soon as you arrive in order to claim your UK pension in the UK again.
- Register with your local GP or Health Practice so that you can use the NHS again without charge.

Appendix

Case Histories

Keith & Hannah Oakley
Ann & Alan Barrett
Bob & Annette Culshaw
Julian Roberts
Anne Scanlon

Case Histories

KEITH AND HANNAH OAKLEY

Keith and Hannah Oakley moved to France 9 years ago when Keith was 55 and taking early retirement. His wife Hannah is now 66. Before moving to France they had lived in the New Forest. Selling their UK property helped to fund their retirement in France though it was not their only source of income. They bought a restored farmhouse near St. Aquilin, 20 km west of Perigeux. Although Hannah spoke 'O' Level French when they arrived, she is now proficient in French; Keith less so but he is still learning. We asked him:

Is property still much cheaper in France than in the UK?
The price of property here in France is a major advantage for anyone moving from the UK to France. It is true that property prices have risen significantly in many parts of France in the past two years, but most people would not expect to pay much more than 50% of the sale price of their UK property for the same property in France.

Some UK immigrants to France say that the cost of living is not much lower that the UK, as they expected? What is your take on this?
Our own experience is that the cost of living is around 10% to 20% lower than in the UK. While direct taxation is higher in France for non-retired people, the same is not true for retired people. You do have to pay *mutuelle* insurance to cover the 30% of health costs which are not met by the government; for us, at our ages, this is €1600 (£1,100) a year for the two of us. On the other hand, in France a couple are taxed on their joint income (unlike in the UK where they are taxed as individuals) and this tends to make them better off than under the UK system. The other direct taxes on income,

the *taxe d'habitation* and *tax foncière* (the equivalent of UK Council Tax) come to €700 (£483) per year which for a large house on a large plot is considerably less than you would pay in the UK. However the same property in a residential suburb of Périgeux would be about €3,000 (£2,000), similar to the UK.

Does the French health service live up to its reputation as one of the world's best?

In common with others who have experienced it, the French health service is indeed excellent, and certainly, in our experience, better than private health care in the UK. Just one example of this: I visit my GP, he decides that I should have a routine check-up with a cardiologist in Périgeux; he rings the secretary, makes the appointment, types a letter and writes the date and time of the visit on the envelope. Within an hour of visiting the GP I have a letter and an appointment. My GP says that it is necessary to give the specialist the results of a recent blood test. He writes out a form listing the tests to be made. Without an appointment, I take it to the local Pathology Laboratory (there is one in every town of 5,000+ inhabitants in France). The sample is taken at 9am (no food allowed beforehand) and I collected a printout of the results at 5pm the same day (or it can be posted). The GP gets a copy, but it is me who takes my copy to the specialist.

When we came to France in 1997, the French health service was not an issue. Having experienced it, if we were to consider moving back to the UK, it would be a significant factor in not returning.

We have heard that public transport is excellent. What is your experience?

Public transport in larger towns is excellent, but in the country it is virtually non-existent due primarily to the low population density. Travel between cities is exceptionally good. Typically, travel by TGV in France is half the price and takes half the time for the same distance in the UK. For example, with a *Carte Senior* (€50 per year) Bordeaux to Paris one-way is €31 (£21) on all trains; journey time 3 hours; distance 600km.

What about eating out?

Eating out locally generally gives very good value for money, but cuisine can be very regional with less variety than you would get in the UK.

Is there anything you would like to add?

In view of the increasing numbers of Britons who have moved to France in the past two or three years, perhaps I would have been more negative about living in France if I could, in order to slow down the exodus!

ANN AND ALAN BARRETT

Ann and Alan Barrett, are in their late fifties and moved to the Dordogne in 2003 from Jersey as part of their plan to take early retirement. The sale of their home in Jersey funded the purchase of a farm with eight acres and four *gîtes* near the village of Tocane, 20 minutes by car from Riberac. The first house deal they made in France fell through, but when they found the place they now live in they realised it was meant to be. We asked Ann:

Most people would consider Jersey a great place for retirement, so why did you move to France instead of retiring there?

As Jersey is a tax haven, our motivation for leaving was not financial. For many people, moving to France is prompted by the fact that money goes further and they can afford a nicer property that they could afford in the UK. This was not so in our case; it was more to do with quitting busy office life and having a complete change of pace and lifestyle.

How long did all the procedures for buying a property take you to finalise?

It took about three months for everything to be completed in France. During that time we bought a camping van and travelled around France, mostly in Brittany. We used to sail the Brittany coast in our boat from Jersey and had only explored the shoreside before. It was fascinating, seeing the place from the landside.

Did you find retiring to France a bit quiet after the active and busy lives you left behind in Jersey?
Not at all. We have four gîtes, which were up and running when we bought the farm. We didn't have to do a thing to them. We have occupancy year round, although summer is busier as you might expect. As a lot of English people come to buy property here, we regularly get longer lets of three or four months as it can take this long for property purchase to be completed and people need somewhere to stay in the meantime.

I thought you said you were retired! Can you make a living from running gîtes?
Many people have unrealistic expectations of the income from gîtes. We do not make a lot of money from them but they help support our comfortable lifestyle. I should say I am semi-retired really, although the work involved is for short bursts and is only really busy on change-over days.

O.K, so it is not full-time work. How do you keep busy the rest of the time?
When the gîtes are quiet, there are always masses of other things to do as we have quite extensive grounds that need tending, so I never have to wonder what to do next.

Presumably, coming from the Channel Islands you already knew French?
Well I'm bilingual actually, but my husband is not. I don't think lack of French is a problem in this (the Dordogne) area as there are so many English-speakers, especially around Riberac, and you bump into them everywhere: in supermarkets and outdoor markets.

What is better about being here in France, rather than on Jersey?
I am no longer governed by time. In fact I hardly glance at my watch at all. When we visit Jersey it is a six-hour drive to St. Malo, but I never think twice about doing it because time has become flexible; it takes as long as it takes. You can also fly to Jersey from Bergerac airport.

Oh, and I like working with my husband for a change.

BOB AND ANNETTE CULSHAW

Bob and Annette Culshaw took early retirement from local government jobs. Bob, who is now 61 was near retirement anyway, but his job was very stressful and he had a heart attack and decided it was time to quit. He and Annette took an unusual approach to retiring abroad, which worked out for them (after one or two hazardous experiences), but might not appeal to others; let's call it the unplanned approach. We asked Bob:

What made you decide to retire to France?
We didn't actually know that we wanted to be in France necessarily. We had spent some enjoyable holidays in France and knew we wanted to settle somewhere abroad, but had not decided where. So we sold our house on the Isle of Wight and bought a motorhome intending to travel around Europe until we found somewhere we liked and then find a property to buy and stay put. You could call it trial and error or even trial and terror. How much time have you got?

So you didn't plan much in advance then?
Well if we had we probably wouldn't have found ourselves in the north of France in mid-winter battered by wind and lots of rain.

Sounds like a bad start. What did you do next?
Fed up with driving in a deluge we decided to head south. We ended up in Carcassonne and there followed a series of burglaries to our motorhome. The first was in Carcassonne, while we were parked opposite the police station! We were robbed again two days later when I confronted a burglar inside the van, and then a third time in Orange near Avignon, when one of our tyres was slashed. The perpetrator followed us to the garage and robbed us while we were in garage's office and the motorhome was on the forecourt. The police we reported the thefts to, pointed out that we were an advert to robbers. We had English plates, and a vehicle that obviously contained a lot of stuff. We told the police we were thinking of heading into Spain and then Portugal. They told us this would be madness, because Spanish robbers were more ruthless than French ones as they have organised gangs who hold

up foreign vehicles at the roadside. So we rearranged our plans and arranged a rendez-vous with my son in Périgeux instead.

How did you find your French home?
We turned up at the campsite in Périgeux in January and as it was a bit dreary, we decided to walk into Perigeux town. We fell in love with it instantly. It has Roman and medieval parts that have been beautifully restored. Within three days we had spotted the house that is now our home in the hamlet of Atuor, 6km from Perigeux. It was the first one we looked at out of about a dozen properties. The couple selling were sadly in mid-divorce, and wanted to complete the sale as fast as possible, which was good for us, as it meant no delays. The house has three bedrooms, about an acre of land, and a swimming pool.

Was it easy to make friends?
Perigeux in the Dordogne has a lot of English residents and there is also an English pub 'The Star Inn' run by Mike and Bev who have lived here for 20 years and operate as an informal base and information centre for residents and newcomers. They helped us a lot when we were starting out. We also met an English-speaking Frenchman in the local garden centre who introduced himself and it turned out that he lives a mile from our house. He 'adopted' us and has helped in all sorts of ways including introducing us to his social circle. The best thing about it is that we have been totally embraced by the local community. We were amongst the first English-speakers to move to this locality and considering how little French we spoke it is absolutely staggering how many French friends we have.

Have you found anything new and interesting to do?
My wife and I joined a local walking club run by French people and we are just about to go on a snow-walking holiday in the Auverge with them. I am looking forward to putting 'tennis rackets' on my shoes; it will be a new experience for me. Our entertainment consists mainly of socialising with our French and English-speaking friends. We have three invitations for one night this weekend, but because we're a community, dates are being changed as we speak, to make sure everyone can go to everything. We still have our motorhome so when we feel

like touring in France we can. We never get tired of doing this because there is an amazing amount to see and lots to learn.

Did you manage to learn French?

My wife had 'O' level French and I even less. We arrived with a pile of phrase books and dictionaries. We tried to find classes locally but were put off by the teachers changing every week. In the end we found a Dutch woman teacher who gives one-to-one lessons. Here I am, 61 years young learning French. We can understand the radio quite well now, but find the television too fast.

What are the advantages?

The French will respect you for trying to learn their beloved language and will take great pains to help you. Not learning the language is one of the biggest causes for sell-ups and failures, as it leaves you isolated. One of the biggest advantages of understanding French is the way that it opens up the whole culture to you and that is immensely stimulating.

Is there anything that is not as you expected it to be?

Our cost of living expectations were not fulfilled. We thought shopping would cost less here, but although we use the local hypermarkets, prices are slightly higher than the UK's. Prices are higher in general except for local wines (€3 a bottle direct from the viticulteur) and diesel petrol is also cheaper at €1.03-€1.17 a litre. Motoring (but not the cost of buying a car) is once of the few things that costs less than in the UK.

JULIAN ROBERTS

Julian Roberts retired from the financial services industry when he reached the age of 65 in 2004. He and his wife had always wanted to retire to France. They now live in the hamlet of St. Michel de Double (pop. 260) between Riberac and Bergerac in the Dordogne and have 'settled in nicely.'

How did you fund your retirement in France?
We first sold our property in the UK and then travelled in France during 2004, looking for a house to buy. We are also now registered in the French tax system. For pensioners on modest incomes without large private pensions etc. you are better off tax wise in France than you would be in the UK.

Did you always want to retire to the Dordogne?
Initially we wanted to avoid it. We looked at a few places on the Mediterranean but it was too expensive and crowded on the coast, and too sparsely populated inland. We also checked out the Charente, and liked bits of it, but it was still not quite what we wanted. By this time, we found that we were approaching the edge of the Dordogne almost by default. We rented some basic accommodation near Angoulême from some Brits. It was November and rather cold without heating.

Didn't you begin to worry that you would never find what you wanted?
It is important to get it right. A lot of Brits come to France for a week or two, look at a lot of properties and choose the least unacceptable one because that's what you have to do if you are only spending a week in France. We wanted to find the best property for us; that often takes time. Being retired means you can take all the time you need.

How did you find the house that is now your home?
We saw it advertised in an estate agent's in Angoulême, even though it is quite a distance from there. The vendors are actually our neighbours. The house is a former gîte and we also bought three-quarters of an acre of their land with it.

Was it easy to settle in and make friends locally?
Our neighbours are a Russian/English couple and we got to know some other people through them. We are not great joiners of clubs except for the Gardening Club at Vertillac, which is an English-speaking club.

How are you keeping busy?
We have explored much of the region, which is interesting historically as it is the remains of a great medieval forest. I am trying to write a local history about it. We have a large garden, and I read a lot, and I am trying to improve my French. I did half an 'A' level course before I arrived. We have had our friends and grandchildren to stay. We are handy for visitors as we are 40 minutes from the airport at Bergerac.

Have you used the French public health system?
We are registered with CPAM. However, we have not taken out top up insurance for the 30% of costs that you have to pay. Because of our ages such insurance is very expensive and so we pay as we go for minor ailments, as that works out cheaper. The cost of expensive treatments such as those for chronic or life-threatening illnesses is in any case refunded 100% by the state.

What are the best things about retiring to France?
I fell in love with France when I came here for the first time in the 1960s. For me, it is like turning the clock back to my 1950s boyhood in England. Where we are, it is virtually crime free, and nearby towns seem to suffer mainly petty rather than serious crime or yobbish behaviour. You never see any litter. There is also more of a community spirit. Every year the commune organises a few events that include a meal, a live band and dancing open to everyone in the community.

Any nasty surprises?
Some very distant acquaintances from Britain turning up on our doorstep like old friends and expecting to be fed and lodged. It can also get very cold and hot here. One night in March last year the temperature went down to −15C and during the summer it went up to 38C.

Would you return to the UK?
No; you can expect me to be buried here. For my wife it's a bit different. She might go back if I turned up my toes. Even as we left here to go to the UK for Christmas I was already looking forward to coming back.

ANNE SCANLON

Originally from Ireland, Anne Scanlon, who is in her seventies, moved to France from Plymouth with her husband in 1989 when he had just retired, aged 60. He died four years later, and she is still there, living in the old farmhouse they renovated together in the village of Faux (pop. 566), 18km from Bergerac, in the Dordogne.

What made you choose France?
Originally, we thought we would go to Spain, because that's where everyone was going, but we had toured in France many times with a caravan and loved it. My son and his family were a factor in the final decision, as France is easier for them to visit by car.

Did you speak or learn French before you arrived?
Neither my husband or myself had learned French at school, but I have been learning ever since; though it is difficult to learn a new language at my age. I go to classes regularly, and also go to conversation groups where we practice speaking English and French with French people. I can get by in French, but I need help with some things. I have English friends here who are fluent and I ask them to help me.

How did you end up in the Dordogne?
Originally we looked in the Vendée, because my husband had a friend with connections there. However, we didn't like it and found it rather bleak. Another friend of my husband's had a connection with an agent in the Dordogne so we came here instead.

Was it easy to find a property?
It took us a week solid of looking at places. The house we chose was a one-room farmhouse when it was built 500 years ago, but over the centuries it had been added to. We were able to renovate it without having to start from ruins, as the conversion had already been done by the previous local owner. It has three bedrooms and two bathrooms. There is also a terraced garden and the original village well. Local farmers come here to fill their water tankers to use on their fields. It never runs dry.

What facilities/amusements are there in the village?
We have a bakery, garage, shop, bar and post office. The post office is located in a room off the bar; a permanent arrangement. We also have several clubs including a Pensioners' Club called *Temp de Loisirs de Faux*; though you don't have to be a pensioner to join it. The Pensioners' Club is run by the local commune and they organise evenings of card games, regular lunches, bingo and so on. The commune also provides an annual four-course Christmas lunch for all the pensioners, which is free.

What about English clubs?
Most of the clubs in this area are English-run, though some attract French members as well. For instance, at Issigeac, 8km away, is a drama club with 260, mostly English members. I know, because I am the membership secretary. We put on two plays a year in the Château at Issigeac, which is the municipality's *Salle des Fêtes* (venue for organised events). The drama club also organises an annual shopping trip by coach, to Bordeaux. There are lots of other clubs; some of them have been going for twenty years such as the Ladies' Club and there is an excellent music club. The Brits in this area organise an annual Christmas Bazaar in Bergerac and the French flock to it; they absolutely love it.

You're quite busy socially then?
I don't seem to have a free moment; there is always a function or soirée on somewhere. We Brits make an evening of it, bringing the food, salads and buffet dishes that we all share. Life here, as anywhere, is what you make of it.

Would you ever consider returning to the UK or Ireland?
I hope never to have to return to live in the UK again. I'm enjoying myself so much. Everything is much more laid back in France. However, A few British women I know are rushing backwards and forwards to the UK because their elderly parents are very ill or dying. I wouldn't want to put my son through that, in reverse as it were. If I couldn't cope here on my own, I'd go back.

What is your advice to anyone thinking of retiring in France?
Well firstly, if you don't want to mix with British people then you should avoid the Dordogne. It's not everyone's cup of tea; we had a couple move to the area from the UK and they said they didn't want to meet English people, only French people. They only lasted here a year.

Secondly, there are no public bus services, except for schools, so it is absolutely essential to have a car and to be able to drive. Widows who don't drive are very isolated. I know two; their husbands drove them everywhere. Now they are reliant on friends and taxis for transport.

Do you travel away from France?
I drive to Roscoff (it takes about 8 hours direct from here) to get the ferry to Plymouth where my son lives. I also drive to Fishguard to get the ferry to Ireland. I love driving because I am completely free to stop when I want to. I often take longer on the way back to make detours to visit interesting sounding places.

Complete guides to life abroad from Vacation Work

Live & Work Abroad

Live & Work in Australia & New Zealand £12.95
Live & Work in Belgium, The Netherlands & Luxembourg £10.99
Live & Work in China £11.95
Live & Work in France.. £11.95
Live & Work in Germany £10.99
Live & Work in Ireland £10.99
Live & Work in Italy £11.95
Live & Work in Japan £10.99
Live & Work in Portugal.. £11.95
Live & Work in Saudi & the Gulf... £10.99
Live & Work in Scandinavia... £10.99
Live & Work in Scotland.. £11.95
Live & Work in Spain £12.95
Live & Work in Spain & Portugal £10.99
Live & Work in the USA & Canada.. £12.95

Buying a House Abroad

Buying a House in France £11.95
Buying a House in Italy... £11.95
Buying a House in Morocco.. £12.95
Buying a House in New Zealand... £12.95
Buying a House in Portugal.. £11.95
Buying a House in Scotland £11.95
Buying a House in Spain £11.95
Buying a House on the Mediterranean £13.95

Property Investment

Where to Buy Property Abroad – An Investors Guide £12.95

Retiring Abroad

Retiring to Australia & New Zealand £11.95
Retiring to Cyprus.. £11.95
Retiring to France... £11.95
Retiring to Italy.. £11.95
Retiring to Spain £11.95

Starting a Business Abroad

Starting a Business in Australia... £12.95
Starting a Business in France £12.95
Starting a Business in Spain £12.95

**Available from good bookshops or direct from the publishers
Vacation Work, 9 Park End Street, Oxford OX1 1HJ
☎01865-241978 * Fax 01865-790885 * www.vacationwork.co.uk**